Additional praise for
Win with Advanced Business Analytics

"JP Isson and Jesse Harriott are outstanding leaders in this field. If you want to succeed with analytics, you must read this book!"

> —Bruno Aziza, Vice President of Marketing, SiSense,
> and coauthor of *Drive Business Performance: Enabling a
> Culture of Intelligent Execution*

"In today's ultra-competitive world, leveraging analytics to help companies manage their path forward is a must. *Win with Advanced Business Analytics* does a great job of providing an understanding of business analytics and creating a framework to build upon. The authors bring great experience and knowledge to help explain a critical and complex topic."

> —Larry Freed, CEO, ForeSee, and author of
> *Managing Forward: How to Move from Measuring
> the Past to Managing the Future*

"At LifeCare, we are passionate about using analytics to drive innovation and business growth. This book provides executives and managers with useful guidance for using business analytics to drive results. I recommend reading and applying the concepts and frameworks of *Win with Advanced Business Analytics*."

> —Doug Klinger, CEO, LifeCare

"*Win with Advanced Business Analytics* provides a blueprint for how analytics can impact the bottom line of an organization and helps business leaders make the most of their analytics investments. It's a must-read in today's big data environment."

> —Michael Krauss, @ C Level Columnist, *Marketing News*,
> and President, Market Strategy Group

"In today's world, an analytical, data-driven approach to business is table stakes. *Win with Advanced Business Analytics* has been written for those of us who need an introduction or an update on the state-of-the-art/science. It is comprehensive and practical. It suggests approaches and concrete real-life solutions to complex business challenges while remaining nontechnical and fun to read. A great reference for today's decision makers!"

> —Louis Gagnon, Chief Product and Marketing Officer, Yodle

"A great overview of analytics and best practices for the business leader. It will be a critical resource for anyone looking to get the most out of their analytics initiatives and is a must-read for both newcomers and seasoned vets."

> —Raj Aggarwal, CEO, Localytics

"Finally, a book that provides straightforward, accessible, and proven approaches to dealing with the massive amount of information collected by companies. Isson and Harriott give managers the analytical tool not only to see the forest from the trees but also to capitalize on the picture."

—Stéphane Brutus, PhD, Professor,
Department of Management,
John Molson School of Business,
Concordia University

"Business analytics focuses on developing new insights and understanding of business performance based on concrete data and statistical methods. This book is a good guide to help you compete and win with advanced analytics."

—Jean-Marc Leger, President and CEO, Leger Marketing

"*Win with Advanced Business Analytics* offers the business leader a clear path of how analytics can impact the organization."

—Joe Carvelli, CEO, Retail Ingenuity

"Whether you work in marketing research, customer relationship management, social media, customer experience management, web analytics, or have to use all of these inputs in developing your organization's strategic planning efforts, this book will open your eyes. The authors present an integrated approach to customer and competitor information analysis. They define the domain, explain the disparate functions, give great and timely company examples, and tie it all together. This book is certain to cause more than one company to reorganize how it approaches analytics."

—Roger Baran, Professor of Marketing, DePaul University

"Retail is a highly competitive industry, and part of our success is due to how we leverage big data and analytics. *Win with Advanced Business Analytics* is a key resource for leaders looking to gain insight and direction regarding how data assets can be used to impact the bottom line of their organization."

—Scott Bracale, President, Tween Brands
Agency Inc., d/b/a Justice

"This book is great for managers and students who would like to learn how to apply advanced business analytics. The conceptual framework and case studies presented here are a must-read."

—Minha Hwang, PhD, Assistant Professor of
Marketing, McGill University

Win with Advanced Business Analytics

WILEY & SAS BUSINESS SERIES

The Wiley & SAS Business Series presents books that help senior-level managers with their critical management decisions.

Titles in the Wiley and SAS Business Series include:

For more information on any of the above titles, please visit www.wiley.com.

Win with Advanced Business Analytics

*Creating Business Value
from Your Data*

**Jean Paul Isson
Jesse Harriott, PhD**

John Wiley & Sons, Inc.

Library of Congress Cataloging-in-Publication Data:

Isson, Jean Paul, 1971-
    Win with advanced business analytics : creating business value from your data/Jean
Paul Isson, Jesse Harriott.
        p. cm.
    Includes index.
    ISBN 978-1-118-37060-5 (cloth); ISBN 978-1-118-41708-9 (ebk.);
    ISBN 978-1-118-42051-5 (ebk.); ISBN 978-1-118-43428-4 (ebk.)
        1. Business planning. 2. Industrial management—Statistical methods.
    I. Harriott, Jesse. II. Title.
    HD30.28.I83 2013
    658.4'038—dc23
                                                                    2012026662

Printed in the United States of America

10 9 8 7 6 5 4 3 2 1

I dedicate this book to Roxane, my daughter, who, despite her young age, was old enough to understand that I was not available as usual and managed to keep busy with her own stuff, giving me time to write. Daddy is finished writing and hopes when you will read this book you will be proud of your patience. A special thanks to Nathalie, who is always supporting me 100 percent in all I do. Thanks, Nat, for being there with our lovely daughter.

—JP Isson

I dedicate this book to my wife, Evelyn, for all her love, support, and great feedback during the writing of each chapter and to my wonderful young children, Jesse and Eva, for their patience and understanding while Daddy sat in front of a computer for days at a time.

—Jesse Harriott

Contents

Preface

Many people have an interest in analytics right now; it's an undeniably "hot" area. After having practiced analytics for 20 years, we are seeing the technology finally begin to catch up to the analytical techniques. We are also seeing a wide variety of organizations and non–analytically trained business people gaining an interest in analytics. Analytics is definitely going mainstream. We are also seeing a lot of books written on analytics, from technical manuals on how to do analytics to works written to help you kick-start your organization's efforts in a particular analytical area, such as Web analytics.

We wrote this book to be different from the available books on analytics, and we are glad you have chosen to read it. The motivation for writing this book comes, in part, from the lack of resources we found that can help a business leader create value from, and make the most of, his or her organization's analytical assets. In other words, this book will help you think about analytics across your organization, will help you evaluate whether you are doing analytics well, and will provide you with frameworks to take your analytics to the next level, creating economic value for your organization in the process. It is not a technical book and is written to be relevant to someone with no analytical experience, as well as to the person with a great deal of analytical experience. Also, unlike many of the analytics books out there, we each have about 20 years of practical analytical leadership experience in more than 50 countries. As such, this is not a book written in an ivory tower. We have been through what we write about in the book, have overcome the pitfalls we outline, and have created successful analytical solutions for a wide variety of global business situations.

The focus of this book is on advanced analytics and how companies can create business value from their data assets. By advanced analytics, we mean analytics that starts with a business goal or question, integrate disparate data sources together, create a prediction for the future, and lead to business actions with measurable results. We provide numerous advanced analytics examples throughout the book, with an eye toward real-world examples that will be of interest to a business leader, as well as to practicing analytical professionals.

One of the key trends we are seeing emerge and that we have incorporated into this book is the integration of previously unrelated data assets together in the organization. For example, it used to be that marketing research was siloed in the marketing department, user-experience research was in the product development part of the organization, Web analytics in the technology group, and customer analytics in yet another part of the organization. We are slowly starting to see these barriers break down within companies. Organizations are realizing that key business questions often cut across departmental silos and that richer and deeper analytics will help an organization compete more effectively. In some companies, this means the formation of a centralized analytics organization; in others, it may not mean a formal organization but instead an informal center of excellence. To reflect this trend, we cover areas of analytics not often seen together in one book. This is an effort to expose you to areas of analytics that may be new, as well as show you how they relate to one another and outline the information areas you need to think about as you create your own strategic analytics endeavor.

This book is written such a way that each chapter builds on the last, but each chapter can be read by itself as well. You will get more out of the book if you read it from beginning to end, but if you are interested in quickly learning about mobile analytics, for example, you can jump right to that chapter. Regardless, we encourage you to start with Chapters 1 and 2, which provide the foundation for the book, as well as outline one of our key frameworks, the Business Analytics Success Pillars.

We are confident that if you follow the principles contained in this book, you will develop a high-impact analytics function and will generate economic value from data for your organization. Many of the practices we outline are not easy to accomplish, but whether you are in a large company or a small one, you can apply your vision for advanced analytics and create business value from your data.

Acknowledgments

We engaged hundreds of analytical business leaders to help in the writing of this book. Whether through interviews, formal contributions, or informal collaboration, we are indebted to many for helping us complete this book. You will see many of their contributions throughout the book, in the form of useful insights in their quotes and concrete examples of how they make analytics work. A few even wrote an entire chapter in their area of expertise. We are thankful to have such esteemed colleagues in the field of analytics; the impact of this book would not be as great were it not for their input. There are too many to list, but we would like to especially acknowledge Dr. Abby Mehta, Dr. Jac Fitz-enz, and Judah Phillips for contributing excellent chapters in their respective areas of expertise. We would also like to thank Sims Hulings, Stephen Kaufer, Elise Amyot, Avinash Kaushik, Steve Krichmar, Alex Yoder, Jon Lehto, Steve Pogorzelski, Sudeep Haldar, Joseph Arsenault, Jim Tincher, Mark McKenna, Tim Ruth, Amy Quigley, Jonathan Mendex, Amel Arhab, Justin Cutroni, Chris Krohn, Karem Tomak, Raj Aggarwal, Josh Chasin, Dr. Latha Palaniappan, Eric Wong, Seth Grimes, and Chris Musto for writing about some of the helpful examples and providing insightful quotes that can be found throughout this book.

JP Isson is especially grateful to Marjorie Bayard for her insightful discussions and support during some major keynote speeches he delivered in Chicago and Las Vegas, keynotes that helped lead to the idea of writing this book. Their early morning discussions and inspiring late-night talks have finally been brought to life.

We also want to thank the reviewers and the friends who supported us during this endeavor and provided valuable feedback during the writing of this book. Pat Turgeon, despite his busy schedule at Figures, was instrumental in reviewing some chapters and generously gave us great feedback and input. Kim Lascelles graciously reviewed the original book proposal, as well as some chapters of the manuscript, offering excellent input along the way. We appreciate Elise Amyot not only for contributing a case study from CMPA but also for reviewing some chapters of the book. We are very grateful to Shelley Sessoms from SAS for quickly seeing great potential from the proposal and fast-tracking the project to a book. In addition, we appreciate Stacey Hamilton from SAS and Sheck Cho and Kimberly Monroe-Hill from John Wiley & Sons, for helping to manage the publication of this book within a very aggressive time frame. We thank Doug Hardy as well, for his continued insight into, and support of, the writing process.

This book would have never been completed without the support and love of our families. A special thanks to them all.

We would like to thank all of our friends and colleagues who helped inspire many of the concepts in this book: Louis Gagnon, Mario Bottone, Mike Nethdercotts Martijn Mengerink, Fedel Chbihna, Karim Salabi, Alfonso Troisi, Caroline Apollon, Raymonde Beaudoin, Oumar Mbaye, Ellen Julian, Deanna Hampton, Karima Arhab, Mark Bienstock, Ezana Razwork, Diawo Diallo, Francois To, Jeff Quinn, Sean Dalton, Sunday Eboala, Paul Jamieson, Eugene Robitaille, Keke Wu, John McLaughlin, Peter Anastacio, Kim Vu, J. W. Milon, Marjolaine Boisvert, and Stephane Britus, just to name a few, because the list is endless. We would also like to thank all of our analytics colleagues at Monster Worldwide for their ongoing implementation of effective advanced business analytics in more than 50 countries around the globe and for embracing the business challenges of analytics. We want to thank all of you for your input, as well as for helping us implement the analytics solutions contained in this book.

CHAPTER 1

The Challenge of Business Analytics

"In God we trust, all others bring data."

—Edward Deming

Those of you who have teenagers in high school living under your roof understand what a transitional life stage this is for your kids. It is a time of many ups and downs, with great memories being created and, in some cases, momentous life struggles beginning. If you don't have teenagers in your home, imagine for a moment that you have a 17-year-old daughter in high school. She's a wonderful kid, very personable and outgoing, and excels at most things she attempts. You're very proud of her—she is on the honor roll, has a lot of nice friends, has the responsibility of an after-school job, has visions of college, and even has a long-term boyfriend of whom you approve. Being a good parent, you also occasionally monitor her computer use and e-mail activity. You notice that she is getting a lot of e-mails from a retailer to encourage her to buy baby and pregnancy-related items and are concerned that the retailer is glamorizing the notion of teen pregnancy and encouraging her to get pregnant. Furious, you storm into the retailer in person, read the manager the riot act, and demand that these e-mails stop. The retailer humbly apologizes and vows to stop the e-mails. Satisfied, you head home and relate entire experience to your teenage daughter. To your surprise, she reveals to you that she is indeed pregnant and is expecting a baby in five months.

According to a *New York Times* story, this is exactly what happened to a customer of the large retailer Target. Practically speaking, Target's business analytics activities informed the father that his daughter was pregnant. Specifically, Target statistician Andrew Pole used data-mining techniques to create a "pregnancy predictor" based on online shopping activity. If a customer scored high enough on the pregnancy predictor, Target would send e-mails with offers for pregnancy-related products:

> As Pole's computers crawled through the data, he was able to identify about 25 products that, when analyzed together, allowed him to assign each shopper a "pregnancy prediction" score. More important, he could also estimate her due date to within a small window, so Target could send coupons timed to very specific stages of her pregnancy.
>
> [Pole] ran test after test, analyzing the data, and before long some useful patterns emerged. Lotions, for example. Lots of people buy lotion, but one of Pole's colleagues noticed that women on the baby registry were buying larger quantities of unscented lotion around the beginning of their second trimester. Another analyst noted that sometime in the first 20 weeks, pregnant women loaded up on supplements like calcium, magnesium and zinc. Many shoppers purchase soap and cotton balls, but when someone suddenly starts buying lots of scent-free soap and extra-big bags of cotton balls, in addition to hand sanitizers and washcloths, it signals they could be getting close to their delivery date.
>
> Take a fictional Target shopper named Jenny Ward, who is 23, lives in Atlanta and in March bought cocoa-butter lotion, a purse large enough to double as a diaper bag, zinc and magnesium supplements and a bright blue rug. There's, say, an 87 percent chance that she's pregnant and that her delivery date is sometime in late August.[1]

Data privacy debate aside, the Target example is a brief illustration of the insights that can be gained through leveraging big data in an effective business analytics practice. If you are reading this book, we assume you see the importance, as we do, of using business analytics to positively affect your organization. You may be a business leader who wants to learn more about how companies use data effectively. You may be an analytics manager who wants to understand pitfalls to avoid that can lead to failure. You may be motivated to learn some of the latest techniques and best practices of how to use different types of information across the enterprise. You may be an analytical professional and want to learn how to take your organization's analytics to the next level. You may be an HR leader who wants to learn about data across the enterprise so you can decide how best to use it to make strategic human capital decisions. Whatever your motivation for reading this book, we assume your organization has business challenges that you hope data and the practice of business analytics will help you overcome.

Effective business analytics is a focus for business leaders across the globe in ever-increasing numbers. A 2011 report by the McKinsey Global Institute projects that the United States needs 1.5 million more data-literate managers to meet the demands of the data-driven enterprise.[2] In addition, during IBM's 2012 IBM PartnerWorld Conference, its CEO predicted that analytics will be the thread that weaves together front- and back-office systems in order to give companies that harness huge volumes of unstructured data a competitive business advantage.[3] Also, a recent International Data Corporation (IDC) report predicts that the business analytics market will grow 8.2% in 2012 to $33.9 billion.[4] It is gradually becoming clear that in today's cut-throat business climate, failing to leverage business analytics effectively in your organization can be the difference between thriving or slow death.

Because business analytics is rapidly evolving and often indicates different things to different people, we think it is important to outline what we mean by "business analytics" for the purpose of this book. We define business analytics as the integration of disparate data sources from inside and outside the enterprise that are required to answer and act on forward-looking business questions tied to key business objectives. We realize this is a fairly broad definition; however, our experience in practicing business analytics, as well as the hundreds of companies that have provided input, indicates to us that business analytics is moving away from an isolated reporting and dashboard mentality and toward an integration of various types of information across the organization in tighter alignment with the business goals of C-level executives.

Even though business analytics is a relatively new field, we see it as having the potential for great organizational impact and importance, much beyond that of the more traditional and isolated reporting function, research department, or "business intelligence"–related activities. Actually, the practice of business analytics is beginning to have a meaningful impact in many companies, some of which we profile in this book.

There are several key components worth noting in our definition that may differ from more traditional definitions of business intelligence, research, Web analytics, information retrieval, data mining, or other related disciplines. First, in our view, effective business analytics must be grounded in key business questions. The amount of data available to businesses is overwhelming and is growing at an exponential rate, and it's easy to enter analysis paralysis or drift into intellectual curiosities. Therefore, organizations must articulate and prioritize the key questions they want business analytics to answer.

Second, we believe that business analytics has the most impact on the organization when it is forward looking—not backward looking. In other words, business analytics is most useful when it is predictive and provides a lens into the future regarding likely business outcomes.

Third, to us, the new age of business analytics requires the integration and synthesis of various information disciplines across the organization, such as marketing research, Web analytics, business reporting, competitive intelligence, customer data, and outside data sources, among others, in order to be effective. If you recall, from our definition, all effective business analytics should be grounded in key business questions and objectives. Those business questions and objectives do not care about your organization's structure—that some of the data are in finance, some are in marketing, and some are in product. Those business questions simply demand an answer, and whichever organization can answer them consistently, with speed and accuracy, will win. Will that be you or your competition?

THE CHALLENGE FROM OUTSIDE

We see several business challenges that led up to the newfound focus on business analytics, as well as several challenges that business analytics must rise to meet.

We all know that the economic environment has been more intense and challenging than ever before. At the time of this book's writing, the global economy is still on unsure footing, consumers are still being conservative about their spending, the real estate market has not fully recovered, and businesses are struggling to understand how to grow effectively, yet profitably. In the first quarter of 2012, the chairman of the Federal Reserve, Ben Bernanke, was still predicting only modest growth during 2012, expecting economic and job growth to remain somewhat muted through the remainder of 2012.[5] Those companies that identify with the Fed's cautious outlook see the economic glass as half-empty and are trying to hold market share, stem losses, and keep their current customers happy.

Yet business and consumer confidence is showed signs of improvement during 2012, and the long-term payroll data trend from the Bureau of Labor Statistics indicates that companies have started to create new jobs. Therefore, optimistically minded companies are eagerly trying to be smart about staying ahead of business trends, as well as about how to capture some of the impending economic growth. Regardless of whether your future business outlook is optimistic or pessimistic, effective business analytics is becoming a required component of business success.

Another business challenge driving the increased importance of business analytics is that business competition has become more intense. It's easier to start a business with little capital and, in some cases, gradually disrupt an entire industry or invent a new one. Take the case of Amazon, the well-known online retailer based in Washington State. Started in 1994, it spurred the rise in the online purchase of books and music and was, in part, responsible for the relatively rapid decline of bricks-and-mortar stores in the book and music industries. These types of examples should motivate most organizations to acquire as much data about competitors and their industries as possible.

Part of addressing competitive threats is to monitor and stay one step ahead of your competition—tracking, analyzing, and integrating everything you know about your competitors into the analytics of your own company. For example, do you know your market share trend over time, the strategies and tactics your competitors use to sell to customers, how your products are perceived compared to theirs, which of your customer segments are more likely to defect to the competition, or why some customers use only your competition and not you? If your organization has timely and thorough answers to these types of questions, then bravo. Many companies rely on informal feedback about the competition and do not have solid analytical systems in place to address these issues.

Another business challenge that's leading to an increase in companies relying on business analytics to drive their strategy is that customers are becoming more fickle, and loyalty to products and services is rarer than ever before. Mark Ratekin from Walker Information Group, a respected leader in the measurement of customer loyalty, indicated, "We, too, have seen evidence of a shift in customer sentiment toward more of the High Risk category. Interestingly, there is a similar trend starting to occur among employees—more and more employees are becoming less engaged, and are planning to look for new work when the recession ends."[6] The decline in employee loyalty is also seen to be affecting the quality of the service provided to customers. Given all of this, it's extremely crucial for businesses to understand customer issues, such as what drives purchase intent, purchase preference, and purchase behavior. Doing this without systematic analytics and voice-of-the-customer input is almost impossible—unless you have only one or two customers. In that case, you may have business challenges to address beyond just analytics.

Given intense business competition, existing companies must continually monitor their customers' behaviors and feedback, remaining on guard for new entrants into the marketplace. Companies are under great pressure to continually and rapidly reinvent themselves and how they offer value to customers, and failing to accurately listen to customers and track their behavior often results in certain and swift demise. Take the case of Polaroid, the well-known brand of instant photographic equipment that failed to capitalize on the growing trend of digital photography. Polaroid was founded in 1937 by Edwin Land and was one of America's early high-tech success stories. The catapult of its success was the invention of camera film in 1948 that developed a photograph in minutes—much faster than other methods at the time. This competitive strategy was successful for Polaroid through 2001, when Polaroid filed for bankruptcy due to the rapid decline in the sale of photographic film. The irony is that Polaroid had been investing heavily in digital photography technology and was actually a top seller of digital cameras into the late 1990s. Yet although Polaroid invested a lot in technology R&D, the company failed to take a business analytics approach and understand that customers were relying more on storing digital photos on their computers, rather than printing a paper copy of each picture. If Polaroid had integrated accurate voice-of-the-customer input and customer analytics into its business analytics strategy at the senior executive level, it may have been able to adapt its strategy away from photographic print film and toward a successful digital photography play.

With customer loyalty elusive, the number of sales and marketing messages seen by your customers is also ever-increasing and is another business challenge driving the importance of business analytics. In the United States, marketers send more than 90 billion pieces of direct mail each year, trying to influence the behavior of customers.[7] Also, the Radicati Group estimates that nearly 90 trillion e-mails are sent each year, and certainly a large percentage of these are from businesses trying to get your customers to try their products.[8] Furthermore, eMarketer expects that U.S. online advertising spending will grow 23.3% to $39.5 billion during 2012, pushing it ahead of advertising spending in print newspapers and magazines.[9] In terms of traditional media, according to Media Dynamics, a media research group, the average American is exposed to a minimum combined total of 560 advertisements each day from radio, print, and television.[10] At the same time that this sales and marketing onslaught pervades our daily lives, the customer's attention span is shrinking, with customers seeking to avoid marketing messages through the use of digital video recorders that can skip ads, e-mail spam blockers, do not call lists, do not mail lists, and other techniques to avoid being exposed to your message. Given these challenges, the world of multichannel customer acquisition requires the effective use of business analytics to untangle the complex patterns of brand and product perception that arise from being exposed to so many marketing messages from so many channels.

At this same time, the promise of new media to help businesses grow and ensure success has reached somewhat hysterical proportions and is another business challenge leading to the importance of business analytics. Mobile usage continues to increase dramatically on a global basis, as does the use of social media and other online content, such as micro blogs. You can even call mobile and social media mainstream media at this point. At the end of 2011, there were roughly 6 billion mobile phone subscriptions worldwide, with some users having service on more than one device.[11] According to the Direct Marketing Association, 36% of consumers now follow brands on social media platforms.[12] Also, the number of social media users age 65 and older grew 100% during 2010, so now one in four people in that age group is part of a social networking site.[13] As an example, one of the authors of this book, Jesse Harriott, has a 94-year-old grandmother who recently purchased a cell phone and started searching Facebook to find people she knows.

This new media is taking a lot of the friction out of learning about a product and about choosing a company brand. Yet with the increase of new media and the multitude of ways to interact online comes a flood of new data into the organization. Every interaction someone has with your brand or product in an electronic medium, such as an Internet search engine, a website, a social media platform, an electronic coupon provider, a blog post, or a mobile device, generates a data trail. Other interaction points are also growing and generating massive amounts of data in their wake. For example, there are unknown quantities of digital tracking sensors in shipping crates, electric meters, automobiles, industrial equipment, and various other devices. In addition, GPS, wifi, and Bluetooth position tracking by mobile devices is widespread and generates massive streams of location data that companies are beginning to harness.

Given that economic pressures remain, that business competition is more intense than ever, that customer loyalty is all but gone, and that new media usage is on the rise, it is no surprise that the use of business analytics is gaining new prominence. These are the challenges for the business analytics discipline, the challenge to help organizations thrive and prosper. It's clear that using effective business analytics is seen as a way to address these key outside business challenges and that business analytics holds great promise to help you understand what your customers want from you, figure out how to acquire new ones, and learn what will lead to a repeat purchase. Yet most organizations we speak with are struggling to make sense of what these data can tell them or how they can use it. Therefore, we have designed this book to help businesses think about, organize, and make the most of the data assets available to them. Throughout this book, we provide examples of companies that are doing it well, along with some that are not.

THE CHALLENGE FROM WITHIN

Whatever your specific outside challenges driving you toward business analytics, there are also challenges for analytics inside the organization. In other words, how do you unleash the power of analytics to address the business challenges that are most critical to your organization, while overcoming typical pitfalls inside your company? If you could only find that brilliant data scientist and woo him or her into your organization, then everything would be all right, and your company could do brilliant things with its data. That one genius could help you segment your market effectively, increase your number of customers, reduce the customer attrition rate, predict what will make new customers buy, predict online customer behavior, and increase your company market cap by 30%, right?

Wrong. Certainly, smart and knowledgeable staff is important in helping you make good use of your data—but that is nowhere near enough. Several other challenges from within your organization need to be addressed before you can reach data nirvana using brilliant data scientists. This book is designed to help you address those internal challenges, but first, let's outline a few of them.

To illustrate some of the internal challenges to business analytics success, let's take the case of executives we spoke with at a company as part of the background research for this book. Out of respect for the company, we won't name it; however, let's just say it is a fairly well-known media company. Executives at this media company expressed some analytical angst to us during our interview. They said they realized a few years ago that their unstructured data were an untapped resource to help their business strategy, as well as help their customers. So they went searching for someone with the requisite degrees and experience who could lead the work with their data to help them unleash the data's potential. They searched for seven months (these people are in demand) and finally found someone with a statistics degree, computer science experience, great references, and a solid track record of helping well-known brands analyze their data. They hired him and put the existing seven analysts already at the company under his management. They were very optimistic with their new key hire and set him immediately to work on analyzing customer segments with a large average order size and a long tenure, versus those without, in order to understand how to better target prospective sales and marketing that would yield profitable relationships with a solid customer lifetime value. They said everything started off well at first—the team was optimistic and energized with its new team member. However, problems gradually started to develop. First, the analytics team went away for weeks at a time, with little data analysis completed, and then when something was delivered, it was usually lots of raw data and a graph or two, all of which were difficult for the business-people to understand. Second, the new team occasionally provided stats that were in conflict with other analytics teams in the company or what had been common company wisdom in the past—setting off ill will between departments and spates of dueling data that often took weeks to untangle. Next, it seems as if the analysts would occasionally come out with numbers that were different from the analysis they had provided just a few months earlier, which frustrated the business to no end.

The executives at the company attributed these challenges to the difficulty of doing analytics and tended to blame the analytics team for the problems. As a result of our interview, however, they gained an expanded view that it was very likely that the overall organizational dynamics within the company may have been the cause of their analytical team's difficulties.

First, we asked what company leadership sponsored the hiring and formation of this analytics team. It was explained to us that a long-tenured VP of marketing commissioned this initiative, and everyone had great faith that she could make the best use of these analytical resources. When we followed up regarding whether the most senior corporate or functional leaders were also in favor of forming this team, we were told that they were not completely sure, because no one beyond the SVP whom the marketing VP reported to was consulted. This illustrates our first internal challenge that business analytics must overcome—weak executive sponsorship. Unless a senior leader within the organization is a driving force behind business analytics and is aware, supports, and believes in the mission of the business analytics discipline over the long term, then it will likely have difficulties thriving and may fail eventually, due to shifting corporate priorities, company politics, and lack of corporate accountability.

Second, we asked what process the company had undergone to make sure its corporate business objectives were in line with the objectives of this new analytics team. We uncovered that the executives didn't really communicate corporate objectives to the new analytics leader or his team, because they thought the team simply needed to analyze data and not worry too much about corporate priorities. This illustrates the second internal challenge that a business analytics function must overcome: failure to communicate and align business analytics priorities against corporate priorities.

Third, we noted that surely technology systems and resources were required to help the analytics function do its work, so we asked how the analytics team worked with the technology team that supported these analytics initiatives. For example, did the technology resources report in to the new analytics team? Was there a direct line of accountability in some other way? We were told that the company did not set up any formal arrangement but relied on the new analytics manager to build a bridge and work across the departments. This illustrates our third internal challenge that the practice of business analytics must overcome: weak alignment and lack of accountability from the technology support function.

Next, we asked whether there was any data quality or governance function within the company to ensure that definitions were standardized and data were accurate. We were told no, but that it was the analytics team's responsibility to make sure that whatever data and analysis were distributed were accurate and reliable. This leads us to the fourth internal challenge: lack of formal data governance. It takes dedicated and diligent effort from business and technology to ensure that data being published from various systems is accurate and reliable, and this cannot be merely an afterthought by a few analysts simply because they happen to be last in the chain of data distribution.

Then we asked how the new analytics team's activities were rationalized against the activities of other analytics departments, such as product, service, finance, or strategy teams. We were told that they did not really communicate with one another formally and didn't initially think it was necessary because those teams were working on different analytical tasks. This illustrates the fifth internal challenge: weak alignment of existing analytical resources within an organization. We explained that in order to reduce the likelihood of a duplication of efforts and of dueling data, as well as to ensure that the company is leveraging the collective knowledge of the analytical resource most effectively, there must be some type of formal alignment across analytical teams. That can take the form of a reporting relationship to a single manager or simply a formal communication and management cadence across different analytical teams throughout the enterprise. The right solution depends on corporate culture and maturity and is definitely open for debate, as we have seen both work well under different circumstances. There are several ways to overcome this challenge, and we will outline each later in the book.

Many internal challenges will crop up on the way. These are just some of the internal challenges a business analytics function must rise to meet in order to become business relevant, fast, insightful, and predictive; have a bias toward action; and become part of the corporate culture. We don't claim this book will solve all of these issues for everyone. Yet we know that the best practices, lessons learned, and assessment tools within will go a long way toward helping you make sure your business analytics is world-class.

This book is organized in such a way as to help you build on your knowledge as you read from chapter to chapter. We have also attempted to define and organize the chapters so that they can stand on their own. For example, if you are primarily interested in learning about how companies effectively use Web analytics across the enterprise, you can jump to Chapter 9, "Leveraging Digital Analytics Effectively." However, if you want to learn about how to successfully evolve an analytics function, then we suggest you read the chapters in order and ask yourself hard questions about whether your company is doing everything it can to *win with advanced business analytics*.

 KEY TAKEAWAYS

- The field of business analytics is evolving. It's becoming less about data silos and more about the integration of different data assets across the company.

- There is a skills shortage for knowledgeable data professionals. It's expected to get worse, not better.

- Business analytics is being driven by several external factors, such as increased competition, decreased customer loyalty, economic woes, and the proliferation of new media.

- Business analytics requires many internal factors to succeed, including strong executive leadership support for analytics, effective technology infrastructure and tools, alignment with corporate priorities, and effective communication across departments.

NOTES

1. Charles Duhigg, "How Companies Learn Your Secrets," *New York Times*, February 16, 2012.
2. James Manyika, Michael Chui, Brad Brown, Jacques Bughin, Richard Dobbs, Charles Roxburgh, and Angela Hun, *Big Data: The Next Frontier for Innovation, Competition, and Productivity* (McKinsey Global Institute, 2011).
3. Ginni Rometty, keynote address speech, IBM Partner World Presentation, New Orleans, February 27–March 1.
4. IDC (January 2012), Worldwide Business Analytics Software Tracker.
5. Ben Bernanke, testimony to U.S. Congress, regarding the economic outlook for the remainder of 2012, Washington, DC., February 29, 2012.
6. Mark A. Ratekin, "What Is the Current State of Customer Loyalty?" *Walker Information Group Blog*, March 2011.
7. *2011 Statistical Fact Book* (New York: Direct Marketing Association, 2011).
8. Radicati Group, April 2010.

9. eMarketer, January 2012.

10. "Our Rising Ad Dosage," Media Matters, February 15, 2007.

11. International Telecommunication Union, November 2011.

12. *2011 Statistical Fact Book*.

13. "Boomers Joining Social Media at Record Rate," *CBS News*, November 15, 2010.

CHAPTER **2**

Pillars of Business Analytics Success

The BASP Framework

"Great things are not done by impulse, but by a series of small things brought together."

—Vincent Van Gogh

Chapter 1 introduced some of the challenges business analytics faces, from both outside and inside the organization. We are sure that by now you have gained a new appreciation for why some analytics initiatives are difficult to get off the ground or why others languish within the organization. In this chapter, we propose and outline a conceptual framework for successfully implementing business analytics in any organization so that your analytics initiatives will flourish and bring positive return on investment to your firm.

Our emphasis in this book is on practical solutions that have shown themselves to work in successful analytically focused organizations. The framework we developed is based on research we conducted with analytics leaders, as well as on our own practical experience, with each of us having been in this field for 20 years. That being said, any framework is merely a starting point for your organization's unique circumstances. Therefore, we encourage you to think about how this framework may be uniquely applied to your company, and we welcome your feedback or stories regarding how the framework has affected your organization.

We created the framework with the intention that it be simple and straightforward, yet have deep complexity beneath the surface, such that it applies to a broad range of organization challenges and situations. We hope the framework will inspire business analytics creativity, as well as heated debate. We believe the framework is responsive to the needs of business analytics customers, as well as business analytics creators. We know it's a framework a CEO can get behind, yet the individual analyst or manager can also use it as a blueprint to take analytics to the next level at her organization.

This chapter is merely an introduction to the elements of our framework. We have provided key practical examples throughout the book, as well as some dedicated chapters on important aspects in order to illustrate the concepts in the framework fully.

Before reviewing our framework, we think it is important to cover the Five Stages of Analytical Maturity that are required in order to move toward being an analytical competitor. The Analytical Maturity model was developed by Tom Davenport, a pioneer in the use of information and analytics effectively across the enterprise, and his coauthor Jeanne Harris in their 2007 work, *Competing on Analytics.*[1] Their outline to becoming an analytical competitor involves five stages, with Stage 5 being the most advanced.

- Stage 1 is labeled "analytically impaired" and is reflective of a company that has some data and management interest in analytics, yet no real center of excellence or organized capability.

- Stage 2 is labeled "localized analytics" and reflects an organization where some isolated managers may support leveraging analytics, but there is no formal enterprise-wide effort or recognition at the senior-most level regarding the importance of analytics.

- Stage 3 is labeled "analytical aspiration" and has some executive level sponsorship regarding the importance of analytics, and some organizational structure and effort have been put in place to leverage analytics within the enterprise. However, analytics is typically siloed to a few areas of the organization and lacks standards, support, and consistency.

■ Stage 4 is called the "analytical company" and involves a company-wide analytics priority that is actively under development, has the support of top executives, and has some standards and systems consistency.

■ In Stage 5, an "analytics competitor," the organization has consistent standards and practices, has thorough data integrity, and routinely capitalizes on all of the business benefits of its enterprise-wide analytics focus and capability.

The framework we developed for this book is designed to move your organization rapidly through the five stages and into becoming a world-class center of business analytics. The conceptual framework is especially helpful to organizations that have expressed interest in making analytics a priority, have made some organized analytics efforts where senior leaders understand the benefits of analytics, and are attempting to push themselves further into Stage 5.

Based on our experience and research and through interviewing other analytics leaders, we have noticed several common themes regarding companies that are successful with business analytics initiatives versus those that are not successful. From this knowledge, we created the framework that we call the Business Analytics Success Pillars (BASP). The BASP captures the key activities and similarities that thriving and successful business analytics functions share. The BASP can be used by the analytics leader as a self-check on what is being done well versus what is not done well. The BASP can also be used by the senior business leader to assess what is working with the analytics functions and what is not.

The BASP framework contains seven pillars that we believe are critical to successful business analytics implementation (see Exhibit 2.1). The pillars are not necessarily going to be followed in a particular order, because some organizations may be strong in one pillar but weak in others. For example, your organization may have a great culture of internal communication and have very little organizational friction when it comes to communicating information across business units or geographies—so the pillar related to communication may not need as

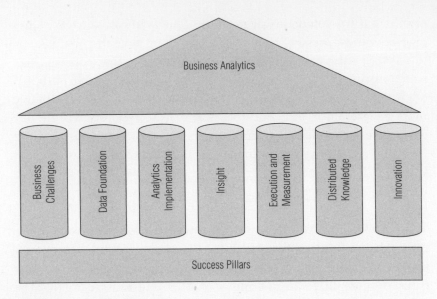

Exhibit 2.1 BASP Framework

much work. Conversely, your company may be very weak in the data foundation, with little integration or standardization of data sources across the enterprise—so a lot of your effort may need to be spent there. Regardless of your specific situation, the pillar framework can be thought of as being similar to the foundation of a house—you need all of the areas of support in order to make the house stand strong and not collapse. Therefore, the goal of the BASP framework is to focus your organization's attention on those areas that are key to business analytics success and will lead to the greatest return on investment.

BUSINESS CHALLENGES PILLAR

In today's challenging business environment, professionals across all industries are being tasked with doing more with less, with limited time and resources to allocate toward individual business analytics initiatives. This makes prioritization imperative and means that a crucial step of any business analytics implementation requires clear understanding of organizational objectives, or "business challenges," to ensure that any solution is aligned with, and addresses, the company's biggest or most pressing needs. This is why we have the first pillar of the BASP framework as "business challenges." This concept may sound obvious to some, but it is a deceptively simple concept that is often difficult to follow consistently. Any business analytics initiative must be grounded in "critical" business challenges. When we say *critical*, we mean challenges or questions for which the answers will lead to the company increasing its revenues or reducing its cost. It's very easy for the analytics effort within an organization to drift gradually into issues of intellectual curiosity or merely be a support function that answers questions at the whim of senior business leaders. This is how an analytics function can gradually turn into a cost center, rather than a function that adds economic value to the organization.

We cover the best practices for how to establish the critical business questions in detail in Chapter 3: "Aligning Key Business Challenges across the Enterprise." However, some of the most common business challenges that analytics may work to address include:

- How can I increase customer acquisition and retention?
- What prospects do I need to target in order to increase market share/customer spending?
- What are the emergent competitive threats, and how can my organization manage them?
- Who are my most profitable customers, and how do I bring in more like them?
- What types of our customers are most loyal, and what can we do to increase loyalty among the others?
- How are customer prospects using our online environment, and how can we increase conversion to a customer in our online experience?
- What are customers saying about us in the marketplace?
- What new products do customers want from us?

Although these challenges are broad, they are common to all industries and businesses. Understanding their priority within your organization and their alignment with your business's mission should allow you to focus your expertise on the most important needs for which to develop a business analytics strategy or solution.

DATA FOUNDATION PILLAR

As with architecture, the strength of any design is incumbent on the strength of its foundation. And similar to architects, business analytics practitioners must engineer an analytics framework that's built to last. With your business challenges outlined, you can start constructing the foundation that's built on data.

From our own experience and the interviews we conducted with analytics leaders, we've noticed a data trend—namely, that disparate data sources once relegated to single departments or to silos within the organization are being integrated into a unified data vision at the most progressive companies. For example, it used to be that HR data were created and stayed within HR, marketing research data were created and stayed primarily within marketing, customer service data were created and siloed in the service department, and so on. Yet executives whom we spoke to at the most successful companies indicated that the traditional lines of data and intelligence are being blurred. More specifically, companies are leveraging data across departments and breaking down traditional data silos, in order to address the business challenges of the organization. In our view, this is a natural evolution of becoming a data-driven organization. Usually, the critical business challenges cut across departments and really don't care where data are located—they simply demand answers. Truly progressive business analytics leaders understand this and set up a data strategy that takes this into consideration. We will cover building the data foundation in detail in Chapter 4, "Big and Little Data: Different Types of Intelligence." However, here is a list of some of the raw materials that are fundamental for building a data foundation for success:

- Inventory all of your internal data sources across the organization, even those you may think to be unrelated to your business analytics practice (for example, survey data, financial data, competitive intelligence data, Web analytics data, customer purchase data, ethnographic data, and so on).

- Conceive of new or derived internal data sources where applicable (for example, revenue per user).

- Inventory all of the data sources produced outside of your organization that provide insight to your market, customers, competitors, or organization (for example, omnibus studies, industry research, investor analysts coverage, demographic/firmographic sources, Web traffic measurement, third-party transaction databases, industry-specific data sources, and so on).

- In collaboration with key stakeholders across the organization, prioritize each of the data sources against the business challenge. You will likely discover that a lot of data produced within the organization does not align to a critical business challenge.

- Eliminate unnecessary or nonactionable data production.

- For the prioritized data sources, create a data inventory by standardizing and outlining three things for each discrete component of the internal and external data sources:

  - The business definition of each metric/information program.

  - The technical definition for each metric/information program.

  - The business action each metric/information program leads (or should lead) to.

- Create a culture of customer data integration, whereby you aggregate various key data from different sources together into one place, showing a comprehensive view of the customer.

- Build a formal cadence, process, and documentation history for data auditing each of the data sources against the standardized definitions and business actions. The data auditing for internal sources will be much more rigorous than the auditing of external sources. Eliminate data sources that do not consistently lead to business action. Evaluate and add new data sources as available.

- Develop a management process whereby the data inventory and the data audit results are shared and input is gathered from senior executive leaders.

Do not underestimate the time and effort involved in the previously mentioned activities. For example, you are likely to get conflicting responses across the company when asking the seemingly simplest of data questions (for example, who is our typical customer, how many customers do we have, who are our competitors, and so on), depending on whether you talk to someone in marketing, sales, finance, or customer service. This issue is often a key source of frustration with most senior executives when they think about business analytics within their company. Without data sources, definitions, and auditing that cuts across departments and silos, companies with well-implemented or advanced analytics will struggle to speak the same language across the organization. This problem is often exacerbated by the inability to agree on a universal definition for each metric. For example, what is considered a "customer" to marketing may be different from what is a "customer" to finance. In this case, championing the importance of business analytics to standardize the language around what is a "customer" across the organization goes a long way toward ensuring that everyone responsible for bringing your business analytics plan to life is looking at the same design and speaking the same analytics language. If this is not done, then your efforts may be undermined and much wasted effort will be spent on reconciling different data sources and dealing with the "dueling data" problem.

ANALYTICS IMPLEMENTATION PILLAR

The third pillar in the BASP framework is to execute the analytics implementation well. By this, we mean how the information-based business analytics solutions are developed and provided to the enterprise. This pillar is obviously broad and complex. However, the most important point for success with this pillar is to start with the end in mind. How will your solutions be used by your customers, and what actions do you hope they will take? This requires you to have a relentless focus on the customer and make sure to keep the end-user experience in mind. Start by imagining how your internal customers, whomever they may be (for example, marketing leaders, sales people, service reps, and so on), might leverage the business analytics information or tools you will provide in support of addressing the business questions.

Putting yourself and your business analytics team into the mind and understanding of the end customer must become your personal challenge, in order for you to be successful. For example, you really need to picture and map the process of how end users will be using the solution from the business analytics function and how you want the entire company to be affected. At this stage, it's also important to coalesce these positive outcomes into a cohesive, unified vision that's more than a business case. It's also a mission statement, a challenge to develop a solution that will improve the world of work for your end users and increase your company's revenue.

At this step, it is often helpful to do a short business analytics customer survey to gauge which tools are used by whom and how they are used. For example, create and send out a survey asking your internal customers to rate the business utility of each tool/output, how often it is used, and what business action is taken, as well how critical it would be were this tool taken away. This may provide your business analytics function with some tough input to hear but will go a long way toward being proactive to make sure the tools and the information you produce meet the ever-changing needs of the business customers.

Whether they're in sales, marketing, or customer service, it's important to consider the end users' experience and how they'll leverage your solution. Yet just as important as imagining individual outcomes is picturing the business impact your solutions will have on the organization. You should lay out clear steps in the analytical implementation toward reaching your end goal of comprehensively addressing the business challenge you've chosen to tackle. Getting a clear understanding of the steps required to deliver an optimal outcome should also help reinforce your business analytics mission of creating real business benefit to the organization.

We will cover the complex and challenging topic of analytics implementation in more detail in Chapter 7, "Analytics Implementation: What Works and What Does Not." However, here are some of the key questions you have to answer in order to have successful implementation:

- What is your business goal for the analytics solution?
- When will you meet that goal?
- What is your strategy to implement your vision?

- How will the solution be implemented?
- What type of information will you be tracking?
- What collaboration and sponsor will you need?
- What impact will the solution have on the organization?
- Who will be involved in executing your plan, internally or externally?
- What tools and software will you need?
- Who must be trained to use any tools that are developed?
- What resources are required to achieve your plan?

Answering these questions and effectively executing the recommended actions will provide you with a blueprint for building the foundation of a successful business analytics implementation.

CASE STUDY

INTERVIEW WITH CHRISTOPHER KOHN, PRESIDENT AND CMO, RESTAURANT.COM

Jesse Harriott had a chance to interview Christopher Kohn, the president and CMO of Restaurant.com, regarding his company's best practices surrounding analytics. Following are some insightful comments he made.

Harriott: What are the most important business challenges that Restaurant. com uses analytics to address?

Kohn: Restaurant.com uses analytics in three primary areas. First, we assess the opportunities and performance of our business in each local market around the country, analyzing restaurant penetration rates, sales force targeting, and account management effectiveness. Second, we use analytics to measure the impact of our B2C and B2B marketing efforts, identifying channel opportunities or customer segment opportunities to profitably grow the business. Finally, we use analytics to build predictive models for financial forecasting and budgeting and to evaluate the ROI of business initiatives and investments.

Harriott: What were some of the factors that led to the decision to align analytics across the organization?

Kohn: At a high level, we made the decision to transform Restaurant.com into a more data-driven organization. As part of that transformation, centralizing analytics resources was the best way to ensure both (A) deep competency in a variety of analytic disciplines and (B) allocation of those analytics resources across the various areas of the business in the most impactful way. A centralized analytics team reporting directly to the president of the company also helps the organization examine data with an unbiased view, rather than what we've seen happen in other organizations, where individual departments can be tempted to align analytics outputs to their own particular agendas.

Harriott: What advice would you give to other organizations trying to get the most out of their analytical capabilities?

Kohn: First, work to obtain a commitment from senior management that data-driven decision making is an organizational imperative. Without that commitment, analytics resources can sometimes risk being perceived as an expensive luxury. Second, build consensus on the tools, sources, and data definitions that will be used so there is consistency across the organization. When finance, marketing, and sales each talk about "net revenue," for example, they should all be using the same definition and be pulling their reports from the same data sources. In addition, it's important to create a prioritization process for analytics projects that forces tradeoffs in allocating resources to different business initiatives and departments.

Harriott: Many organizations tell us they have too much data and not enough understanding of that data. Would you agree, and if so, how has Restaurant.com worked to leverage its data in a way that leads to understanding?

Kohn: While this can certainly be an issue, we actually feel that we have the opposite problem. We have a fairly good understanding of our data and the limitations of our existing data. We have identified our top customers and their behaviors, for example, but we are still working to get all systems in place to take coordinated marketing and management actions based on that knowledge. In addition, we are prioritizing data collection initiatives so that we can augment the data we already have and data management initiatives to improve our data integrity and data security. That being said, the process of turning data into business insights and insights into informed management actions is a journey, not a destination. We will always be working hard to better understand the data we already have.

(continued)

Harriott: How important are analytics to the restaurant industry and how do you see analytics being used currently and in the future?

Kohn: Historically speaking, the restaurant industry has been bifurcated between large national brands that leverage extensive analytic capabilities and smaller independent restaurants that have limited analytic capacity. Increasingly, restaurant owners are realizing that such factors as diner repeat purchase rates, food cost management, labor scheduling efficiencies, marketing investments, and other key aspects of their business can be improved by insights coming out of analytics. At Restaurant.com, we are partnering, on the one hand, with restaurant owners and brand managers to use analytics to improve their profits and, on the other hand, to help diners choose the right restaurant for their needs, regardless of dining occasion.

INSIGHT PILLAR

The key to business impact, and often the most difficult task, lies in the ability of your business analytics team to take raw data and turn it into a compelling narrative that addresses specific business challenges and results in business action. As a result, "insight" is our fourth pillar in the BASP framework. Like any architect, you've got to know who you're building for before you start construction. In business analytics, fulfilling any commission starts with statistical storytelling—addressing what's happened, why it happened, and, most important, what's going to happen.

Watching a business analytics initiative yield insight is a little like parenting, a parallel one of the coauthors, JP Isson, often draws since his daughter, Roxane, was born seven years ago, around the same time he was working to implement business analytics at Monster Worldwide. Watching both children grow up has meant knowing that they're not going to be up and running without first taking tentative baby steps, and each evolution toward self-reliance is worth celebrating and reflecting. Soon enough, like Roxane on roller skates, it's even hard to keep up, but you can let go knowing that you've done enough to guide your vision to a life of its own. Of course, independence takes a little hand holding. Many groups within the organization may prove initially resistant to analytics, a fear that is most easily overcome by tying these analytics to a tangible tool. Speak in terminology that speaks to them, building on the data they probably already know: metrics on sales acquisition versus basic key performance indicators, for example, or more advanced analysis, such as cube and interactive call to action reports.

At Monster, for example, we created the Job Optimizer tool, providing our sales reps and our customers with the analytics that matters to them—and their bottom line. This solution measures the relative performance of job advertisements against industry benchmarks and actively intervenes when any given job starts performing below average—giving our end users actionable insight into what to do in clear, stark graphics that are easy to interpret but are created with data that's impossible to misinterpret.

We will cover how your analysts can extract insights from data in detail in Chapter 5, "Who Cares About Data? How to Uncover Insights." However, it is helpful now to review a framework one of the coauthors, Jesse Harriott, developed and has used for more than 15 years when training analytical staff on the path to providing insight. The acronym is IMPACT, and it's a cycle that represents the stages to high-impact analytics: Identify, Master, Provide, Action, Communicate, and Track. The core premise is a simple one: When analytical output or tools are produced by the business analytics function, you can think of several discrete stages toward having an impact with that output.

First, you must Identify your key business questions that are important to your business partner. Then there is the mastery of the facts that have been uncovered or calculated, which may be presented in the form of a raw data table, a regression equation reflecting the relationship between a few variables, or a graph or some other data visualization technique. For example, creating a model with a good fit that scores customer prospects in terms of their likelihood to convert to customers and creating visuals to accompany your model would fall under the mastery-of-facts stage. Unfortunately, all too often even highly skilled business analytics professionals stop at this stage and think they have done their job and want a pat on the back at this point. The reply should be "no." The mastery-of-facts stage is a necessary, yet not sufficient, step along the path toward insight. We are reminded of the old philosophical thought experiment: "If a tree falls in the forest, but no one is around to hear it, does it make a sound?"

Business leaders are paying your business analytics function to analyze and interpret the data for them, as well as to provide guidance on what the data are telling them regarding their businesses. Generally speaking, your internal customers have not the time, the inclination, or the skills to interpret the raw data you provide them. If you don't bridge the divide between the data and the business utility, you are making them work too hard for the data payoff, and you might as well not have made the effort to analyze the data in the first place.

This leads us to the next step in the path to high-impact insights: provide the meaning. It is crucial that data be brought together, interpreted, and put in an appropriate context for your business audience. This is often a challenge to do, because sometimes the business person is not at all data literate, and sometimes the analytics person is not at all business literate. Regardless, it is a required step in order to extract business value from your data. For example, in the case of creating a customer-scoring model, examples of providing the meaning might include that something such as this: We noticed that companies with between 10 and 50 employees respond most favorably to our e-mail campaigns when the content of those campaigns is business advice, or we noticed that companies most likely to leave us after one transaction are purchasing our low-cost product *and* do not receive a follow-up service call 20 days after their purchase.

The next step in the path to insight is action. This is often the most difficult step for the business analytics function, because it requires truly thinking about the broad needs of the business, understanding what is important to the business leaders across the organization, and learning how the organization operates. If your business analytics function has done a good job with the first pillar of the BASP framework, business challenges, then proposing actions is a bit easier. Examples of actions from our previous customer-scoring example might include a suggestion to create a monthly small business customer newsletter that includes contributed content from small business leaders or a suggestion such as to bundle complimentary product service and support with each first purchase. What we always tell our analytics teams is that the recommended actions do not need to be perfect and exactly what the business decides to do. The criterion for a successful recommended action is whether it is thought provoking and stimulates some form of business action from the business analytics exercise. Even if the business thinks the suggested action would never work for this or that reason, that's okay; it's an opportunity for the truly consultative business analytics function to probe and ask what would be a good course of action as a result of the new knowledge that has been provided.

The remaining steps of the IMPACT cycle to create high-impact analytics is to communicate and track. These are often overlooked steps, yet are a must for long-term analytical impact. Specifically, you must communicate your analytical findings and their recommended actions across the company. Certainly, this must be done with leadership cooperation and approval—however, evangelizing your work is often a step where many analytical teams fall down. The last step is to track the business outcomes of your analytical findings. What was done as a result of your work? What business impact did it have? How did it increase revenue or save costs? These are important questions to answer as you grow and refine your business analytics discipline.

EXECUTION AND MEASUREMENT PILLAR

Execution is the step where your business analytics vision becomes a reality, wowing end users through creating powerful tools that solve real business problems and needs and that lead to real business impact. When we talk about that "wow factor," we think of our first iPod and the amazing ability to transport an entire music library wherever you go. Talk about a revolution—and a moment of breathtaking realization.

For one of the coauthors, JP Isson, one of his greatest moments of execution as a business analytics professional was implementing an end-to-end Customer Lifetime Value (CLTV) during his time in the telecommunications industry. Before he implemented the CLTV, his vision was to align customer service and sales based on customers' CLTV segment score, offering premiums and incentives for the most valuable customers, knowing who they were, and scoring that value relative to the rest of our customer base.

Determined by the CLTV score, CRM activities were subsequently based on this project, but more important, he recommended providing customer service staff with a kind of premium caller ID, which showed the staff not only the customer's name and number but also his or her underlying CLTV information.

Suddenly, customer service staff could see at a glance the caller's churn risk, product offering, and segment score—information that could be acted on in real time. This is an example of execution—creating an integrated solution that leads to a business action and supports the outcomes necessary to achieve a positive impact on the entire business and drive it forward.

The second piece of the execution and measurement pillar is measurement. Peter Drucker, the famous management consultant, coined the phrase, "If you can't measure, you can't manage," and nowhere is that aphorism more applicable than in business analytics. Measurement can be a scary word, but in this case, it simply means tracking the results of the execution of your business analytics vision and initiatives.

Measurement provides a barometer that shows the real results behind your vision in action, good or bad, reflecting end user adoption and its result on the bottom line. These measurements provide a powerful and compelling argument for allocating future resources and budget and can be the difference between buy-in and bowing out.

If the business analytics implementation successfully addresses business challenges, the benefits should be tangible across the organization and measurable against a simple benchmark: where you were before your vision became a reality compared to where you are now.

Here are some elements to remember when providing the business and your customers with an accurate before-and-after analysis:

- Describe what was happening without/before the solution.
- Describe what is happening with the solution in place.
- How has the solution increased business revenue (for example, retention, acquisition, CLTV, and so on)?
- How has the solution improved business productivity (such as sales per rep, average order size, calls per service rep, customer satisfaction, and so on)?
- How satisfied are the internal customers with the solution (for example, satisfaction ratings, anecdotal quotes, and so on)?

Focusing on execution and measurement not only showcases your work but also suggests whether your mission was truly accomplished, indicates what might have been done differently, and ensures that business analytics is repeatedly showing a positive business impact.

DISTRIBUTED KNOWLEDGE PILLAR

The sixth pillar of the BASP framework is that of distributed knowledge. The core idea behind this pillar is that there must be a conscious and concerted effort to communication and disseminate as much business analytics insights and enterprise value across the organization as possible. Traditionally, analytics has taken an old-fashioned "typing pool" approach, whereby a business leader submitted a request to the analytics team for some specific information or the answer to a question. The analytics team members would go away to their secret lair and then magically appear with the data a week or two later. The person requesting the information said, "Thank you," and that was the end of the information exchange.

The distributed knowledge pillar focuses business analytics in a new direction, toward using the wisdom of the organization to create greater enterprise value from its data, as well as to propel the organization more rapidly toward the truth and away from the myths and legends of the corporate Kool-Aid. For example, there are sales people in your organization who likely know more about the competitive threats your company is under than anyone in strategy and development will ever know. Also, specialists in your product organization can quickly make sense of Web analytics data that might take a pure analyst a lot longer to interpret. This can be challenging in a command-and-control managed company, but by distributing the knowledge and the data across the organization in a thoughtful manner, you can ensure that your business analytics will have a more positive impact on the organization and will benefit from the collective wisdom within your company.

There is not only one correct way to distribute the knowledge of business analytics across the organization effectively. Unfortunately, there are many incorrect ways to do so as well. We cover various effective communication strategies and tactics in Chapter 15, "Effective Analytics Communication Strategies." In the meantime, remember these key points for distributing the knowledge of your group's business analytics activities across the enterprise:

- Follow the hub-and-spoke model of centralized data excellence, yet of distributed users.

- Designate one business "navigator" from analytics for each key customer group (for example, marketing, product, sales, and so on), who is dedicated to ongoing communication with, and can represent the needs of, that customer in business analytics activities.

- When communicating, always focus on the business impact first and on the data/information second, not the other way around.

- Communicate important information and initiatives in multiple ways, repetitively, to your key audience.

- Make well-designed data tool access as wide and broad as possible.

- Be prepared to train your business users on data tools . . . again, again, and again.

- Regularly review the usage statistics and feedback of your distributed knowledge tools in order to iterate and evolve them as the organization changes.

INNOVATION PILLAR

The last pillar in our BASP framework is innovation. Innovation sounds like common sense and is even a bit trite; however, we are continually surprised at how many business analytics functions fail in this area. It seems to be too easy for a business analytics function to fall into the trap of providing the same information to internal customers because it's what has been provided historically or because someone asked for it monthly eight months ago—yet the analyst cannot explain, specifically, whether and how the information is being used by the business today.

As a point of illustration, when we interviewed more than 100 companies regarding their business analytics practices for this book, about 85% described their analytical techniques as innovative; however, only 15% described their business analytics function as "innovative" in meeting the needs of the business. So it seems as if there may be an overemphasis on new and innovative analytical techniques, yet not enough innovation and creativity in how business analytics can help the enterprise. In our view, this is a missed opportunity and one that requires action by the business analytics community. Specifically, innovation in how we work with our business partners should be an ongoing activity. There are many ways to be innovative, and we will discuss them in more detail in Chapter 17, "Analytics and Innovation."

CONCLUSION

We believe that living by these seven pillars is key to driving business analytics success across the enterprise. Using the pillars, your solutions will inform your next business challenge and will inspire you to create a successful solution that makes a meaningful difference for your end users and your bottom line.

KEY TAKEAWAYS

- Ongoing alignment of the business analytics function with the mission and the goals of the organization is critical for success.
- Lay the data foundation for your business analytics function in a rigorous and thoughtful manner. Include a centralized and audited data governance function to ensure data reliability and validity.
- Successful analytics implementation must start with the end in mind. In other words, what is the impact you want business analytics to have on the organization? What should be the business outcome?
- Follow the IMPACT cycle to create high-impact analytical insights, putting an emphasis on being customer-focused with your analysis, as well as on answering the critical business questions directly—not merely providing data.
- It's a must for the business analytics function to communicate wide and deep into the organization. Knowledge is power, and the organization becomes more powerful as knowledge is distributed throughout its many departments.
- Challenge your business analytics team to innovate relentlessly, always thinking critically about how past activities can be done better and how the team can affect the business in new and different ways.

NOTE

1. Thomas H. Davenport and Jeanne G. Harris, *Competing on Analytics: The New Science of Winning* (Cambridge, MA: Harvard Business School Press, 2007).

CHAPTER 3

Aligning Key Business Challenges across the Enterprise

"Accept challenges, so that you may feel the exhilaration of victory!"

—George S. Patton

I n today's unstable economy, business analytics in some form has become almost ubiquitous in the corporate world. Companies doing business in highly competitive marketplaces seek to identify and harness their customer acquisition, customer retention, and customer wallet share growth strategies by leveraging analytics. Depending on their analytics maturity, they may take the business analytics road at different stages of development.

At the same time, many companies are now inundated with a large volume and velocity of data from multiple locations and sources: B2B data, B2C data, traffic data, transactional data, third-party vendor data, macroeconomic data, and so on. On top of the more traditional data sources, Web data, social media data, mobile data, and new third-party sources have added another layer of complexity to the big data puzzle that companies are eager to resolve. Although some don't even know where to start in dealing with their data avalanche, others are still struggling to move from beyond basic reporting.

This is where the process of aligning key business questions across the enterprise can help. Business analytics must prioritize its resources and activities, as well as help the overall organization get the highest return on investment for its analytical efforts. As we outlined in Chapter 2, we believe our BASP framework provides a blueprint for successfully implementing any business analytics initiative across an enterprise. The first pillar of the BASP framework is to continually identify, and gain agreement on, the critical business challenges across the organization that business analytics should address. This can be an extremely difficult task in some companies and may require a great deal of struggle, especially if you have a decentralized management structure or your corporate strategies are not well defined.

In this chapter, we explore some steps for understanding and identifying those business challenges, as well as offer tips to make the process as easy and smooth as possible. We first start with the concept of a company mission statement, then lead into company business challenges, introducing some examples of business challenges. We then discuss how to validate and prioritize those business challenges in the context of business analytics using our IRIS framework. We also review common business questions by functional group (for example, marketing, sales, product, service, finance) that can be used in your process to gain agreement across executives on critical business challenges. We then tackle the early steps of bridging the gap between the business challenge and the analytics solution by reviewing our Business Analytics Recipe Matrix, which can be a useful tool as you identify how business analytics can help the business challenges across your company.

MISSION STATEMENT

Before you tackle any business analytics initiative or project, it is imperative to understand your organization's top priorities, as well as the company's mission. A mission statement is a statement of the value proposition of a company or an organization. The mission statement guides the actions of the organization by laying out the company's goals, and it aids in decision making. It also provides the framework under which the company's strategies are formulated and is the foundation of the company's "raison d'être," or reason for existence. Peter Senge, the director of the Center for Organizational Learning at the MIT Sloan School of Management, said it best: "Mission instills the passion and patience for the long journey."[1] Your organization's mission statement is the core from which business challenges will be derived for your business analytics efforts.

Examples of Company Mission Statements

Monster Worldwide: "Inspire people to improve their lives."

Microsoft: "At Microsoft, we work to help people and businesses throughout the world realize their full potential. This is our mission. Everything we do reflects this mission and the values that make it possible."

IBM: "At IBM, we strive to lead in the invention, development and manufacture of the industry's most advanced information technologies, including computer systems, software, storage systems and microelectronics. We translate these advanced technologies into value for our customers through our professional solutions, services and consulting businesses worldwide."

Google: "Google's mission is to organize the world's information and make it universally accessible and useful."

Facebook: "Facebook's mission is to give people the power to share and make the world more open and connected."

Yahoo: "Yahoo!'s mission is to be the most essential global Internet service for consumers and businesses."

Apple: "Apple is committed to bringing the best personal computing experience to students, educators, creative professionals and consumers around the world through its innovative hardware, software and Internet offerings."

SAS: "SAS delivers proven solutions that drive innovation and improve performance."

Nike: "To bring inspiration and innovation to every athlete in the world."

Bristol-Myers Squibb Company: "To discover, develop and deliver innovative medicines that help patients prevail over serious diseases."

The aforementioned statements are the company missions from which business goals and business objectives should be derived. It's imperative for the business analytics teams to have the company mission and goals in mind and at their fingertips. Corporate business goals are usually defined and revised on at least a yearly basis, whereas the mission rarely changes. The best-managed companies remain tightly focused on their mission and deliver quality in a competitive market. To achieve that objective, companies clearly define goals and priorities that need to be addressed or solved under the mandate of the mission—these are their business challenges. And when business challenges are properly addressed, in part by the business analytics function, it will lead to the accomplishment and furthering of the organization's mission.

BUSINESS CHALLENGE

In early 1999, when one of the coauthors first joined Fido (Rogers Wireless company), the leading Canadian wireless service provider, a pressing problem at that time was the increasing customer attrition or churn and the related cost of trying to reactively save defecting customers. At that time, the company mission was to deliver a no-contract service to its customers, counting solely on quality, service, and customer loyalty to prevent subscribers from leaving to use a different wireless provider. The Fido No Contract mission was successful during its early years but later turned out to be cost prohibitive for the company, and customer profitability suffered. Fido was somehow flying blind at the time, counting on the goodwill of the subscriber base, but the increase in churn soon became obvious and evolved into the most pressing business problem. It quickly became the primary company business challenge that it was eager to address on all fronts: from service marketing sales and finance to executive leadership.

When JP Isson joined the company and met with the marketing and service teams, this was communicated as the top priority, the main business challenge the company had on its docket. Given this, JP decided that this was the right birthplace to build and put business analytics to work. We will go back to this churn project and the related cost savings from leveraging customer lifetime value models and the proactive attrition campaign in Chapter 10, "Winning with Predictive Analytics." However, the key point for now is that churn was the critical business challenge that led to the systematic investment in, and adoption of, business analytics across Fido. JP knew that any business analytics insights would be welcomed at the time and immediately put in action. As a customer behavior modeler, JP was thrilled and relished this business challenge of helping Fido reduce customer churn and increase customer loyalty and profitability.

As you can imagine, understanding the business challenge is often a powerful motivator for your business analytics team, because it helps team members understand the context of their efforts. Therefore, as a leader, you should make every effort to communicate how your analytics work ties in to the business challenges. Unfortunately, more typically, analysts are often disconnected from the strategy and the business priorities of the company. In our research of more than 100 companies for this book, 37% indicated that their business analytics function was not tightly aligned with the strategic priorities of the organization.

IDENTIFYING BUSINESS CHALLENGES AS A CONSULTATIVE PROCESS

When we hire analytical staff, we often look for prior consulting experience. This tells us that the analyst likely knows how to communicate effectively and relate to different types of business people and understands what it means to be customer-focused and a strategic business partner. Marshaling your business analytics team to identify the business challenges for your organization is often a great opportunity for your analytics function to demonstrate to the company that it can be a consultative and strategic partner with your internal customers. This will show that the team has value beyond merely analyzing data but also conveys that they understand and can relate to the overall needs of the business.

For example, in late 2009, JP Isson was invited to speak at the IDC and SAS CIO of the year event in Denmark. On his way to Copenhagen, he had a layover in Amsterdam. While in Amsterdam, he went to grab some coffee in order to stay awake during the short flight to Copenhagen. There was a line to the airport café that was known to deliver the best morning espresso, and while waiting in line, he struck up a conversation with a lady that quickly turned into business, after the common airport greetings: "Hi, how are you? Where are you heading to?" The woman's name was Amber. She started talking about work, because she was going to Copenhagen for a business meeting and soon shared her pressing objective with JP.

Amber: I am currently in charge of multinational business customers for the largest bank here in Amsterdam. I will have a pretty good 2009. I should total $12M with 15% YoY [year over year] growth.

JP: That's great!

Amber: But next year I have been asked to increase my 2009 figures by 25%; I don't know how I'm going to do that. I have been told that the economy will not be that good.

JP: Yes, 25% is quite an aggressive number in the current economic conditions.

Amber: I have a lot of good clients who renew.

JP: Do you know where your $12M is coming from? Who bought what?"

Amber: "I know we have a lot of data about our customers, but I don't really understand much of it.

Amber continued to explain that they were inundated with data but did not have an easy way to gain access to or understand it. JP then told her that it sounded as if her organization had a gold mine of banking data that could give her a comprehensive 360-degree view of her customers, and he mentioned that she should not only focus on retaining existing customers but also use the data to decide where to target and capture new opportunities. Amber's reaction was positive, but her immediate concern was, "How do you do that?" JP then articulated some basic points about how to leverage the power of business analytics to drive sales productivity.

Amber replied, "I know we have an analytics team, and they send us a lot of reports—it's just not something I have paid much attention to."

JP then replied that she should talk to the team members, tell them about her business challenge, and get answers to the following questions:

- What is the total universe of opportunity in your territory?
- What attributes describe your current customers? (New vs. existing)
- What attributes distinguish those that bought from the company from those that did not, and what are they likely to buy?
- Which customers should be top priority for retention and up-sell?

They finished up the conversation by exchanging business cards, and JP asked Amber to let him know how her 2010 sales went and her work with the bank's analytics team.

A year later, in January 2011, Amber sent JP an e-mail to share her great news. She wrote, "I made it; I was able to leverage analytics and grow by not only 25% but 32%!" She underscored, *"Without leveraging the data, I was flying blind. The four questions we discussed were addressed and gave me actionable insight to prioritize my activities."*

In this example, Amber's business challenge was to increase the sales by 25%. It was her most pressing business problem and served as an opportunity to uncover a likely common business challenge in the organization, while providing business analytics consultative value along the way. The result was a win for the business analytics function at the bank, as well as for Amber, because she was able to outpace her goal by leveraging her analytics team to win against the competition.

IDENTIFY AND PRIORITIZE BUSINESS CHALLENGES

In today's challenging business environment, professionals across all industries are being tasked with doing more with less, having limited time and resources to allocate against individual business analytics initiatives. This makes prioritization imperative and means that the first step of any business analytics implementation requires clear understanding of organizational objectives, or "business challenges," to ensure that any solution is aligned with, and addresses, the company's biggest or most pressing needs.

In order to better identify business challenges, we have provided the following list of typical business challenges. Although these business challenges are broad, many are common to all industries, sizes of companies, and geographical locations. Examples of some of the most common business challenges that business analytics may be asked to address include

- Increase market share (customer acquisition).
- Increase customer intimacy.
- Increase customer satisfaction and retention.
- Increase customer wallet share growth.
- Increase customer profitability.
- Increase traffic and conversion.
- Increase employee productivity and performance.
- Reduce cost.
- Manage and anticipate competitors and gear up for new competition.
- Increase customer loyalty.

Understanding and validating business challenge priority within your organization and aligning with your business's mission will allow you to focus your analytics expertise on the most critical challenges that will have the greatest impact for the analytics effort. Many models have been proposed over the years in order to identify and evaluate key business challenges within an organization, including MOST,[2] SWOT,[3] PESTLE,[4] 5 WHYS, and several others, all of which are beyond the focus of this book.[5] In order to capture the key activities the business analytics function must undertake to identify and align with the key business challenges, we created the IRIS Business Challenge framework for business analytics, which we explain further on.

With increasingly limited resources and time to deliver, business analytics projects and initiatives are challenged to stay current with the fast pace of business changes and new data tools. Therefore, getting a good and current understanding of your organization's top pressing business challenges is a must. As part of starting this process, it is recommended that you informally sit down with a few people who represent three of the most important customer-focused departments in your organization: sales, marketing, and customer service.

Meeting with sales, marketing, and customer service is a first step that will help you get acquainted with the critical business objectives and what is happening across your organization. Other departments must also be engaged, but sales, marketing, and customer service are often under the greatest pressure to support the organization's revenue goals and to position your organization's product and value proposition. Those groups need to be involved at the beginning of your goal to align analytics with the critical business challenges of your organization. Why meet with sales? People in this department will likely be acting on the insights provided by analytics and will give you a direct line regarding the most pressing challenges of selling into the market. Why meet with customer service? Service reps are the ears and eyes of the business and will provide unfiltered information and feedback from the customers' perspective. It is likely that customer service will use some of the analytics solutions you develop, and you may also leverage this group for proactive customer outreach for activities, such as to prevent customer attrition or to increase up-sell opportunity. Why meet with marketing? People in marketing will provide a good perspective regarding the pressing strategic customer acquisition problems, as well as on what's working or not working as a means to communicate with customers.

When you meet with key stakeholders across the organization in an effort to understand the critical business challenges, it is sometimes helpful to start your discussion with some business questions. This can start the dialogue in a positive way and help to identify information gaps that may lead to the critical business challenges, especially when departments may not be able to articulate challenges to you immediately. The following is a list of some key business questions you can use to start the conversation that will help lead to the critical business challenges:

■ Is our organization maximizing the return on investment (ROI) of our marketing spend?

■ Are our organization's products best-in-class and delivering results?

■ Is our organization hiring and retaining top talent?

■ What is our organization's financial performance?

■ Is our organization outperforming the market and our competitors?

■ Are our organization's sales reps maximized for productivity?

■ Are customers satisfied with our organization's products?

■ Is our organization providing best-in-class service?

■ What is the ROI of our tech investments?

■ Is our organization acquiring and retaining customers?

After informational meetings with some internal stakeholders, you will be armed with new knowledge on your corporate business challenges and ready to take the next steps to truly prioritize a comprehensive list of business challenges. Below we outline the four steps in our IRIS Business Challenge framework for business analytics to use as a process to go deeper in identifying the top company business challenges and as a starting point toward aligning them with your business analytics priorities and projects. If possible, begin these steps around the same time the organization as a whole is undertaking an annual strategic planning exercise and revisit the IRIS process at least annually, more often if possible.

■ Identify a senior-executive advocate/partner outside of business analytics that will sponsor or at least support your efforts to others in the organization.

■ Review any available existing strategic planning documentation in order to educate yourself and your team.

■ Interview key individual contributors in the organization from as many functional teams as possible (e.g., marketing, product, service, sales, finance, business development, HR, and so on) regarding their perspective on the top business challenges for the team and the organization as a whole. Use the list of business questions where appropriate. As a result of these interviews, create a preliminary but consolidated list of top business challenges for the company. Remember to emphasize those challenges where you think business analytics can help the most. Also, tie a hard dollar figure to any revenue improvements or cost savings associated with the challenge.

■ Socialize this preliminary list through in-person meetings with senior leaders as high as possible in the organization from as many functional teams as possible, as well as with the individual contributors you interviewed. Seek input on whether the list is accurate and reflects their understanding of the organizational challenges. Prioritize a final list based on your socialization activities, revenue impact and where analytics can do the most good. Use the final list as a basis for developing your business analytics data strategies and tool implementation plan, which you will socialize later across the organization and modify as needed.

ANALYTICS SOLUTIONS FOR BUSINESS CHALLENGES

After you create and socialize your prioritized list of business challenges, it's time to begin brainstorming and developing the business analytics plan of action you believe will lead to increased revenue and saved costs for the company. This is no simple process and will be covered in more detail throughout the book. However, as one example of tailoring a business analytics solution for a critical business challenge, let's turn to Avis.

Avis Rent a Car System, LLC, is an automotive rental company headquartered in New Jersey. Avis, Budget Rent a Car, and Budget Truck Rental are all units of Avis Budget Group, and they have rental operations in North America, Latin America, the Caribbean, India, Australia, and New Zealand. Avis is the second-largest car rental agency in the world, providing rental car services to travelers at major airports around the world.

Avis engaged a new breed of metrics-based digital ad agency, WebLiquid to help it with a key business challenge.[6] WebLiquid is a UK-based organization whose focus is on understanding clients' business goals and translating them into the metrics that make a difference to the bottom line. It is focused in this area and does not evaluate its growth in annual billings. Rather, WebLiquid charts its clients' revenue and ROI. Avis UK approached WebLiquid to help with the business challenge after it noticed that revenue had fallen dramatically year over year in the UK. Avis partnered with Web Liquid to identify the possible sources of the revenue decline and to define a strategic plan of action.

To identify the possible sources of the decline, WebLiquid undertook an extensive analysis of the travel and rental car market in the United Kingdom to ascertain whether online travel brokers were responsible for the drop in UK outbound business over the period in question, as had been suspected by some, or whether it was just a market anomaly. The study revealed that while Avis was a dominant brand in the UK online rental car market, its overall share of voice had been affected by

1. Increased consumer research via broker sites.

2. A longer consumer purchase cycle.

3. A single-minded focus on demand-meeting initiatives by Avis, as opposed to demand-generation activities.

WebLiquid presented the findings of the analysis to the board of directors, which included identifying a series of recommendations such as the launch of a demand-generation campaign aimed at leveraging the upstream and downstream traffic of broker sites and Avis.co.uk. The campaign leveraged behavioral targeting in an effort to re-target users who had visited Avis.co.uk and completed a quote check but not a reservation. The campaign generated 890 incremental outbound bookings and a considerable increase in site traffic during a three-week period.

Another example of turning a business challenge into an analytically based business solution is British Airlines, another WebLiquid customer.[7] British Airlines is a UK-based carrier airline that serves some 36 million passengers each year, making it one of the world's largest airlines. When British Airways was launching its new premium airline, OpenSkies, its business challenge for WebLiquid was to provide an integrated measurement of the online roll-out. Working with multiple stakeholders at British Airways, ranging from the finance to the marketing teams, WebLiquid began the process by identifying the key performance indicators for OpenSkies, based on British Airways' business goals. WebLiquid also plotted the offline and online consumer interaction path against key data variables and data sources. Through this initial consumer and data mapping, WebLiquid was also able to identify technical dependencies for the project. Following the consumer and data mapping, WebLiquid undertook a detailed technical cost and capability audit of all major measurement platforms. The audit was undertaken following a review of OpenSkies' technical infrastructure, including its content management system platform and customer transactional database. The findings from the analysis were put forward to all decision makers with a recommended analytics implementation road map, as well as future enhancements. The resulting solution allowed OpenSkies to have an integrated view of advertising, site, and ecommerce data on launch, which facilitated reporting and the dissemination of data across different internal teams and countries. As a result, OpenSkies was able to quickly identify and capitalize on the levers that led to a successful launch.

When you are thinking about how to translate your own business challenges into successful analytics solutions, whether they be tools or metrics, we think it is important to have some guiding principles. Toward that end, we have adapted 'Doran's original SMART model toward something more appropriate for business analytics.[8] By SMART, we mean an analytics solution that is

Specific: Having a clear mandate and goal, defined by clear expected benefits.

Measurable: We can easily track performance.

Aggressive and Actionable: A solution that could be quickly put into the organization and that leads to clear action.

Realistic: A solution that avoids overpromising or overestimating the value added of the outcome.

Time bounded. The solution should have a clear time line to deliver the business benefit to the organization.

With this framework in mind, our recommendation based on experience and research is to address each business challenge following a baby-steps, or incremental, approach. A baby-steps approach enables a smooth path to be set up, to better manage adoption and track the performance of the analytics solution along the way, without overpromising results to the business. As Kouzes and Posner mentioned in their book *The Leadership Challenge*, "Major change is a process of small wins."[9] We believe business analytics should be successfully implemented through realistic baby steps based on your organization and data circumstances.

To spur your thinking, in the following section we provide an Analytics Recipe Matrix. It is a table that illustrates examples of possible business analytics solutions for typical business challenges. By no means is this a comprehensive list; it is merely a tool to get your teams started on the creative process of designing analytics solutions from the business challenges that will have the greatest business benefit.

Analytics Recipe Matrix

Business Challenge	Analytics Solutions	Benefits
Acquire new customers.	Target Response Model	Bring in more customers for the same costs.
Retain your profitable customers.	Customer Churn/At Risk Model	Increase customer wallet share and overall profitability.
Up-sell and cross new and existing customers.	Customer Lifetime Value Model	Identify long-term profitability.
Avoid high-risk customers.	Risk and Approval Model	Identify credit risk among credit applicants. Detect and minimize the effect of fraudulent claims or transactions.
Increase sales.	Acquisition Up-Sell and Retention Models	Increase market share and customer profitability.
Win back your lost customers.	Win Back Models	Increase sales and profitability.

Business Challenge	Analytics Solutions	Benefits
Increase customer satisfaction.	Market Research and Customer-Profiling Models	Deepen your understanding of current and prospective customers through survey research.
Recruit new talent cost effectively.	Predictive HR Analytics Model	Talent and personnel management.
Increase employee retention.	Employee Satisfaction Survey and Predictive HR Analytics	Manage personnel turnover and retain valuable talent.
Increase conversion.	Seeker and Visitors Segmentation	Increase the usability and strategic value of your Web properties.
Expand in new markets.	Global Acquisition Model	Global footprint diversification of revenue.
Understand the characteristics of your customers.	Customer Profiling and Customer Segmentation	Improve customer profitability and CRM optimization.
Manage and anticipate competitors and gear up for competition coming from uncharted territories.	Proactive Competitive Intelligence Analytics	Win against the competition.
Streamline your pricing.	Pricing Optimization Models	Increase revenue and gross margin.

In the upcoming chapters, we will cover analytics solutions for specific business challenges in detail. We will also provide examples of how forward-looking companies have been successful in leading with analytics and how their actions illustrate the BASP framework and how it can help your organization win with business analytics.

KEY TAKEAWAYS

- In this chapter, we've underscored that business challenges are the starting point of implementing any business analytics solution. Ironically, analytics are often not aligned with the corporate priorities or business challenges.

- Before starting any analytics initiative, you must define your analytics road map by identifying the most critical business challenges across the enterprise. In other words, those business challenges where overcoming them will result in either incremental revenue or cost savings and where analytics can have the greatest potential impact.

- Listing every business challenge across the company can be overwhelming. We recommend you follow the IRIS framework to ruthlessly prioritize the most critical challenges that analytics will address. Execute this process regularly, ideally within the same cycle, as your corporate strategic planning.

- We also recommend providing SMART business analytics solutions to address your business challenges following a baby-steps, or incremental, approach. This should help underscore the value of the analytics solution to the business without over-promising.

- Finally, we provided an Analytics Recipe Matrix that includes most common business challenges, with examples of underlying analytics solutions. Use this matrix to develop your own list of business challenges and analytics solutions that can be socialized throughout your company.

NOTES

1. Peter Senge, "The Practice of Innovation," *Leader to Leader*, 9 (1998): 16–22. doi: 10.1002/ltl.40619980907.

2. Strategy Consulting Ltd., "Exploring Corporate Strategy Using M.O.S.T. Analysis."

3. Albert Humphreys, Presentation at the Seminar in Long Range Planning, Zurich, Switzerland, 1964.

4. Chartered Institute of Personnel and Development, PESTLE analysis history and application, http://www.cipd.co.uk/hr-resources/factsheets/pestle-analysis.aspx.

5. Taiichi Ohno, *Toyota Production System: Beyond Large-Scale Production* (Portland, OR: Productivity Press, 1988).

6. WebLiquid Group, "Avis Europe: Delivering ROI Across 11 European Countries," online case study, http://www.webliquidgroup.com/index.php?id=91, accessed March 2012.

7. WebLiquid Group, "British Airways OpenSkies: Launching a New Airline," online case study, http://www.webliquidgroup.com/index.php?id=81, accessed March 2012.

8. G. T. Doran, "There's a S.M.A.R.T. Way to Write Management's Goals and Objectives," *Management Review* (AMA Forum), 70(11) (1981): 35–36.

9. James M. Kouzes and Barry Z. Posner, *The Leadership Challenge*, 4th ed. (San Francisco, Jossey-Bass), 2007.

CHAPTER **4**

Big and Little Data

Different Types of Intelligence

> *"Sometimes too much to drink is barely enough."*
>
> —Mark Twain

I t's amazing how the amount of data to analyze has grown so dramatically during the last 20 years. We remember the days before the Web, before big data, before social media, and before mobile, when an annual customer survey, a customer database with basic information, retail purchasing data from a third party, or credit reporting information was about as rich or as detailed as the data would be that a company hoped to analyze. Back then, it was possible to build a nice information-based business from something as simple as conducting regular benchmark surveys and selling the results to companies. At that time, companies were flying by on less information than they needed, and there was simply no flow of deep customer, competitor, and industry information compared to what exists today. Gut feel, or instinct, was a prized business characteristic, and it, rather than data, drove many corporate leadership decisions.

Compare that to today, where now almost every aspect of life can be tracked in one way or another by someone, whether it be data from

Web behavior, mobile phone usage patterns, in-store shopping activity, public surveillance videos, GPS tracking data, automotive driving patterns, physical fitness data, social media data, satellite imagery, video streams, or car telematic data, and the list goes on and on. As a result, data are the business focus "du jour." Companies now all say they are "data-driven" and make only quantitatively based business decisions. Yet companies are now also overwhelmed by the data that lie in front of them—the data at their disposal to analyze against critical business questions. The issue today is not the lack of data, but rather how to prioritize, gain access to, and use the deluge of data in real time to achieve the greatest impact on the business. As a result, an entire industry of technology and business people see the challenges and are working hard to enable deeper and faster data access. For example, Joe Dalton, the CMO of MarkLogic, an enterprise database provider in Silicon Valley, said, "If you took a snapshot of the information that was being processed 30 years ago and a snapshot of the information that needs to be processed today, you'd have two very different pictures. Today's information is in a variety of formats, it's more complex, and it's coming from a multitude of sources, inside and outside of the enterprise."[1]

Add to this avalanche of information the fact that the analyst firm Gartner predicts data will grow 800% during the next five years, 80% of which will be unstructured data. Gartner analyzed the historic trend of the explosion of available data and concluded that the volume of data generated only in 2009 was greater than in the preceding 5,000 years combined.[2] Another perspective comes from IDC, which estimated that the volume of data is growing at 50% a year and more than doubles every two years. IDC predicts that digital content volume will balloon by 2.7 zettabytes in 2012—a 48% boost over 2011 levels.[3] A zettabyte is a trillion gigabytes. For a little perspective, that would be the data produced if every person in the world received 215 million high-resolution MRI scans per day, or the amount of data needed to fill 57.5 billion 32GB Apple iPads. That many iPads would create a wall of iPads 4,005 miles long and 61 feet high extending from Anchorage, Alaska, to Miami, Florida.

Along with the proliferation of data, you have the increasing diversity of data sources and types that an enterprise needs to analyze.

As a result, one of the trends in information management is the blurring of traditional lines regarding where specific data reside and the business owners of different data types. Traditionally, and it is still the case in many companies, different data are scattered across the enterprise. For example, marketing campaign data may be contained only in the marketing department, customer service metrics and feedback are managed and maintained only in the service department, historic customer spend data are maintained in finance, and so on, and so forth. As a result, getting data to inform strategic decisions that cut across departments and data sources can sometimes be a painful process for executives. In addition, in the silo organizational approach, typically data assets are managed by a more junior staff leader who is focused primarily on his or her specific data asset and on his or her department objectives. For example, the sales operations data on sales representative productivity, talk time, and other sales metrics may be managed by a metrics professional or a small team in sales with 5 to 10 years of experience in a sales operations or metrics capacity. That person is typically focused on how sales teams operate, function, and thrive. This can be a successful approach for some issues; however, typically the sales operations data are used for tactical sales decisions at the manager level and do not regularly and often make their way to executive leadership to help with such strategic company issues as sales force optimization, cost of sales compared to the industry norms, employee productivity and morale, and market prioritization.

Furthermore, as a result of a silo data approach, data integrity, standards, and quality will often vary greatly across the organization, with one data type very well managed and other data types poorly managed. For example, customer feedback data may be very well organized and accessible, with high standards of quality, whereas website analytical data are not. Therefore, when a business question involves the merging or bringing together of these two data sources, the company can suffer delays and inabilities to answer certain questions that cost the company money or result in missed opportunities.

As a result, many of the most progressive companies are rethinking their data and information strategies and trying to consolidate their data assets. As an example, one of the coauthors, Jesse Harriott, conceived and created an integrated data and research function at Monster in 2002, years before it was more widely accepted or practiced. At the time of joining Monster Worldwide in 2002, Jesse immediately realized that Monster had massive amounts of valuable big data, from information such as the site behavior it captured as a high-engagement website with millions of monthly visitors to the flow of supply-and-demand labor market data it captured in the hundreds of millions of job searches each month to the millions of employer customer records it contained, to the unstructured customer feedback it tracked—among other data. At the time, however, information was scattered across the company, contained in disparate systems, managed by different people, and kept to different quality standards. As a result, getting answers to business questions took much longer than needed. Jesse proposed creating a center of research and data excellence with close ties into other departments globally across Monster. It took time and great effort by multiple people across Monster, including the other coauthor, JP Isson, but eventually the global Monster insights team became a well-respected and crucial team at Monster, helping enable big data successes in global sales, marketing, product, customer service, finance, investor relations, business development, and for Monster customers over the years. It helped enable faster decision making across the company and positioned Monster's big data assets as premiere in the minds of Monster customers.

When Jesse formed the global insights team, he had a strong emphasis on data quality, in terms of both reliability and validity. As a result, Jesse created a formal Data Governance Team as part of insights organization, whereby consistent data standards were put in place for business and technical data definitions, along with regular data audits and security issues that were addressed. This was essential in helping the company scale and effectively leverage its data assets to make decisions in real time.

As we have mentioned, a key theme of this book is the integration of previously distinct information types and analytics in order to answer critical business questions for the enterprise. For example, it has been a corporate tradition to have Web analytics analyzing the "what" of site behavior in one department, customer feedback analyzing the "why" of customer attitudes in a separate department, and competitive intelligence in yet another department analyzing market dynamics. Rarely did these departments work closely together; however, the avalanche of available data types during the last few years and the ubiquity of data use across organizational departments has resulted in the need to synthesize disparate data sources into a unified view of customer and market forces. Analytics vendors have foreseen this trend and now offer analytical services that blur the lines between disciplines such as customer analytics, Web behavior, and competitive intelligence.

For example, Keynote Systems, a global leader in Internet and mobile cloud testing and monitoring, has developed a customer experience measurement methodology that integrates data such as customer feedback, click-stream data from Web behavior, and competitor performance information to understand which factors will drive a desired site behavior, such as making a purchase or opening an account. According to Chris Musto, the general manager for Keynote's Competitive Research Group, their methodology answers questions such as

- Which sites are most effective at generating positive brand perceptions and increasing the likelihood of acquiring a customer?
- What aspects of the online experience predict brand affinity and customer acquisition?
- Which are the leading sites in the category, and why?
- What are the opportunities to improve the effectiveness of the experience on its site?

According to Chris Musto, the goal of the Keynote methodology is "to assess the entire online experience in practical terms in order to focus companies on those aspects that will drive their desired outcomes." To do this, Musto and his team track online users as they complete tasks on multiple sites in a category (for example, credit cards, travel, and so on), asking questions along the way, as well as analyzing their comments and feedback. Out of all of these data, Keynote uses principal components analysis to understand which factors are most important to drive behavior and brand preference, as well as to compare sites to one another along several indices, such as a Brand Impact Index, an Acquisition Impact Index, an Online Adoption Index, and a Customer Satisfaction

Index. Keynote makes recommendations from data on more than 80 dimensions, identifying the elements that drive the desired user behaviors for each site, such as opening an account or making a travel reservation. According to Musto, these recommendations provide "tangible elements the company can change to directly improve the key performance indicators of their site, and as a result, grow their business."

Throughout this chapter, we will introduce different types of data that can be commonly found across the enterprise that you may consider integrating in one form or another into your business analytics efforts. For some of you, this may mean the establishment of a formal data function; for others, it may mean a decentralized approach to the business management of data assets. Whatever your ultimate approach, we will provide a perspective that will help you think about your data assets and make the right decisions for your organization, as well as illustrate what some leading companies are doing to deal with these issues. For many of the information types reviewed in this chapter, we also provide greater detail later in the book. Certain chapters are dedicated to a specific information type, such as competitive intelligence, Web analytics, customer profile information, social media analytics, and customer feedback, to name a few. In this chapter, we will also provide steps to help you achieve data governance success so you can improve your own data-management practices.

As a starting point and to provide some context, we would like to review a Customer Knowledge Framework (CKF) created by Jesse Harriott in 2000 while he served as the leader of the Gomez Advisors consulting practice, an early ecommerce firm that helped many successful Internet companies in their early days, such as Orbitz, Yahoo, and WebMD. The model ascribes that an organization's data and business analytics strategy must put the customer at the center and must consider all of the different factors, direct and indirect, that may influence a customer's use (or nonuse) of your product or service. Only after you create an information strategy that captures ongoing intelligence and understanding for each of these factors can you truly build a strong operational practice that strives to strengthen the customer relationship and customer loyalty and drives maximum customer lifetime value. The framework, presented in Exhibit 4.1, includes three

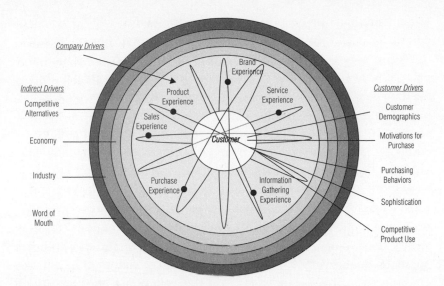

Exhibit 4.1 Customer Knowledge Framework

major components: customer drivers, company drivers, and indirect drivers. We will review this framework in subsequent chapters, but it will be helpful to keep it in mind as you read this chapter.

BIG DATA

Big data is the hottest catchphrase to hit the tech and Internet world since *social*. So, what does it mean? *Big data* tends to be a broad and overused term that is varied and ill-defined when you actually ask people to explain what it means to them. Some people define it as Web data; others define it as a large data set that cannot be handled by traditional database software; still others define it as data that flows in real time. All definitions have their weaknesses, but we like one promoted by IBM that asserts that big data has volume, velocity, and variety.[4] Although we can argue with some aspects of this definition, it's a helpful way to think about and understand how big data may differ from other data sources and how you need to think about it differently.

Volume is the attribute most people mention when they think about big data. The idea here is that you are dealing in large quantities of data, usually larger than a normal person can get his or her head around or that can be processed using traditional tools. The exact criteria for what is considered large volume is a moving target, because the technology is improving so rapidly that yesterday's large-volume data set is today's typical-size data set. Monster Worldwide has always dealt in very high-volume data. For example, each month the site has tens of millions of people engaging in career development and job search activities, with more than five million job searches conducted each day. This type of activity creates unimaginable flows of data volume. The main appeal in using larger volumes of data is that it allows you to predict behavior using statistical models with much more accuracy than smaller volumes of data would allow. However, volume presents unique challenges of its own to many conventional IT tools and systems. Data volume calls for scalable storage and a distributed approach to querying. It's more common for companies to have large amounts of archived data stores, but they often lack the capacity to process it effectively. Companies that can process large volumes of data rely on more than conventional relational database infrastructures. They sometimes rely on parallel data processing architectures such as Hadoop. Hadoop is a platform for distributing computing problems across a number of servers; it was first developed and released as open source software by Yahoo. It implements the MapReduce approach pioneered by Google in compiling its search indexes and involves three steps. The first step is the "map" stage, which is where data are distributed among multiple servers and compiled. The partial results are then recombined in what is known as the "reduce" step, in order to simplify the data. The last step is the "retrieval" step, in which the data models are retrieved from the Hadoop file system and used. For example, Hadoop is one of the tools Facebook uses to be able to personalize its site experience for you.

The second element of the definition put forth by IBM is that big data has velocity. Velocity simply means that data have an ongoing flow and a fast speed coming into your organization, which is sometimes referred to as "streaming." Unfortunately, as the volume of data has increased dramatically across the enterprise, so has velocity. This is primarily due to the growth of the Internet and mobile usage, such that data are flowing 24/7, every day of the year. Therefore, if you are an Internet company, your data architecture and tools must accommodate the processing of high data velocity and volume all the time, nonstop. As a result, companies such as online retailers are able to compile large histories of customers' every click and interaction, not only the final sales. Successful companies are able to use that information in real time by recommending additional products and services. For example, Walmart began using a 10-node Hadoop cluster as a way to analyze the online shopping experience and to make it more personal. It worked so well for Walmart that it is moving to consolidate ten different data processing platforms into one 250-node Hadoop cluster to deal with the increased streams of data it needs to process in order to create the strongest possible online customer experience.[5]

The third important concept to consider in big data is variety. In today's complex world of multiple points of customer interaction and data streams, data come in a standardized form and are ready for processing. Given this, a common theme in big data systems is that the data sources and formats are widely diverse and don't fall into consistent structures that can be easily used by a company for processing or analysis. Examples of the variety of big data flows with high volume and velocity might include customer comments on a social media website, search terms on a website, click-stream data from an online shopping experience, location data from GPS or wifi tracking, and image or video uploads, among others. The main advancement in the data management world related to the principle of "variety" in big data is that traditional structured data are now able to be joined with semistructured and unstructured data. In big data, variety is just as important as volume and velocity. Put all three of those concepts together (volume, velocity, and variety), and you start to understand the challenges and opportunities of big data.

To provide an example regarding the evolution of organizations using a wider variety of different types of data, both big and little, take the telecommunications industry. Traditionally, the telecommunications industry would leverage three major dimensions of customer data when doing customer segmentation and predictive modeling. However, as we can see from Exhibit 4.2, telecommunications has moved to more than eight dimensions as the behavioral environment and the tools available have changed and evolved. With that change of the customer ecosystem in telecommunication, companies realized that they needed

Current Customer Data	Customer Data Before

Interaction
   In person (point of sales)
   Voice (over the phone)
   E-mail
   Internet
   Social media
   Smartphone
	Interaction
	   In person (point of sales)
	   Voice (over the phone)

Preferences
   Build up landing page
   Newsletter
   Choice
	Preferences

Feedback
   In person
   Customer service rep
   E-mail
   Social network
	Feedback
	   In person
	   Customer services rep

Site Behavior
   Page view
   Landing page
   Visit duration
   Exit page
   Ecom orders
   Number of visits
	Site Behavior

Social Media	Social Media
Services	Services

Usage
   Voice
   Data
   Video/pictures
   Text
   Internet	

Exhibit 4.2 Customer Data Sources, Telecommunications

to adapt if they wanted to keep, protect, and capture new customers. The ecosystem moved from customer services plan usage data to Web interaction, preferences, feedback, social media, and buying behavior, among others. Telecommunication companies also quickly realized that they needed to listen to what customers were saying about their brand, their product, and their services, even when customers were not communicating directly with the company. Companies also understand that they need to capture, collect, and keep more historical information about their customers' feedback and sentiments—and, more important, proactively act fast on that intelligence.

Although there is a great deal of excitement about analytics and big data and their potential to deliver a complete understanding of each customer, companies are still trying to figure out many organizational challenges. For example, joint research between Columbia Business School's Center on Global Brand Leadership and the New York American Marketing Association (NYAMA) found that organizational hurdles and barriers to data implementation were some of the biggest challenges to leveraging big data.[6] More than half (51%) of the companies studied said their biggest big data challenge was the lack of sharing of data among company departments. Furthermore, 42% said it was still too difficult to tie data back to individual customers, and 39% reported difficulty in collecting customer data fast enough. Without the ability to fully leverage different types of data in an integrated and effective manner through business analytics, some companies will continue to falter, resulting in poor customer experiences and lost customers, at the expense of companies that are able to succeed in advanced analytics. The companies that first succeed in using business analytics will eventually have a clear edge over companies that are unable to tie information to action.

LITTLE DATA

Little data is our term for anything not considered big data. Although big data is in vogue, little data sources are just as crucial for successful business analytics and answering the critical business questions. If we refer back to Exhibit 4.1 and our Customer Knowledge Model, we can see very quickly that multiple "little data" sources and types are required for a company to operate business analytics in a customer-centered manner. For example, the voice of the customer feedback is a must for understanding the attitudes of your customers, monitoring industry and market developments is essential for you to understand the context under which your customers make their buying decisions, and analyzing customer demographics and buying patterns is key for segmentation and predictive modeling. The trend in many companies that successfully leverage business analytics is the integration of different types of data across the enterprise. To this end, expect that as you lead with business analytics, you may need to understand and integrate unfamiliar data sources and types in order to have the most positive impact on your organization.

As you begin to take stock of the data across your enterprise, it's important to outline the different types of data ("big" and "little") that are needed to address your chief business objectives. As a way to spur your thinking, in the next exhibit we briefly outline some of the data types you might consider making part of your business analytics efforts. We go into many of these in more detail throughout the book.

LAYING THE DATA FOUNDATION: DATA QUALITY

Data are the most important raw material for building and implementing successful analytics solutions. A Gartner research report on Customer Data Quality and Integration claimed: "CRM solutions are good as the quality of the customer data that feeds it."[7] In the previous chapter, you learned about the importance of clearly defining and developing your critical business objectives across the enterprise. Now you need to start constructing the data foundation. Like fine residential architecture, the strength of your business analytics solution will depend on the strength of its foundation. And similar to architects, business analytics practitioners must engineer a data foundation that's built to last. Rem Koolhass, a famous architect, often reiterates, "It's not about form or function, it's about performance." This applies not only to residential architecture but also to business analytics. Whether your business objective with business analytics is to increase customer retention, identify new markets to penetrate, grow market share, develop new and successful products, or achieve some other purpose, data remains the foundation of your business analytics solutions.

Because data are the starting point of any business analytics solution, the quality and quantity will ultimately reflect the quality and quantity of your business analytics effectiveness and insights.

Consequently, the success of business analytics depends mostly on the quality and quantity of data that are available for utilization. As an old adage says, "Garbage in, garbage out." The lack of accurate or valid data will likely lead to bad business decisions and will definitely undermine your business analytics efforts.

Let's review two examples to illustrate how bad data could lead to undesirable decisions and outcomes. The first example is regarding an e-mail campaign execution and the second is related to a survey that attempted to predict a presidential election in United States. Regarding the first example, one of the authors, JP Isson, remembers this e-mail campaign execution as if it were yesterday, thought it happened nearly 20 years ago, at the beginning of his career. We all know that aggressive sales retention strategies are usually directed only toward customers we believe are likely to leave, because they typically involve steep price discounts that may cost the company money in the short term, in the hopes of recovering that money during the course of a lifetime for customers who decide to stay. Unfortunately, a CRM manager with very good intentions mistakenly sent a proactive retention e-mail campaign with an aggressive pricing discount to *all* existing customers, including those who were *not* likely to churn. This happened as a result of the CRM manager using the wrong field for selecting his customer list. Because the CRM manager did not understand the data, it led to events that had serious consequences for the company's profits. The undesirable outcome of that campaign sent a very bad message to customers—that pricing differs for various categories of customers—and made many feel as if they had not been getting a fair price in the past. That campaign led to a mass customer reaction and resulted in many customers turning to the competition; the damage was huge.

This next example comes from historical market research. The 1936 presidential election was an important race. It not only shaped the nation's political future, but it also shaped the future of opinion polls. The *Literary Digest*, a prestigious and well-respected magazine of the time, had correctly predicted the outcomes of the 1916, 1920, 1924, 1928, and 1932 elections through its use of polls. These polls were an important audience draw for the *Digest*, the results of which were promoted heavily in other media of the time. In 1936, the *Digest* used the responses of more than two million returned postcards to predict that Landon would beat

Roosevelt with 57% of the vote.[8] However, the actual result of the election was that Roosevelt won by a big margin: 62% to 38%.

Why was the *Literary Digest* so wrong? It seems like common sense to us today that it was likely a sampling bias issue. Yet although the *Digest* had been in the business of predicting elections for many years, the magazine never took the time to critically evaluate its own biases. As in years prior to 1936, the *Digest* based its prediction on a sample universe of 10 million people, with about 2 million responses to the mailed questionnaire that was sent. The names and addresses of these people who responded to the survey came from lists that included telephone books and automobile club membership, in addition to the magazine's own list of subscribers, who fared well enough to subscribe to the magazine during the Depression years. Therefore, the sample had a strong bias against the poor, because they were unlikely to belong to clubs or to have phones or to subscribe to the magazine.

The outcome of the election showed a split that followed clear economic lines: the poor voted for Roosevelt, and the rich were with Landon. The second bias was regarding the nonresponse, with only 24% of those surveyed responding—the magazine assumed that the nonresponders had the same voting pattern as the survey responders. These two main sources of bias (selection bias and nonresponse bias) and the resulting public relations debacle eventually led to the demise of the *Digest*.

With the aforementioned examples, we can see that the lack of knowledge about the data quality or how the data are collected and analyzed can lead to undesirable decisions, predictions, and outcomes. We can also see with those simple examples that the data foundation is the heart of business analytics. Our goal in this book is to provide you with the best practices that you need to consider before using the data. For those wishing to get additional and broader information on data management, there are several books that cover the topic, but we also recommend that you look into some business intelligence maturity models. Maturity models are covered by Gartner, TDWI (The Data Warehousing Institute) and SAS. Those maturity models offer additional perspectives on how data should be organized and managed effectively.

We have underscored the importance of data, both little and big. Now we turn more specifically to the following concepts as you lay your data foundation:

1. Data sources and locations

2. Data definition and governance

3. Data dictionary

4. Data visualization sanity checklist

5. Customer data integration

6. Data privacy

DATA SOURCES AND LOCATIONS

The simplest way to think about the data you will use for business analytics is that the data will be from either an internal or an external source. Look at Exhibit 4.3 and the sample types of data you might use, and it becomes fairly clear which would be considered internal

Web traffic	Mobile traffic	Sales operations data (talk time, number of calls, performance by rep, etc.)
Customer loyalty	Market share and wallet share	Web search keywords
Website satisfaction	Competitive intelligence	E-mail open rate and conversion
Product performance	New and returning customers: # and $	Product satisfaction
Sales	Economic trends	Market size/opportunity
Win-loss by channel	Customer focus group results	Media mentions/sentiment
Brand awareness and equity	Customer lifetime value	Revenue
Website and product usability metrics	Advertising copy testing	Concept test results
Customer demographics	Satisfaction with service	Employee satisfaction
Media mix performance data	Customer survey data	Shopping behavior data
HR metrics (turnover, exit interviews, etc.)	Customer e-mails and call transcripts	Customer satisfaction with competitors' products

Exhibit 4.3 Example of Data That Can Be Valuable for Business Analytics

(compiled from inside your company) and which would be considered external (compiled from outside of your company). Most internal data are inherent to an organization or derived from its infrastructure. For example, enterprise data warehouse, CRM history, orders management and billing systems that include Web data or transactional data would be examples of internal data. External data, in contrast, can be purchased from outside vendors and can include information such as

- **Firmographic:** For example, Dun and Bradstreet, Experian, Axcion, Info USA, Info Canada, Jigsaw.
- **Macroeconomic:** For example, US Census, BLS, StatsCan, Eurostats, IMF and, APAC.
- **Audience and survey data:** For example, BBM/Infosys, PMB, Comscore, AC Nielsen, Ipsos.
- **Psychographic or demographic data:** For example, Claritas, Environics, GenFive Info US.
- **Financial:** For example, Equifax, Trans Union (very useful for business to consumer businesses predicting churn or risk management).

What's crucial for you to do as a first step in laying your data foundation for business analytics is to take a thorough inventory of the types of data available to you, both in your organization and outside your organization. This inventory can be done before you gain consensus on your critical business objectives; however, doing so after you have an understanding of your objectives will be more productive.

CASE STUDY

HEALTH CARE: MEDICAL DEFENSE ORGANIZATION, CMPA

The Canadian Medical Protective Association (CMPA) is a not-for-profit mutual defense organization that provides its physician members with medico-legal advice, risk management education, and legal assistance related to their clinical practice.

The CMPA database is a centralized administrative database that contains extensive data collected during its 100-year history, which provides a unique

Canadian repository of information about medico-legal difficulties. Over the years, the aims of the data-capture activities have evolved from membership and claims management support to a broader risk management and education mandate. These mandates contribute to efforts toward developing a safer medical practice in Canada.

Business Challenges

The main challenge in using advanced analytics in a medical defense organization resides in the complexity of the data collected. The capture of the health-care episodes that are the subject of the claims is called medical coding. Medical coding involves the review of a medico-legal event and the assignment of industry-standard diagnostic, procedural, and contributing factors codes that depict the event.

Adverse events found in claims can take place over several days, months, and perhaps even years, across multiple care episodes, and can involve multiple health-care providers and sometimes multiple patients. The objective of medical coding is to identify who was involved, what happened, when it happened, how it happened, and what was the outcome. Medical coding allows the identification and capture of all fail-safe issues and contributing factors, which, if properly analyzed and disseminated, can help prevent or mitigate future adverse events.

Solution: Data Capture

This first challenge the CMPA faced was to develop an appropriate approach to capture medical events in a "cause and effect" manner.

To achieve this, we developed the Sequencing Graphical Interface (SGI) application to graphically depict medical adverse events and electronically capture the relationships between event components into our medico-legal claims database. Interfaced with a commercial encoder for medical coding, the SGI draws on the *International Statistical Classification of Diseases and Related Health Problems, Tenth Revision, Canada (ICD-10-CA)*, and the *Canadian Classification of Health Interventions (CCI)*, and an in-house taxonomy describing the adverse events' contributing factors. Contributing factors include fail-safe issues in diagnostic, performance, medication, administrative, and communication areas. The pictograms and the structured data that are generated using the SGI represent the clinical states of a patient during the care episodes and the contributing factors as reported in the

(continued)

claims documentation. The structured data that are created enable pattern searches across all adverse events within our database.

Solution: Pattern Detection

Our focus is to uncover which combination of adverse event components led to the patient's adverse outcome. We call this process pattern detection. Pattern detection is in fact a data-mining process, enabling the identification of common factors that contributed to several adverse events. Pattern detection may be based on a relatively small number of variables, representing the patient's condition and the treatment provided during the care episodes. More specifically, patterns based on a patient's underlying presenting conditions, comorbidities, interventions performed, complications, and intervening critical incidents (performance, diagnosis, etc.) can be found. An adverse event may be characterized as a combination of diagnoses and interventions occurring in the presence of one or more critical incidents and resulting in complications with varying degrees of patient disabilities.

Using commercial statistical software, the data-mining process identifies potential adverse event patterns from common event component combinations. From these patterns, the researcher can drill down into the individual cases that exhibit the patterns. Aggregated statistics of the cases within patterns (profiling), comparison between patterns, and other predictive risk analyses (impact of risk patterns or relative risks) can then be performed.

Benefits

On examining these risk patterns, clinical experts can develop risk-management strategies and educational programs to promote safer medical care.

References

Canadian Institute for Health Information, *ICD-10-CA/CCI—International Statistical Classification of Diseases and Related Health Problems, Tenth Revision, Canada (ICD-10-CA) / Canadian Classification of Health Interventions (CCI)* [CD-ROM] (Ottawa: Canadian Institute for Health Information, 2009).

E. Amyot, P. J. Finestone, Yin Bin, Julie Milton, and Ho Tuan, *Adverse Event Analysis: Pattern Detection*, (Union of Risk Management for Preventive Medicine, 2008 [2]).

Source: Contributed by Elise Amyot, director of research at the Canadian Medical Protective Association.

Outlining the location of the various internal data elements is the next important step in your quest for effective business analytics. It is imperative to document clearly where your data are located so that it will be integrated readily into subsequent analyses. The most common locations include

- Legacy systems
- Operational data stores
- Data warehouses
- Data marts
- Excel files
- Word processing documents
- Tapes
- CDs
- Videos (for example, focus group or customer interview videos)

One of the authors, JP Isson, remembers when he started working for Monster in Canada several years ago, and the company executed a very successful viral marketing campaign called "Rate Your Boss," whereby a tool was created to capture feedback on how workers perceive their bosses and provide industry benchmarks from those ratings. This analytics-based marketing campaign was so successful that it won an award from the Canadian Marketing Association. Ironically, for what ended up being such a successful campaign, the marketing VP (Louis Gagnon) handed JP a CD with the data and asked him to try to figure out "What can we get from that?" (Yes, his data was an online survey on a CD.) "Rate Your Boss" ended up being an exceptionally creative viral campaign that really gained the attention of Canadian employees and employers everywhere, and from data on a simple CD came a CMA award.

DATA DEFINITION AND GOVERNANCE

It's crucial to have standard definitions, both technical and business, for the data you use for business analytics. Your business analytics work will flow across the organization, and the lack of a consistent and common data definition will undermine the credibility of your team's work. For example, let's say your team conducts a well-thought-out and thorough analysis of customer retention by industry segment in an effort to identify industries that needed additional attention, and as part of that analysis, you calculate the average customer retention rate. You give the analysis to executive leaders, and they are thrilled and impressed with the insights. Yet two days later, the findings are being discussed with a junior analyst within the sales operations function, and she indicates that the customer retention rate you provided is wrong, compared to the data that have been reported each month for the last few years. This is not due to an error on your part, because you simply used a slightly different definition than the sales organization did. As a result, however, the executive team now looks at your entire study with skepticism. This is an all-too-common situation of "throwing the baby out with the bath water" that could be avoided if technical and business definitions had been standardized.

Keep in mind that sometimes even the simplest data definition questions will result in your receiving conflicting responses, depending on whether you talk to someone in marketing, sales, finance, or customer service. Without a shared definition, an organization and its departments will make decisions, sometimes different decisions, in silos. In fact, even many companies with well-implemented or advanced analytics struggle to speak the same language. When one of the authors, JP Isson, was in the telecommunications industry, he remembers asking a simple question soon after he started with the company: "How many customers do we have?" Guess what? He got four different answers from four cross-functional groups:

1. For marketing employees, customers meant the number of clients in the universe where they could send marketing campaigns.

2. For people in sales, it meant the number of customers they have sold to during the last 12 months.

3. For services, it meant the number of clients they have in the pipeline to serve.

4. For people in finance, customers were simply clients they have billed.

This "simple" issue of getting a common definition for a "customer" can be a challenge and could become even more complicated for a company with a global footprint operating in multiple countries. In these global companies, cultural differences, more departments, and other ways of doing business could widen the definition gap.

Given this, it's then important for you to keep the information chain as flawless as possible across the company. It's essential to have people speak and mean the same data language. To achieve this, we recommend putting in place corporate definitions that everyone can use and become aware of. We recommend doing this through a formal data governance function/team. The data governance function should reinforce the compliance of data utilization for business analytics across the organization.

Data governance is an emerging discipline with an evolving definition. The discipline embodies a convergence of data quality, data management, data policies, business process management, and risk management surrounding the handling of data across your organization. Through data governance, organizations are looking to exercise positive control over the processes and methods used by their data stewards and data custodians to handle data.

Data governance is a set of processes that ensures that important data assets are formally managed throughout the enterprise. Implementing data governance will ensure that your data can be trusted and that people can be made accountable for any adverse event that happens because of poor data quality. Your data governance function should champion the definition standardization and identification of data across the enterprise. Keep in mind that data governance requires working effectively across the enterprise to discuss and agree on data standards, not to dogmatically dictate them. As an example, leaders of successful data governance programs declared at a recent data governance conference in Orlando, Florida, that data governance is between 80% and 95% communication.[9]

Understanding the data is a key step before any usage of a single variable. It's critical to understand what a field means by the information it contains. If the CRM manager in our example cited earlier who sent out inappropriate offer e-mails to customers actually understood the data she was pulling and the *Literary Digest* understood the bias of its data, their outcomes might have been different.

DATA DICTIONARY AND DATA KEY USERS

After you have implemented some form of data governance function, you can now start building the wish list of variables and analysis tables that will feed some of your recurring and ongoing business analytics needs. Therefore, the next step in your quest to lay the data foundation is to find out whether a data dictionary exists for each of your key data elements and, if not, create one. Word documents, relational databases, CD, Excel, or any documents could help you understand the structure and the meaning of the data. Sometimes you will get lucky, and this will be in a standard format. Most often, however, you will be creating or modifying it to suit your needs.

After you get acquainted with the existing documentation, it is very important to meet with people who are currently using the data. Oftentimes, not everything will be documented, and they will give you a better sense of what is being used and what not to use. In many cases, certain data could be available in the organization, but because people "in the know" are aware of its inferior quality, it is not used. It is always good to rely on the data experts in your organization, because they are more likely to discover and be aware of data issues, compared to you, because you are starting over with an investigation from the beginning.

SANITY CHECK AND DATA VISUALIZATION

Linda L. Briggs, in her 2010 TDWI article, interviewed Dannett McGilvray, a former data quality expert at Hewlett Packard, and he mentioned that "Data quality is a measurable and ongoing process effort."[10] Before building any data table for business analytics, here are some standard sanity checks that we recommend your team undertake:

- Missing value percentage: Avoid keeping any variable with more than 50% missing value.

- Outliers: Extreme value when looking at, for instance, age—140 would definitely be suspicious; we recommend getting rid of extreme value or simply adjusting them.

- Suspicious definition and unknown value coding.

- Invalid or erroneous data.

- Data distribution: Understand how your data are distributed and how it affects your business. Are your customers leaning to be younger more than older? Is their average spending higher or lower?

- Inconsistent values: A field containing both defined at character and integer data types.

On top of this sanity check list, it is important to visualize the data. Most business analytics companies offer a variety of visualization tools. Visualization would help you quickly spot data inconsistencies. We will cover data visualization in more detail in a separate chapter.

It is also essential to understand the process by which the data are created in a given system. In the end, familiarization with the extraction and transformation processes, as well as with other data hygiene steps, is vital for you to be confident in the data you are using.

When you perform sanity checks, "baby steps" is still the way to go, in order to avoid becoming overwhelmed. The key to success will be to start small, test and learn, and then expand as your approach to becoming successful.

CUSTOMER DATA INTEGRATION AND DATA MANAGEMENT

As mentioned throughout this chapter and reflected in our Customer Knowledge Framework, organizations are getting customer data from multiple sources, both internal and external. Yet to be useful and meaningful, customer data from multiple sources must converge into one place. In fact, customer data should be integrated to ensure a "single view of the customer." If the data are not integrated, there will be multiple conflicting views of the customer, and it will most likely lead to weak analytics and conflicting perspectives and recommendations.

Your company should integrate data from multiple sources in one place to enrich the customer insight and market knowledge, ultimately offering the right services to the right customers in the right markets via the right channels. As Jill Diche said in her great book *Customer Data Integration*: "There is no excuse for an executive to fly blind. Customer Data integration is a must, not an option."[11]

Note that customer data integration is a continuous process, one is never done. Data quality, of which integration is a component, can make or break your business. As a result and as we have discussed, your data need to be understood, defined, and managed using formalized processes and skill sets.

DATA PRIVACY

In today's era of globally connected customers and consumers, the strength of any business is based on the size and loyalty of its customer base, as well as on its value proposition carried to the market by sales, customer service, marketing, and product teams. However, customers are connected to one another and are sharing their opinions in widely open Internet and social media environments. With this in mind, companies can't afford any failure to protect their customer data. Companies must protect their customer information vigorously. If they fail to do so and there are some data leaks, repercussions and damage could lead to highly undesirables consequences, such as

- Customers could be offended and might turn to the competition.
- Competitors could poach customers from the data leak.
- Your company brand and image could be tarnished.
- Malicious individuals could take fraudulent actions against your customers in your name.
- Data leak victims could sue your company.
- Your company could lose the confidence and trust of its customers.

Because of the expanding volume of data from multiple sources, data privacy and data risk management have become very complex and should be part of a formal, ongoing effort so that your company can stay on top of the latest legislation and can ensure that data privacy tools are up to date. The most effective privacy and risk practices focus on preventing data privacy breaches, as well as on scenario and operational planning should a breach occur. Although data privacy for your organization is likely not the mandate of your business analytics function, you should be aware of, encourage, and ensure that your team follows the data privacy policies that are set forth by your organization.

 KEY TAKEAWAYS

- In this chapter, we underscored that data are the most important raw material and the foundation of any business analytics solution.
- We outlined a Customer Knowledge Framework (CKF) for how to think strategically and organize the data assets in your organization.
- With the explosion of different data sources, companies must successfully build a solid data foundation based on consistent governance and standard setting across the organization.
- Creating an effective data foundation is a long-term competitive advantage for attaining company success and will become increasingly more important over time.
- A bad data foundation is likely to create harm or missed opportunities for your company.
- The standardization of data questions across your organization (such as "What is a customer?") is required in order to effectively leverage business analytics.
- The quality and quantity of data will drive the quality and quantity of analytics that are derived from it.
- Big data encompasses three dimensions: volume, velocity, and variety.
- The proliferation of data has created an analyst labor shortage, which will get dramatically worse over time, with McKinsey Global Institute predicting that by 2018, the US market will have a shortage of around 1.5 million people with the know-how to use analytics to make effective decisions.
- Data knowledge maturity is a gradual process that involves data exploration, governance, integration, and management across the organization.
- We introduced data privacy and underscored the importance of systematically protecting it from leaks and security breach. Any failure in data privacy may create irreparable financial harm to your company or tarnish the company's brand.

NOTES

1. MarkLogic On-Demand Webinar, "Managing the Information Explosion," July 27, 2011.

2. Gartner, Symposium Conference, "Infrastructure & Operations: Top 10 Trends to Watch," David Cappuccio, October 2010.

3. IDC Digital Universe Study, sponsored by EMC, June 2011.

4. Paul C. Zikopoulos, et al., *Understanding Big Data: Analytics for Enterprise Class Hadoop and Streaming Data* (New York: McGraw-Hill, 2012).

5. GigaOM Interview with Stephen O'Sullivan, Walmart senior director of Global e-commerce, March 23, 2012.

6. David Rogers and Don Sexton, *Marketing Measurement in Transition Study*, Columbia Business School's Center on Global Brand Leadership and the New York American Marketing Association, March 2012.

7. Ray Paquet, "Technology Trends You Can't Afford to Ignore," Webinar, Garner, January 2010, http://www.gartner.com/it/content/1503500/1503515/january_19_tech_trends_you_cant_afford_to_ignore_rpaquet.pdf.

8. *Literary Digest*, October 31, 1936.

9. Peter Hopwood, "Data Governance: One Size Does Not Fit All," *DM Review Magazine*, June 2008.

10. Linda L. Briggs, "Why Data Quality Is a Measurable, Ongoing Effort," *TDWI* Blog, www.tdwi.org, May 2010.

11. Jill Diche and Evan Levy, *Customer Data Integration: Reaching a Single Version of the Truth* (Hoboken, NJ: John Wiley & Sons, 2006).

CHAPTER 5

Who Cares about Data?

How to Uncover Insights

"When I ask you what time it is, you tell me how to build a clock."

—Sheriff, in the 1959 movie *The Giant Gila Monster*

In Chapter 4, we discussed the different types of information your organization may have, as well as the importance of integrating it effectively in one way or another. We also explored different ways to make sure these data are valid and reliable. As we hope you also now believe, data are the foundation on which you will have an impact on your business. However, data are necessary but not sufficient in order to unlock business value for your organization. For this, meaning is required. We speak to business leaders on a regular basis about their data assets and challenges. It never fails—a common sentiment we hear consistently is that their organizations are drowning in data but lacking in understanding and action from that data. Said a different way, they have a lot of numbers and stats but aren't really sure what they mean or whether the companies are getting the most business action from these data. As a result, data at some companies remind us a bit of the spices in your kitchen. Generally speaking, people are happy and comforted that the spices are there—all of the fancy dishes we could create! However, when push comes to shove, most people don't really know what to do with them and end up cooking the same five to six simple meals they have always known and are comfortable creating.

For example, take the case of one of our clients, a large well-known technology company that was trying to understand where to locate a new customer service center. Its customer service needs were growing rapidly, yet the company did not have the staff or the systems in place in their West Coast corporate office to support the customers' needs. Therefore, the company was looking to open a new service center in a different city that would allow the company to provide excellent service but at a reasonable cost. The SVP of HR wanted to understand which of seven locations would be best for the company in order to have relatively low staff-recruitment costs, low labor costs, high-quality workers, and low turnover. During the discovery period of our engagement, we inquired whether the company had done any analysis internally. The company executives indicated that a lot of internal work had been done—but it had not been a good process or provided any answers. Specifically, they worked with their internal HR teams and their finance teams for recommendations of places. However, they told us that each time they asked for recommendations and/or analyses, they would get back Excel spreadsheets with data that were confusing and that they needed to pore through. This was frustrating to the senior team, and they told us they concluded that "our internal teams are not able to effectively help us with this issue."

Honestly, it may have been case that their internal teams had the capability and knew exactly how to analyze the data in order to uncover meaning and answer the business question. It may have also been the case that their internal team would have done an excellent job and made a brilliant recommendation. However, for whatever reason, the analytics team chose to stay focused on the data, thinking that it was what the senior leaders wanted. As a result, the analytics professionals lost credibility in the minds of the senior leaders and helped define their future existence solely as purveyors of data, rather than as insightful and strategic business partners.

We see this happen all too frequently with analytical professionals. It goes something like this: Analysts usually enjoy the process of pouring over the data, looking for a way to understand and summarize the data that is new, meaningful, and insightful. It's also a comfort zone for many analysts. Many are able to easily see what a data set, a chart, or a table is telling them. It is a learned skill that sometimes stems from a natural ability—much like that of a star athlete or an emotionally moving orator. Furthermore, for many analytical professionals, "analyze the data" means to run the best statistical technique, derive the model with the greatest parsimony, and create the best data visualization to get your points across. However, to the nonanalytical business professional, "analyze the data" usually means "tell me what you think I should do in response to my business question," "advise me on the best course of action based on your read of the data," or "tell me what the data are showing so I don't have to analyze it myself."

All too often, this can cause a disconnect between the analyst and his or her customer. Some nonanalyst businesspeople get headaches and feel frustrated when you give them a chart or a graph. Many don't even like looking at data—they'd rather visit the dentist. Analysts sometimes forget that many nonanalyst businesspeople don't want to see graphs, charts, or data tables—that's why they have analytical professionals in the organization.

THE IMPACT CYCLE

So, how do you get your analysts to pull their heads up from the data and focus on the business? It's not always an easy task, and it's a bit of art and a science. Based on our combined 40 years of experience in analyzing data, as well as input we received from researching best practices of other analytical professionals, we have developed and used a practical framework to guide you through the process of ensuring that your analysts are insightful business partners, rather than just purveyors of data. We call this the IMPACT cycle (see Exhibit 5.1). During the remainder of this chapter, we provide an outline of the IMPACT cycle, as well as examples of it in action.

In an effort to drive the point home to analysts that they really need to think as much about what their customers want as they do

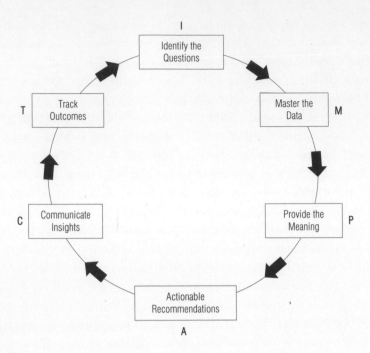

Exhibit 5.1 The IMPACT Cycle

about the data, one of the coauthors, Jesse Harriott, sometimes relays two examples from seemingly unrelated disciplines in order to get the analysts thinking about how they can best serve their customers as analytical professionals. This exercise can be done individually or in a group setting. First, he asks them to think about a time that went really well when they needed to take their car to a mechanic for service. He then asks them to relate that experience and describe what made it successful. He repeats back what he hears to the person telling the story, and it inevitably comes down to some form of "the mechanic fixed my car, and it ran well after that." He then asks them to think of another experience with a mechanic, but this time relay a situation that did not go well, when they were not satisfied. He repeats back what he hears, and it is usually some form of "the mechanic kept going round-and-round with me and did not really understand and/or fix my issue."

Jesse then summarizes that in both cases, the positive and the negative outcome do not hinge on any form of technical knowledge taught by the mechanic. For example, nobody says, "My mechanic experience was great because the mechanic told me how the exhaust manifold draws air into in the engine cylinders as a precursor to the combustion of gas." Jesse then outlines that both the positive and the negative experiences hinge on whether the mechanic satisfies the need to fix the issue in a timely manner and communicates effectively. You don't really care too much about learning the systems of an automobile and how he or she was able to fix the car—you just care that it was done. Jesse explains that this is a good analogy for how your internal and external customers think about the analytical work your team does. They pay you to analyze the data and help them achieve their business objectives, not to provide them with data or a technical overview of how you got there. Typically, nonanalytical business professionals don't care about how you arrived at your conclusions, only what the conclusions are and what action you recommend that they consider. The goal is to make their lives easier, not to make them go through a bunch of mental gymnastics to get to the conclusion.

The second analogy Jesse often draws is that providing analytical services is somewhat like being a professional translator. In business, people may hire a Chinese language translator to help them communicate with someone from China in order to do business. They do not hire the translator because the businesspeople have the time, inclination, or ability to learn Chinese themselves—they just want the Chinese translator to tell them what their Chinese business partner is saying. By the same token, analytical professionals are usually hired to translate what the data are telling the business and turn it into relevant conclusions that answer important business questions or critical business objectives. Nonanalytical business partners do not have the time or the desire to learn about the data and how it was analyzed. To be blunt, they often do not even care.

The IMPACT cycle addresses these issues by providing the analytical professional with a guiding framework for thinking about all of the steps in being an effective analytical consultant or adviser to their business partners. We outline the steps in detail later in the chapter, but a brief description of each stage in the IMPACT cycle is listed here:

- ■ **I**dentify the question. In a nonintrusive way, help your business partner identify the critical business question(s) he or she needs help in answering. Then set a clear expectation of the time and the work involved to get an answer.

- **M**aster the data. This is the analyst's sweet spot—assemble, analyze, and synthesize all available information that will help in answering the critical business question. Create simple and clear visual presentations (charts, graphs, tables, interactive data environments, and so on) of that data that are easy to comprehend.

- **P**rovide the meaning. Articulate clear and concise interpretations of the data and visuals in the context of the critical business questions that were identified.

- **A**ctionable recommendations. Provide thoughtful business recommendations based on your interpretation of the data. Even if they are off-base, it's easier to react to a suggestion that to generate one. Where possible, tie a rough dollar figure to any revenue improvements or cost savings associated with your recommendations.

- **C**ommunicate insights. Focus on a multipronged communication strategy that will get your insights as far and as wide into the organization as possible. Maybe it's in the form of an interactive tool others can use, a recorded Webex of your insights, a lunch and learn, or even just a thoughtful executive memo that can be passed around.

- **T**rack outcomes. Set up a way to track the impact of your insights. Make sure there is future follow-up with your business partners on the outcome of any actions. What was done, what was the impact, and what are the new critical questions that need your help as a result?

CURIOSITY CAN KILL THE CAT

You know the old saying, "Curiosity killed the cat." Well, in the case of business analytics, it can. We see it too often on analytical teams—analysts really enjoy exploring the data. Exploring data often leads to more questions, which lead to more exploring of the data, which leads to . . . okay, you get the idea. This usually results in unmet expectations from the business and eventually the business seeing the analysts as purveyors of data, rather than as strategic business partners. It's essential that your analysts get out of this self-stimulating intellectual spiral and focus their efforts on uncovering the meaning that's related to clearly defined business questions when they are exploring the data. In the corporate world, there is rarely any time for intellectual curiosity. Intellectual curiosity is to be satisfied in the academic world or on your analyst's own time. Business analytics is ultimately about helping the company increase revenues or save costs, either directly or indirectly. Therefore, analytical work should drive toward these two goals. Analyzing business questions or exploring data that does not have as its ultimate goal to either lower costs or increase revenue is not where the focus of your analytical team should be. The previously mentioned reasons are why the IMPACT cycle for the analyst focuses its first two phases ("identify" and "master the data") on dealing with these issues.

The first phase of the IMPACT cycle is to identify the critical business questions. It's fairly common for a business partner to call up an analyst and ask for "this" data or "that" data, with little, if any, business context provided. We always hope that the basis of asking for data is a legitimate business question; however, that is not always the case. Sometimes it can be an attempt by the business person to acquire data to justify to someone else in the organization a decision that's already been made. Other times, data are needed to justify a political move within the organization. Occasionally, data are requested to satisfy random curiosity or a question the business partner has but that is not tied to a critical business objective or question. The job of the analysts on your teams should be as consultative partners, to work with the business to identify and answer the critical business questions.

One point to keep in mind: High-level communication skills, creative thinking to identify business questions, and analytical prowess to dive into the data do not often come together in a single person. Therefore, we have often found it more successful to split these roles in our analytical teams, such that one analyst is the primary client contact before, during, and after the project, and one analyst is the primary person cranking through and uncovering the data insights. This can set up your team for success, as well as make the whole process more rewarding for everyone involved. It will be most successful if you rotate the people a bit across different projects, such that each analyst has the opportunity to develop and work in each role, both as the primary client contact and as the primary data investigator.

The process of identifying the business question for the project, if done well by a skilled analyst, will largely depend on how well the nonanalytical business partner has thought through his or her business questions. Identifying the business question can be quick and easy if someone contacts your analysts and says, "We need to decide which e-mail marketing campaign strategy was most effective for getting small businesses to try our product. Can you help?" In this case, the process is really effortless on the part of the analyst and simply involves repeating back what was heard, in order to make sure there is a clear understanding. Yet it is usually not this easy. Frequently, the nonanalytical business partner will call up with a vague description of a need, often delegated to him or her from someone else. For example, a typical call might be, "Our SVP of marketing asked me to look at our e-mail strategy and see what we can do to improve it. Can you get me some data on this by Friday?" At best, this is a vague articulation of a truly clear business question in the mind of the nonanalytical business partner. At worst, the nonanalytical business partner isn't even sure what the SVP of marketing wants and hopes your analyst can shed light on the issue for her by providing some "data." In this case, your analyst must tread lightly and help the nonanalytical business partner see that more clarity is required, in order to provide her with the most effective analytical help.

When your analysts are trying to uncover or get clarity on the critical business questions for a project, we recommend using the following questions as the basis for a creative and interactive discussion:

- Can you describe what business situation(s) led up to your need for this information?
- Can you explain what a successful business outcome looks like to you, if we are able to give you the most relevant information?
- Who is the audience that will see the information related to this issue?
- Can you describe what action you plan to take with the insights we provide?

The key to success at this stage is not to ask questions in an interrogative way, but rather, to have a supportive discussion and offer suggestions if the business partner has trouble answering these types of questions. For example, your analyst can say something like, "It sounds like you want to understand how our e-mail strategy is working. Are you trying to understand something specific about the types of e-mails sent, the groups or the conversion behaviors after the e-mails, or something else?"

After your analyst has identified the business questions, it's crucial that he or she quickly document and send them back to the business partner to make sure there was a clear understanding regarding questions to be addressed. In addition, it is key at this stage to also give some indication regarding a rough time line for how long the project will take and what work will be involved. All too frequently, non-analytical business partners will underestimate the time and effort required to develop business analytics insight—so setting expectations early will make the entire process much smoother.

TRIPADVISOR

CASE STUDY

Jesse sat down to discuss the importance of meaningful business analytics with Stephen Kaufor, the cofounder and CEO of TripAdvisor, the world's largest travel site. TripAdvisor helps travelers learn about and plan for their trips through advice and reviews from other travelers, as well as by enabling travel reservations through multiple booking tools. TripAdvisor manages and operates websites under 19 travel media brands in more than 30 countries and contains more than 60 million reviews and opinions written by 20 million-plus members. As a result, says Stephen Kaufer, "Analytics are central to what we do as a business. Whether helping our advertisers understand the return on investment for their marketing spend with us or by helping our travel merchants understand what consumers are saying about their establishment, meaningful analytics are critical."

TripAdvisor's success with consumers hinges on its ability to anticipate and exceed the fickle demands of the traveling public. As a result, it must do extensive testing of any new product idea or site change to make sure it will meet the TripAdvisor standard, as well as satisfy the travel-conscious consumer. However, Stephen is insistent that TripAdvisor's analytics efforts focus on providing high-impact business meaning, rather than letting the company be overwhelmed with data. "We don't have time to get drawn into

(continued)

analysis-paralysis. Our analytics are designed to be done as quickly as possible and lead to practical business insight and action."

For example, because new products are expensive to build and do not always lead to success, Stephen advocates for what he calls "the 404 test" to understand the business impact for site enhancements or new feature ideas. Basically, this involves linking to a new product or feature on TripAdvisor's site in order to gauge user interest. The catch is, when a user clicks on the link for the new product or enhancement, it doesn't exist, and the user is taken to a "404—Page Not Found" error page. Because TripAdvisor has such a large volume of visitors, it can tell in minutes or hours by measuring the 404 error page traffic whether there is likely to be user interest in the proposed site enhancement or the new product before it is even created. "It gives us a fast and effective way to decide whether we should invest the time and effort to create something for our TripAdvisor community without wasting company resources to develop things people do not want." Although some user-experience purists may criticize testing in this way as a bad experience for TripAdvisor visitors, Stephen says the tests are always done quickly, with limited impact to users. One cannot argue with more than 10 years of TripAdvisor's success or with the fact that, according to comScore, TripAdvisor-owned properties continue to attract more than 69 million visitors each month.

MASTER THE DATA

The second stage of the IMPACT cycle is to master the data. Here is where the analyst hopefully shines, uncovering and analyzing all of the data thoroughly that will help answer the critical business questions. The amount of data is vast, and there are many innovative companies that have created data tools and sources that make the analyst's job easier. Also, high-impact data tools are no longer found only in the large enterprise, so your analysts should have no excuses for not mastering the available data. For example, we had a chance to sit down with Steve Pogorzelski, the CEO of ClickFuel, a company that provides SaaS-based campaign performance dashboards that enable small- and medium-business (SMB) customers to track the effectiveness of their marketing spend. Steve indicated that analytics in the small business segment, like those provided through the 25,000 dashboards for ClickFuel's customers, is evolving rapidly. Pogorzelski said, "We believe that data provided to SMBs and product providers alike can change the paradigm of how online products and services are sold and purchased in this multibillion category by using information that leads to action. That is, moving from a process experimentation and intuition to one of predictability and analysis."

A FACT IN SEARCH OF MEANING

After the critical questions have been identified and the data have been analyzed and mastered with some sophistication and care, it's time to move to the third stage of the IMPACT cycle: "provide the meaning." This is the beginning of the true "translation" into something the nonanalytical business partner cares about. Uncovering the meaning of data is a creative and subjective process and is addressed in multiple examples throughout this book. However, as a basis, we advocate that your analyst focus on addressing the critical business questions that were given by thinking about four principles when doing his or her analysis of meaning:

1. What is happening/has happened?
2. Why is it happening/has it happened?
3. What will happen in the future?
4. How can the company maximize any opportunities?

In a business context, the focus of the data meaning should be putting it into discrete, easy-to-digest parts. Therefore, we have found that in the world of business, it's often best to have your analysts articulate their interpretation of the data in short bullet points, rather than a more narrative write-up. This is done for two reasons. First, it helps force the analysts to put their interpretation into concise, crisp language that is hopefully quick to read, easy to understand and to-the-point. Second, it helps the analysts focus and make sure each bullet point supports the critical business question(s) being asked, without irrelevant data interpretation.

The next part in the search for meaning is to ask the analyst to put those bullet points of meaning in order of importance with regards to how each bullet addresses the critical business question that was originally asked. At this point, it's time to ask for some cross-review by other trusted analysts and internal business partners. Two questions Jesse often asks analysts, to see whether they have done their best to provide the meaning of their data for a nonanalytical business audience, are:

1. Could the analysts give the write-up without any background or additional information (e.g., graphs, charts, data) to a nonanalytical businessperson outside the client's organization? and

2. Could that person understand what was meant by the conclusions drawn by the analysts?

If the answers are no, then there is more work to do to make the meaning clear, concise, and business relevant. If the analysts are unsure, a litmus test for these questions can often be a spouse or a significant other.

ACTIONS SPEAK LOUDER THAN DATA

Data should not be a substitute for business decision making, but rather a torch to help illuminate which business actions are likely best. Unfortunately, all too often, nonanalytical business leaders and analysts think the analysis is the action, and analytical work can sometimes end with the presentation of the data. Strong companies know that the work is just beginning when the analysis is done.

As the fourth stage of the IMPACT cycle, we advocate putting forth "Actionable" recommended business initiatives stemming from the analytical work. In other words, your analysts should take a stab at answering the critical business questions based on their analysis of the data for the nonanalytical business partner. For example, they should give some clear and direct answers/options to questions such as

- What should we do to improve the e-mail conversion of small business prospects?
- Where should the new call center be located?
- How can the company increase average order size?
- How should we segment our customers?
- What is the sales model that maximizes profitability at the lowest cost-of-sale?

For many analysts, this is an uncomfortable exercise. Their critical thinking skills turn inward to doubt, and they wonder things such as

- How could they possibly know enough to make a solid recommendation for action?
- How could they know enough about the business function (such as marketing, product, sales) to give a recommendation that makes sense?
- They don't know about everything going on in the company, so how can they be in a position to recommend business action that doesn't conflict with other priorities?

These are all excuses, cop-outs, or mind tricks that prevent the analyst from taking accountability as a true business partner. It's easier and more common to provide analytical work and walk away with an attitude that "it's up to you what you do with the information." Instead, you should challenge your analysts to have a stake in the businesses' success by giving their best recommendation based on the knowledge they have. The worst outcome is that the business will reject it, in favor of a different idea. However, more often than not, your nonanalytical business partners will appreciate that your analysts gave them something other than only data or merely telling them how to interpret the Web behavior of the site visitors, for example. If your analysts consistently give business insights, advise their business partners regarding what to do, and make their partners' jobs easier, they will receive nothing but gratitude.

"EAT LIKE A BIRD, POOP LIKE AN ELEPHANT"

The above well-known quote from the former chief evangelist of Apple, Guy Kawasaki, reflects the communication philosophy your analysts should have after a project.[1] Namely, they should take little from the business in time, attention, and resources, yet give back plenty. Toward that end, having your analysts "communicate the insights" of their analytical activities will be key and is the fifth stage of the IMPACT cycle. Unfortunately, it is somewhat common for analysts to be more comfortable with analyzing and less comfortable in communicating with business leaders. However, in order for your analytics to affect the business, they must be communicated effectively.

By communication, we don't mean giving an oral presentation to executives as moving and insightful as the famous minister T. D. Jakes. No, what we mean is that your analyst uses multiple means of communicating to get her findings across the company to as many people as possible, with the appropriate management approvals, of course. Knowledge is power, and the more people across the organization who have the knowledge, the more powerful the organization becomes. For example, once the data have been analyzed against the business questions, the meaning succinctly interpreted, and the business actions outlined, your analyst must create and gain approval on a documented communication plan that lists the three or four ways the analyst will evangelize what has been learned to others in the company.

We will discuss communication strategies in more detail in Chapter 15: "Effective Analytics Communication Strategies"; however, following are some examples of creative tactics your analysts can use to communicate their findings across the organization:

- Create a Web-based interactive tool that is self-service for others across the organization.
- Hold "lunch and learn" meetings, where the analytical team provides the food and guests bring their interest and creativity.
- Conduct a copresentation via Webinar with an internal functional group (for example, sales) that believes in your analysis and thinks it will have an impact on the organization.
- Create posters of the main insights and recommended actions, and put them up around your office locations.
- Partner with your training team to integrate your most significant insights into "new hire training" in your organization.
- Create assessment tools for the most important insights and suggest that key staff members across the company become "certified" on those insights by taking the assessment test.
- Create a team newsletter to provide your latest insights to key managers across the company.

- Create a page on your corporate intranet, in order to showcase the latest insights and findings.
- Ask to be put on the agenda of functional team meetings (marketing, sales, service, and so on) to outline your insights.

We have created multiple Web-based interactive tools that disseminate analysis and insights across the business and have found this to be a favored, effective, and scalable communication method. For example, we have created interactive tools on projected market share through conjoint modeling, real-time competitive profile information, detailed searchable customer intelligence, global market intelligence, website performance insights, and customer wallet share spend, among others, some of which are described throughout this book. Regardless of your favorite, we suggest that your analysts focus on a multipronged communication strategy that will get your insights as far and as wide into the organization as possible. Maybe it's in the form of an interactive tool others can use, a recorded Webex of your insights, a lunch and learn, or even just a thoughtful, yet terse, executive memo that can be passed around.

TRACK YOUR OUTCOMES

The last stage of the IMPACT cycle is to ensure that your analysts track the influence of their recommendations over time. For example, did your analysts suggest targeting small businesses in Cincinnati with half-price offers, in order to drive business in Ohio? If so, what was the outcome? Did the company make money or lose money as a result of what came from your team's analysis? You must think about this type of tracking early on in the project to make sure your business partners are in a position to provide you with the necessary information, in order to make an educated assessment of whether the initiative made the company money or saved costs.

For example, one of the coauthors, JP Isson, created a customer segmentation model for a telecommunications company in Canada. There was some initial resistance from the sales team to roll out the segmentation model that recommended targeting only certain customers, while forgoing others. However, JP insisted it would work and set up tracking to see the results in a pilot test with some sales teams. After six months, it turned out that the sales teams were seeing larger average order sizes and less customer attrition for sales reps that followed the segmentation model recommendations versus those that did not. As a result, JP was able to convince other leaders regarding the effectiveness of his recommendations, and his segmentation model was adopted by the entire organization.

THE IMPACT CYCLE IN ACTION: THE MONSTER EMPLOYMENT INDEX

We have used the IMPACT cycle with many organizations over the years. However, one case study that put it into action was the development of the Monster Employment Index by one of the coauthors, Jesse Harriott. The leaders of Monster Worldwide, the largest online recruitment company in the world, came to Jesse and indicated that they wanted to do something public with data and wanted him to think about what could be done. There was little initial direction at that point, so Jesse worked with the CEO at the time, Andy McKelvey, to identify the key business objectives. After some discussion, it turned out that the goal was to develop some ongoing information that could be used to generate interest in Monster and could position Monster as an authority. Jesse set the expectation to give him three weeks, and he would come up with some options and an analysis that would help the CEO make some decisions. Jesse spent much of the time poring over various types of industry data, as well as Monster's data. What he discovered was that little standardization existed across Monster or the industry at that time. Jesse also saw that no public information existed regarding online recruitment activity. At the time, there was only print recruitment data and backward-looking government statistics on the labor market from the Bureau of Labor Statistics.

As a result of analyzing the available data, Jesse concluded that Monster had a unique opportunity to provide thought-leading and real-time labor market information to the market. During the coming weeks, he created a methodology to create an industry-wide online recruitment index using systematic data collection, not only from Monster, but from millions of job postings across the Web. On meeting with the CEO again, he recommended that Monster create, publicize, and own this index as a thought-leadership activity, in order to position Monster as a labor market authority. He did not go into great detail regarding the index methodology at the time, choosing to focus more on how an index could have business impact and could help Monster position itself as a labor market leader. The CEO liked the idea and gave the project the go-ahead. In the next few months, Jesse worked across Monster to create the methodology and process and communicate the importance of the Monster Employment Index. As result, the U.S. Monster Employment Index was a success and won the PRNews Platinum Award for "Application of Research for Thought Leadership." Since then, the Monster Employment Index has expanded to Canada, more than 25 European countries, India, and several Gulf countries and is now an economic indicator widely followed by millions of people each month, creating hundreds of millions of dollars in free advertising value for Monster Worldwide.

 KEY TAKEAWAYS

- Train your analysts to think outside of themselves.
- Focus on the steps of the IMPACT cycle.
- Start with the business challenge, objective, or questions.
- Set clear expectations for the work and the time involved to address the questions.
- Outline only the facts that answer the business questions.
- Analysts are the translators between data and the business.
- Focus on the meaning of the data, not on the data itself.
- Provide recommended business actions, despite how difficult this may be.
- Communicate your insights broadly and deeply into the organization.
- Track and quantify the business impact of your analytical insights.

NOTE

1. G. Kawasaki, *Rules for Revolutionaries: The Capitalist Manifesto for Creating and Marketing New Products and Services* (New York: HarperBusiness, 2000).

CHAPTER 6

Data Visualization

Presenting Information Clearly: The CONVINCE Framework

"The greatest value of a picture is when it forces us to notice what we never expected to see."

—John W. Tukey

In Chapter 5, we discussed the need to have your team focus on data meaning and context, rather than on just the data itself, when addressing your critical business questions. In this chapter, we extend that notion and highlight the importance of creating high-impact data visualizations. Representing your data visually can be a powerful way to make your business analytic efforts high-impact and convey meaning with the least amount of effort on the part of your audience. In addition, some of us learn and comprehend things more rapidly when we have a visual aid. This is sure to be true for some of your nonanalytical business partners. Therefore, the importance of creating high-impact visual representations of your data becomes a key translation tool to bridge the gap between the data and your business audience.

What do we mean by *data visualization*? Really, data visualization can take the form of a simple graph to a complex infographic. Regardless, data visualization involves painting a visual picture that reflects the results of your data analysis. Vitaly Friedman describes data visualization this way:

> The main goal of data visualization is to communicate information clearly and effectively through graphical means. It doesn't mean that data visualization needs to look boring to be functional or extremely sophisticated to look beautiful. To convey ideas effectively, both aesthetic form and functionality need to go hand in hand, providing insights into a rather sparse and complex data set by communicating its key-aspects in a more intuitive way. Yet designers often fail to achieve a balance between form and function, creating gorgeous data visualizations which fail to serve their main purpose—to communicate information.[1]

It is our belief that the best data visualization in a business environment will not only communicate the information's meaning clearly but will also stimulate audience attention and encourage engagement. As a result, the highest-quality data visualization requires a mix of graphic design, information architecture, information technology, and data analysis skills. This is a rare combination to find in one team in an organization, so we encourage your business analytics function to leverage other skill sets across your organization when creating data visualizations that will be seen by a large audience and/or are expected to be high impact. For example, perhaps you have a graphic design department, an IT department, or an information architecture staff that can help your team as it creates high-impact and rich data visualizations.

During the remainder of this chapter, we review our CONVINCE Framework of principles for effective data visualization, as well as provide examples of good and poor data visualization. Our framework is based on what we have seen work in a corporate environment, and we take a very practical approach to successful data visualization. The reality is that in a business context, your data visualization techniques must be simple, must convey meaning clearly, and must be easy for your audience to digest. Our CONVINCE Framework addresses these issues, among others, as you seek to make your data visualization techniques effective and high impact. We have also provided a list of additional resources at the end of this chapter, if you would like to dig deeper into the topic.

Our CONVINCE Framework has the following principles of data visualization:

Convey meaning

Objectivity

Necessity

Visual honesty

Imagine the audience

Nimble

Context

Encourage interaction

Each is explained in detail in the remainder of this chapter.

CONVEY MEANING

This may seem like an obvious point, but you would be surprised at how many examples we have seen in our 40-plus collective year career of analysts putting together graphs or charts that have no clear or obvious meaning attached to them. Analysts sometimes are too close to the data and lose perspective when putting the data visualization elements together, resulting in the audience being unable to grasp the meaning and feeling confused. Some data visualizations lean toward intellectual curiosity and lack clear business meaning. In our opinion, the meaning of each data visualization graphic should be obvious to the reviewer, without a lot of explanation or background. Each graphic should stand on its own.

For example, bring your attention to Exhibit 6.1, which shows the relative market shares of Sotheby's vs. Christies over time.[2] The market share remains relatively stable over time, so it's really not clear what the meaning of the graphic is or what the designer is trying to represent. There was clearly thought and effort behind the creation of the information graphic; however, besides showing the reviewer that

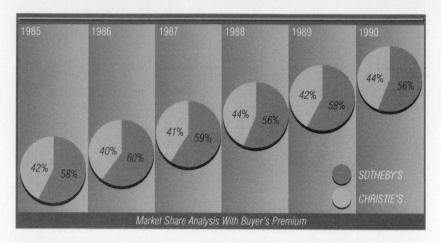

Exhibit 6.1 Sotheby's/Christie's Worldwide Sales: Market Share Analysis

market share is increasing over time, there doesn't seem to be any clear meaning.

In contrast, Exhibit 6.2 shows the relationship between automobile speed and traffic ticket price. From a review of the graph, it's clear that as automobile speed increases, traffic ticket price also increases. One does not need any additional information, explanation, or background

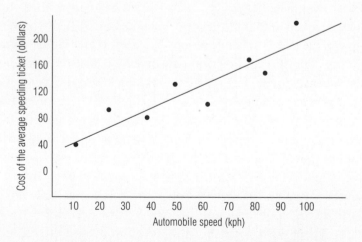

Exhibit 6.2 Dependence of Traffic Ticket Cost on Automobile Speed

to understand the meaning of the graph and the point it's attempting to make. It is simple and to the point. This is the approach you should take with your data visualization for your business audience. Convey meaning clearly, succinctly, and without ambiguity.

OBJECTIVITY: BE TRUE TO YOUR DATA

This is one that is difficult for some analysts to follow. In many business analytics projects, there may be some pressure to show findings in a certain way or to ascribe a certain meaning to your data analysis. For example, people in your marketing department may expect that your analysis will show that their recent spend of $2 million on an online media campaign was very effective at driving a large audience, or your product department may pressure your team to show an analysis that proves that its new product results in higher customer loyalty, average order size, and retention rates. It is sometimes tempting to go along with the group and skew the data presentation slightly to most favorably represent the conclusions that the business might like to see. Data visualization techniques offer many opportunities to do this. However, your business analytics team must aggressively avoid this at all costs.

Take a look at Exhibit 6.3, which shows a less obvious (and therefore more insidious) way to create a misleading impression with your data.[3] William Playfair is considered by many to be the creator of statistical graphing techniques, and his charts are often considered fine examples of how to convey information through images. However, in the case of Exhibit 6.3, which shows the relationship between wheat prices and worker wages, his chart leaves something to be desired. He shows three time series—weekly wages, wheat prices, and the reigns of British monarchs. Unfortunately, he used separate scales for wages (0–100) and prices (0–30) in order to convey his message that "never at any former period was wheat so cheap, in proportion to mechanical labour, as it is at the present time." However, the relationship between wages and prices would change dramatically if either was rescaled.

As a contrast, Exhibit 6.4 shows the activity patterns of employed workers during a typical workday.[4] The time series is clearly laid out

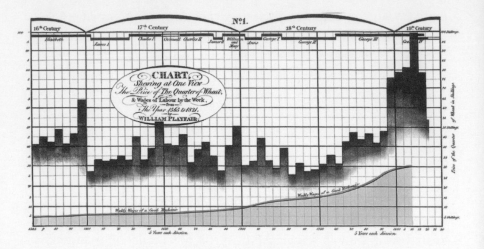

Exhibit 6.3 The Relationship between Wheat Prices and Worker Wages

in a consistent manner, and the data are presented objectively. In addition, interpretation and meaning are easily discerned from this graph. For example, it can be seen that some employees leave work early in order to participate in leisure activities and that the most common work pattern is from 9 a.m. to 5 p.m. This graph is well done, with a clearly labeled scale and a consistent interval. As you are developing your own data visualization, it can sometimes be tempting

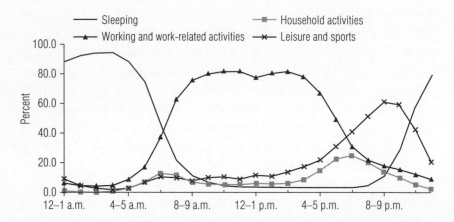

Exhibit 6.4 Percent of Employed Persons Who Did Selected Activities on Workdays By Hour of the Day
Source: Bureau of Labor Statistics, American Time Use Survey

to skew the data, but in order to maintain your team's credibility, you must remain true and objective to the data.

NECESSITY: DON'T BOIL THE OCEAN

The next principle in our CONVINCE Framework for data visualization is Necessity. Here, we mean that you should challenge your team to visualize only data that helps tell the story of the data and ties back to your core business objectives. It's easy to get lost or even overwhelmed in the data and think everything is important. However, your team must focus and tie back to the original business challenges and questions when constructing data visualizations. You must be a beacon and a continual reminder that in order for your business analytics to be effective, each data visualization must tie back to the business needs and support the critical business questions being asked. Including unnecessary information is especially common among inexperienced analysts, who will often include everything and the kitchen sink when presenting the data.

For example, take Exhibit 6.5. It is a poor and overwhelming word cloud and shows too much information, confusing the observer.[5] If you have no idea what a word cloud is, a word cloud represents word usage in a document by resizing words in the document proportionally to how frequently they are used and then assembling them into some sort of an arrangement. This technique was first used online in the 1990s as "tag clouds," which have been described as "the mullets of the Internet" and were originally used to display the popularity of keywords in bookmarks.[6]

Contrast that to Exhibit 6.6, which shows a clear and concise heat map of where users are clicking on different portions of a Web page.[7] This data visualization shows enough information to convey meaning, but not so much as to overwhelm the observer. It also becomes intuitively clear regarding which are the most popular areas of the page.

The bottom line is that if you can remove graphics, data, words, or any other elements from a data visualization without losing the meaning—by all means, take them out.

Exhibit 6.5   Word Cloud

Exhibit 6.6   Web Page Heat Map

VISUAL HONESTY: SIZE MATTERS

The next principle is that you must be careful in the visual representation of your data that you do not unintentionally skew the data and how they are represented. Specifically, you must represent the data in scales that are consistent, present the data truthfully, and do nothing to obfuscate the truth and accuracy of the data. As an example, take a look at Exhibit 6.7, which shows a simple representation of the number of milk cows over time.[8] One must wonder whether the designer of this image had deception in mind or whether it was just ignorance. As we can see from the image, poor choices or deliberately deceptive choices in data visualization can result in a distorted picture of data and the relationships they represent.

It's a more common problem than you might think for charts to be designed in ways that hide what the data might tell us or distract the observer from discerning the true meaning of the evidence presented in the data visualization. In our example in Exhibit 6.7, the two numbers from the data are roughly 3 times the magnitude of the other but are represented by two cows, one of which is 27 times larger than the other! The exhibit depicts the increase in the number of milk cows in the United States, from 8 million in 1860 to 25 million in 1936. The larger cow is represented as three times the height of the 1860 cow. However, the larger cow is also three times as wide, taking up nine times the area of the page. Furthermore, the graphic is a depiction of a three-dimensional figure: when we take the depth of the cow into account, she is 27 times larger in 1936. Based on examples similar to this one, Edward Tufte developed the "Lie Factor," which is simply a ratio of the data distortion.[9] In this case, the data distortion Lie Factor

1860   1936

Exhibit 6.7 The Crescive Cow
Source: From How to Lie with Statistics, by Darrell Huff, illustrated by Irving Geis, Copyright 1954 and renewed © 1982 by Darrell Huff and Irving Geis. Used by permission of W. W. Norton & Company, Inc.

This line, representing 18 miles per gallon in 1978, is 0.6 inches long.

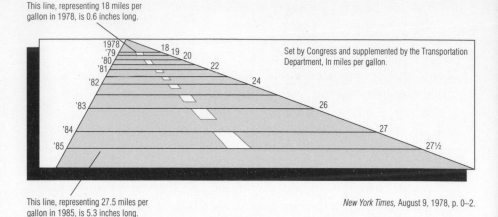

This line, representing 27.5 miles per gallon in 1985, is 5.3 inches long.

New York Times, August 9, 1978, p. 0–2.

Exhibit 6.8   Fuel Economy Standards for Autos
Source: New York Times, August 9, 1978, p. D2

is a 9, because the numbers have an actual 3 times difference in magnitude, yet the image shown is 27 times different in magnitude. Exhibit 6.8 shows another example of a graph with low graphical integrity. According to Tufte's standard, the Lie Factor of this graph is 14.8, because a numerical change of 53% is represented by a graphical change (size of horizontal lines) of 783%.

IMAGINE THE AUDIENCE

In the context of analytics in a business environment, this is one of the more important principles. You really must design your data visualizations with the end in mind, and part of that requires you to think through the audience that will receive and review each project. Analytics professionals sometimes have a difficult time understanding this, but a sizable percentage of your nonanalytical business partners don't have the ability, the time, or the interest in expending cognitive effort trying to figure out what your graphs mean. They want answers fast, and they want you to get to point quickly and succinctly. For this audience, each graph must be simple and clear and must make an obvious point.

You must also consider the role your key audience has in the organization when you create data visualizations. Is your primary audience a sales representative, a senior executive responsible for a marketing department, a customer, or some other group? The perspective your audience members bring with them in interpreting your data visualizations should drive your design. Exhibit 6.9 illustrates how Web marketing managers think about allocating resources among search engine optimization (SEO) tactics.[10] Content creation stands apart in the cluster of tactics, for both its difficulty and its effectiveness. Good content creates buzz and attracts links. For this reason, marketers who commit to the effort that is required in creating quality content can improve their SEO positions. This is a graph that would be appropriate if your audience were a manager a couple of layers down within the marketing organization who needs to plan and make decisions regarding the company's search engine optimization efforts. However, it would probably be too detailed a graph and not business relevant to review with your CEO, even though your team may find it interesting and impactful.

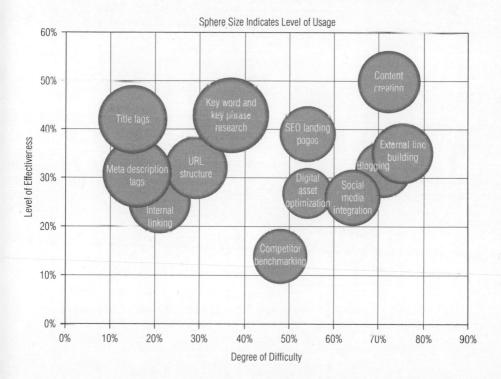

Exhibit 6.9 Effectiveness of Search Engine Optimization Tactics

Turn your attention to Exhibit 6.10, which shows lead quality and conversion rates by SEO practice maturity level. The graph clearly shows that the efforts of strategically SEO-minded organizations pay off through a larger percentage of high-quality leads from organic search traffic, but they also convert more of these leads into action. When looking at median conversion rates, the strategic organizations tend to convert about 150% more leads than do organizations without a formal SEO discipline. Compared to Exhibit 6.8, this graph may actually be business relevant to a more senior audience in your organization, possibly your chief marketing officer or your chief executive officer, assuming he or she is trying to make a decision about whether to invest in an SEO practice within your organization.

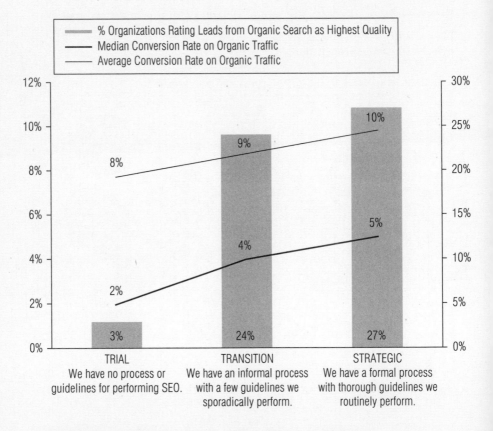

Exhibit 6.10 Effectiveness of Search Engine Optimization Strategies
Source: MarketingSherpa

NIMBLE: NO DEATH BY 1,000 GRAPHS

Business executives dread nothing more than the long PowerPoint presentation with multiple slides that have dozens of eye charts, overwhelming graphs, and unnecessary information. Hopefully, your business audience will be interested in your analytical topic, as you are tying back to a critical objective for the business, as we have discussed numerous times throughout this book. Yet people have only a limited attention span to give to your team's analysis and accompanying data visualization. Some analysts may be put off by this; however, it truly is a matter of competing priorities and cognitive capacity. Next time one of your analysts is upset because the VP of product wasn't patient enough to review the 10 graphs he put together on product adoption, teach him about the idea of cognitive overload and that scholarly research shows that the more effort you require of someone to process your graphs, the less likely the person will accurately understand the meaning you are trying to convey.[11] That point of cognitive overload is a moving target and will be a function of your audience's conceptual understanding and previous knowledge when interacting with your data visualization. However, it's best to assume overload will happen quickly and include only as few data visualizations as possible. Reducing the number of graphs and charts, while maintaining the key points you must convey, is a principle that a business audience will always appreciate.

CONTEXT

It's important to always include "context" in your data visualizations. Context can be any element that helps the audience put the data and the conclusions into a broader concept, thereby resulting in a deeper understanding of the data's meaning. For example, if you are creating a simple time series graph showing the percentage of cases when your customer service organization resolves a customer issue after it has been contacted, consider including context, such as a benchmark for your industry or even just an internal goal for the percentage of resolution the company is aiming to achieve. These numbers will help your audience put the time series of customer service issue resolution into context, allowing for a deeper and more thorough understanding of the data.

A great way to make a chart more useful and interesting and to provide "context" is to include additional information in the background of the chart. Remember not to overwhelm your audience; be stingy with the additional facts you include. If done well, however, the additional information will provide a better perspective for the data that are presented. As a result, your audience's understanding of the information presented will be deeper—and likely more convincing. Furthermore, the entire graphic will be more interesting. Take Exhibit 6.11 as an example, which shows the Case-Shiller home price index over time for 10 major cities in the United States as of 2009.[12] There is a lot of helpful context provided in the graph, including the fall in prices on a percentage basis and the expected forecasted fall in values to come, as well as a prebubble real estate sales trend line. All of the context helps to argue convincingly that real estate prices still had more room to fall.

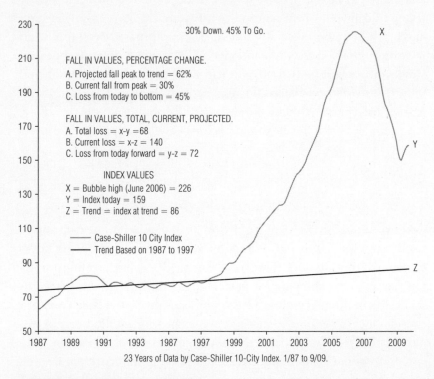

Exhibit 6.11 Residential Property Values
Source: Graph by NewObservations.net

ENCOURAGE INTERACTION

Every data visualization should encourage interaction and exploration of the data. This will make your data more convincing and will also deepen the understanding among your audience. There are many ways to encourage interaction with the data. The simplest method is to include provocative statements and/or questions on your charts and graphs. For example, if you are creating a chart showing customer loyalty data over time for you and your competitors, and the trend for your company is declining, you could include a question as the title of the chart, "How long does it have to go before we act?" or "Customer loyalty is dropping fast; will we take action?" Another relatively simple way to encourage interaction is to host a live presentation of your findings, record it, and then place it in a controlled online environment, where it can be easily passed around within your organization.

The best way to encourage interaction with your data visualization is to create an online interactive data experience. For example, create a Web-based data tool that allows users to explore different data under different conditions. Returning to our Case-Shiller housing index, the *New York Times* also has an online data tool whereby a user can click on a specific location within the United States to get information about that area's local housing trend.[13] (The Web address is included in the reference section at the end of this chapter.) This tool enriches the data experience for the viewer and facilitates a deeper understanding of housing price trends.

If your team follows some of these examples to encourage interaction with your data visualizations, the team will be more successful at influencing the organization and helping to address your company's critical business objectives.

CONCLUSION

As we have discussed throughout this book, effective business analytics is about integrating different types of information across your organization, in order to address critical business questions. Data visualization is a key component of that process and, when done well, enables you to bridge the gap between the data and your nonanalytical business audience. Now that we have reviewed all of the principles in the CONVINCE Framework for data visualization in more detail, let's step back and remind ourselves of the eight principles:

Convey meaning

Objectivity

Necessity

Visual honesty

Imagine the audience

Nimble

Context

Encourage interaction

Hopefully, this chapter has provided you with a way to evaluate whether your business analytics team's data visualizations are hitting the mark or whether there is room for improvement. As we mentioned earlier, data visualization is a half-creative and half-analytical exercise that requires graphic design, information architecture, information technology, and data analysis skills. In an effort to embrace the creative aspects of data visualization, we encourage your team to iterate on designs often and gather feedback frequently. Iterating on your designs allows them to evolve and enables you to try new visualizations quickly, before they are deployed to a larger group. Interestingly, in our experience, we have found that one of the most helpful tools is the tried-and-true pencil and paper; it allows for rapid prototyping and changes as you creatively design new data visualizations.

KEY TAKEAWAYS

- Data visualization is both a creative and an analytical discipline that requires multiple and disparate skill sets, including graphic design, information architecture, information technology, and data analysis.

- Data visualization must clearly convey meaning. People cannot process data easily, so each graphic must be clear in letting observers quickly understand what the data are telling them.

- All data visualizations must be 100% objective. Don't fall into the pressure trap of skewing your data images or selectively choosing data to reflect the agenda of what a constituent wants to see. Stay true to the data and remain objective.

- Include the data visualization only for data that are absolutely necessary, in order to address the critical business questions. Don't boil the ocean.

- Be careful not to unintentionally use data visualization techniques that may skew the data or make differences seem greater than they actually are.

- Know your audience, their appetite for data, and what they care about, and keep the data visualization content appropriate.

- Keep the amount of data that you visualize to a minimum. Don't overwhelm your audience with too many graphs, charts, and images.

- Make sure your data visualizations include context, such as benchmarks or comparisons to prior analyses, in order to help the audience understand the data.

- Design your data visualizations to encourage interaction and exploration of the data, such as using Web-based data visualizations or mobile tools or simply asking provocative questions with your data visualizations.

FURTHER READING

Lengler, Ralph, and Martin J. Eppler. "A Periodic Table of Visualization Methods," www.visual-literacy.org/periodic_table/periodic table.html.

"Mapping Tools in Overview," http://www.visual-literacy.org/pages/maps/mapping_tools_radar/radar.html.

Tufte, Edward. *The Visual Display of Quantitative Information, 2nd ed.* Cheshire, CT: Graphics Press, 2001.

Yau, Nathan. *Visualize This: The Flowing Data Guide to Design, Visualization, and Statistics.* Hoboken, NJ: John Wiley & Sons, 2011.

NOTES

1. Vitaly Friedman, "Data Visualization and Infographics," in *Smashing Magazine*, Smashing Media, January 14, 2008.

2. Nihon Kurieit, *Diagraphics II.* Japan: JCA Press, 1994.

3. William Playfair, "A Letter on our Agricultural Distresses, Their Causes and Remedies: Accompanied with Tables and Copper-Plate Charts, Showing and Comparing the Prices of Wheat, Bread, and Labour, from 1565 to 1821" (London: William Sams, 1821).

4. The American Time Use Study, "Time Use on an Average Work Day for Employed Persons Ages 25 to 54 with Children," Bureau of Labor Statistics, 2010.

5. Kit Eaton, "WikiLeaks Word Clouds: Iraq and Cablegate," blog post, November 29, 2010, www.fastcompany.com.

6. Jeffrey Zeldman, "Tag Clouds Are the New Mullets," blog post, April 19, 2005, on Zeldman.com.

7. Image on website. www.crazyegg.com; http://www.crazyegg.com/external/images/overview2/heatmap-big.jpg.

8. Darrell Huff, *How to Lie with Statistics* (New York: W. W. Norton, 1993), 72.

9. Edward Tufte, *The Visual Display of Quantitative Information* (Cheshire, CT: Graphics Press, 2001).

10. Kaci Bower, *MarketingSherpa's 2012 Search Marketing Benchmark Report*, 2011, SEO Edition, MarketingSherpa.

11. P. Shah, and P. A. Carpenter, "Conceptual Limitations in Comprehending Line Graphs," *Journal of Experimental Psychology-General* 124(1) (1995): 43–61.

12. Michael David, "Case-Shiller Still Predicts Massive 45% Fall From Today's Values," blog post, November 24, 2009, Newobservations.net, http://blog.ml-implode.com/2009/11/case-shiller-still-predicts-massive-45-fall-from-todays-values/.

13. Kevin Quealy, and Jeremy White, "Housing's Rise and Fall in 20 Cities," *New York Times*, accessed March 27, 2012, http://www.nytimes.com/interactive/2011/05/31/business/economy/case-shiller-index.html#city/IND20.

CHAPTER **7**

Analytics Implementation

What Works and What Does Not

"Knowledge rests not upon truth alone, but upon error also."

—Carl Jung

C hapter 2 introduced the Business Analytics Successful Pillars (BASP) framework that provides insights for leaders when undertaking or evaluating the business analytics function in an organization. In this chapter, we will address one of the success pillars in detail, analytics implementation. The analytics implementation pillar deals with the notion that business analytics initiatives must be executed in a manner that enables insight and action to deal with your critical business challenges. More specifically, the way you align your staff, technologies, tools, and other resources can make your analytics implementation more efficient and effective. Failing to align them effectively can result in many wasted work cycles, frustrated staff, and ineffective analytics. However, if you think through all of the elements of the analytics implementation pillar, you will execute analytics effectively within your organization.

As a reminder, the BASP framework is made up of the following pillars:

- **Business challenges.** Align business analytics initiatives to the most pressing business problems your organization needs to address.
- **Data foundation.** The data foundation that will support the business analytics process must be strong in terms of reliability, validity, and governance.
- **Analytics implementation.** Ensuring that business analytics solutions are developed and provided to the enterprise with the end goals in mind is crucial for success.
- **Insight.** Business analytics must transform data from information into intelligence and insight for the organization.
- **Execution and measurement.** Business analytics must be put to work and must lead to organizational action, as well as provide guidance on how to track the results of the actions taken.
- **Distributed knowledge.** Business analytics must be communicated in an effective and efficient manner, as well as made available to as broad a group of stakeholders as is appropriate.
- **Innovation.** Business analytics must be relentlessly innovative, both in analytical approach and in how it affects the organization, by developing solutions that will "wow" customers.

This chapter focuses on the analytics implementation pillar. We will provide detailed information about ten elements that will result in a successful analytics implementation, as well as warnings of which traps to avoid.

As some of you are already aware, putting analytics to work effectively in any organization can be an overwhelming challenge. According to research by the analyst firm Gartner, 70% to 80% of corporate business analytics projects fail.[1] According to Gartner, this is due, in part, to two factors. First, poor communication between IT and the business results in unmet expectations, failure to execute, and poor use of IT and analytics resources. The second primary factor in the failure of business analytics projects is the failure to ask the right questions of the internal stakeholders and, as a result, fail to adequately understand the real needs of the business.

To ensure that analytics implementation and usage will not be relegated to a single team or person or will simply fail, we introduce the successful implementation model we've been using across multiple industries and in different types of corporate cultures. Our discussion will be enriched with commentary from several of the companies we interviewed. We will also cover various recommendations, such as the importance of keeping the right perspective on project outcomes and having a comprehensive checklist with a proper planning process to ensure that we do not get so deep into the analytics that we lose sight of the forest and only see the trees.

This chapter will include a comprehensive plan to implement analytics effectively. The implementation plan will help ensure that every component of an analytics implementation is considered and that you are able to plan for successful project outcomes. The implementation model proposed also provides key milestones of the analytics execution plan that we need to keep in mind and constantly review, to avoid common implementation mistakes and subsequent failures.

Some of you may have witnessed potentially great analytics initiatives and projects not move to complete fruition or full business impact for various reasons. During our interviews, companies shared with us that the main reasons they failed to make forward progress included:

- **Lack of executive sponsorship.** The failure of senior executives to recognize that analytics is important and to resource and empower the analytics function appropriately will result in the eventual failure of your analytics implementation.
- **Lack of analytics leadership.** Team leaders who have neither effectively communicated nor driven strategic analytics projects based on the value of analytics will see their analytics implementation wither and slowly lose momentum. Analytics leaders must champion their analytics *vision* across the organization.

■ **Lack of a clear implementation strategy.** Despite great analytics ideas and solutions, if there is no strategy to put analytics into action across the organization, it will eventually fail.

■ **Lack of support.** If end users, internal customers, and other stakeholders don't understand the value of analytics and don't support the project, your analytics implementation will suffer.

■ **Lack of internal customer experience.** An analytics solution cannot be developed without thinking deeply about the customer experience. Unless customers have been involved throughout the process, it will be hard to get them committed to using the analytics solutions or insights you develop.

■ **Lack of collaboration across organizational groups.** Analytics "is everyone's business." Therefore, if your analytics solutions do not involve multiple functional groups, they are less likely to succeed.

■ **Lack of integrated processes.** If information and knowledge are scattered in silos across the organization, your analytics implementation will be much more challenging.

■ **Lack of skilled and focused human capital.** If your teams don't have the skills and the bandwidth to execute and cannot prioritize effectively, your analytics implementation will fail.

■ **Lack of measurement or metrics to track outcomes.** The outcome key performance indicators (KPIs) should drive the analytics plan and implementation. If outcome KPIs are not clear, the implementation might lead to missed opportunities.

Before we go through the aforementioned reasons for failure and the success factors for the analytics implementation model, it is important for you to really understand the mandate of business analytics and ensure that your teams work within that mandate. Analytics must stay focused and committed in order to deliver the solution that aims to address the critical business challenges. Let's consider the following example of a broad and fairly generic analytics mandate: "Develop customer knowledge and provide actionable insights to sales, marketing, product, and service teams for profitable actions." Within that statement, we quickly see that building analytics tools that do not focus on action will lead to limited impact for business analytics. In this case, the solutions need to lead not only to any actions but actions that make the company profit as well.

ANALYTICS IMPLEMENTATION MODEL

In the following section, we provide an outline and details for each factor that you must consider when implementing your analytics solution within your organization. Exhibit 7.1 outlines the comprehensive

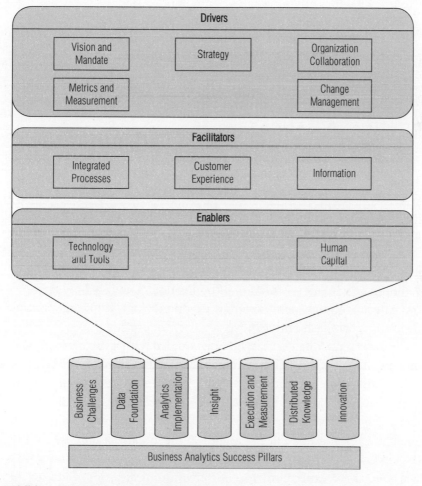

Exhibit 7.1 Analytics Implementation Model

analytics implementation model that resulted from our interviews with different companies and based on our own experience. When each factor is addressed with analytics best practices, your analytics implementations will be very likely to succeed. During the remainder of this chapter, we will outline the analytics implementation model in detail.

Business analytics implementation factors can be broken down into three types:

1. Drivers of your analytics implementation.
2. Facilitators of your analytics implementation.
3. Enablers for your analytics implementation.

We cover each of the 10 analytics implementation factors in the remainder of this chapter.

VISION AND MANDATE

As with any great realization, having an impact begins with a visionary: someone with a mental picture of how the world could change with the delivery of a new solution. In analytics implementation, a visionary is someone able to foresee how the analytics will address pressing business issues in the future. The analytics vision is really about what inspires the analytics leader. What do you need to do to address the business imperatives and challenges for your organization? It should be a broad articulation of hope and dreams for how analytics can affect your business, keeping in mind what your organization needs to accomplish and achieve.

It's about crafting the framework, coupled with a successful model, on how analytics will be implemented across the entire organization or a cross-functional pool of resources. The senior management team must also take the leadership in creating and sharing the data-driven and analytics vision for the company, and this vision will be the guideline for the analytics strategy of the organization. At stake is the creation of an analytical culture and the vision of one and how it will affect the organization. You must communicate your vision for the value of analytics, in order to ingrain the culture of analytics across the organization.

A good example of analytics implementation vision is from Monster Worldwide. In 2005, JP Isson was hired to build predictive analytics from the ground up, because Monster had an executive vision to implement business intelligence and predictive analytics across all regions where it operates. As a global company, Monster operates in more than 55 countries and recognized the opportunity to leverage its global footprint even further by implementing business analytics. The company decided to pilot analytics in Canada and, if successful, expand abroad. The successful vision for this approach was based on the following guiding principles:

1. Start small (one country). Starting small limits and reduces the cost of failure.
2. Test and learn before expanding.
3. Track the performance and the results.
4. Improve the approach and develop best practices.
5. Expand the implementation in other countries, once viability is ascertained.
6. Expand across the world to ensure worldwide analytics coverage.

The senior management team sponsored the project to build an internal predictive analytics team—a team that would help the company bolster the massive volume of data it had and evolve data from the information stage into the intelligence stage. The executive sponsors had clear hopes and dreams of the value that analytics could bring to the entire organization and had the vision to hire people with analytics knowledge and the mind-set to build what later became the global predictive analytics team at Monster. With the global footprint in mind, Canada became the testing and learning ground for analytics. The best practices derived from the successful Canadian experience were then spread across all Monster organizations and regions: from Canada to the United States, Europe, developing markets, and then Asia Pacific.

STRATEGY

Analytics implementation strategy puts in place the master components of the road map created in the vision stage. The strategy must define the objectives for attaining that goal and the activities required to get there; business intelligence projects can take months and years, so it is important to prioritize the phases needed that will be of benefit to the organization. The strategy must also define metrics that will be used to monitor progress on the objectives. The analytics implementation strategy directs the objectives of other operational and sales strategies, as well as the customer relationship management implementation strategy.

Two elements are extremely important to a successful analytics implementation strategy: focus and commitment. The first element of an effective analytics implementation strategy is to focus on addressing the company's business challenges in order of priority. We covered this topic in detail in Chapter 3, so you understand the importance. However, in developing the analytics implementation strategic plan, it's especially important to look back and make sure you are aligned with the company's critical business challenges with each analytics project. This will ensure that projects remain focused and avoid expanding in scope unnecessarily. For example, let's imagine that a critical business objective for your company is to expand the number of different products that companies purchase from you. Therefore, when implementing an analytics project to score customers on their likelihood to purchase additional products, don't be tempted to add more features to your project or tools that do not drive singularly toward that goal. It will be a distraction for your team and will lessen the powerful impact of business analytics on the critical business objective.

The second element that the analytics implementation strategy should have is the commitment of people outside of the analytics team. Commitment from others means they are more likely to devote the time, the budget, and the resources to the analytics project and have the will to see it through. Senior executive leaders are the most essential group from which to engage and secure commitment. However, teams such as sales staff and the collective group of customer-facing employees are also important groups from which to gain commitment. Most successful analytics projects will have at least one other functional group enthusiastically on board.

When developing your analytics implementation strategy, we also suggest creating a one-page executive summary for each project, which will help communicate quickly the key components and

Project Description:				
Value Proposition				

Target Customer & Segment:	Dependencies:
Target Company Size:	Competition:
Benefit:	Risks:
First Customers:	Documentation:

	Year 1	Year 2	Year 3	Yrs 1–3 CAGR
Est. Revenue:				
Est. Total Market Opportunity:				
Est. Cost Savings:				
Est. Customer Satisfaction Impact:				

Exhibit 7.2   Business Analytics Project: Executive Summary

associated benefits to other functional groups in a very straightforward way. This document can be used as needed to reemphasize each project's importance, to introduce new people to the project, and to secure the budget in situations where not everyone understands the impact of analytics. Exhibit 7.2 shows an example of a template your team might use to create the one-page highlight document for each analytics project.

ORGANIZATIONAL COLLABORATION

You can easily find examples of projects that didn't get far because one or two functional groups did not cooperate or were not engaged with the vision. Getting collaboration from all key groups in the organization is a critical factor for bringing your analytics implementation to fruition. In our case, while at Monster.com, we had meetings with the marketing, sales, product, and services teams to get their buy-in and support in the change management process of analytics implementation. We mobilized each group by getting the subject matter expert from each department to become involved in the process from the beginning.

Changes to organizational practices through process, metrics, incentives, and skills must be made to deliver the vision for the ultimate analytics customer experience. Continuous quality improvement through ongoing change management is the norm to bring about an analytics culture. This will ensure that the organization achieves the status of being considered an analytical competitor. Don't start any analytics implementation if you don't have the collaboration of other functional groups and key stakeholders.

HUMAN CAPITAL

Implementing analytics effectively requires a dynamic multidisciplinary team to be in place and available, in order to achieve the ultimate goal of executing the plan and achieving your business objectives. Talent is a requirement to deliver on every phase of the business analytics solution. Depending on the goals for each of your initiatives, your business analytics implementation team for each project may need to include the following skills:

- Project management
- Data modeling
- Data programming in SAS, SPSS, R, SPlus, and so on
- Database extraction and manipulation
- Multivariate statistics
- Data mining/exploration
- Data visualization
- Machine learning
- Marketing analytics
- Web analytics
- Unstructured data analytics
- Marketing research
- Competitive intelligence
- Data quality/governance

It may not be necessary for you to hire people with all of these skills into your organization full time. You may be able to hire independent contractors for some of this expertise, using analytics vendors or individual consultants. Either way, it's important that you map out the skill/capability needs of your organization, based on your critical business goals and corporate culture, so that you may make key analytic staff hires accordingly. Analytical talent is in demand, so it is also extremely important that you offer a clear and compelling career path within your organization for analytics staff members so that they remain engaged and have the opportunity to be rewarded for their performance and talent.

METRICS AND MEASUREMENT

Your analytics implementation must have metrics and measurement as a key component in order to track your analytics successes. The metrics will translate the business challenges into operational measures that can be monitored over time, not only for analytics impact, but for the entire company. If the metrics are well defined, they will be an objective means by which your company can measure progress and business analytics impact. Your company should use these metrics to quantify broad business objectives, such as "be the category leader in online travel," into more specific and measurable objectives, such as "becoming the most visited site in the U.S. travel category, targeting 20 million unique visitors per month." Other examples may include

- Increase productivity
- Increase market share
- Increase retention rate
- Increase wallet share
- Increase conversion rate
- Increase customer satisfaction
- Increase average order size/number of products
- Increase average spend per customer
- Decrease operational costs
- Decrease time-to-decision
- Optimize human capital

Your established metrics for each project will demonstrate the benefit of analytics implementation and will motivate cross-functional teams as your project progresses. Measurement should always be part of the implementation process, in order to track how the analytics solutions are performing and to address the question: are we getting the expected value and ROI from our analytics investment? Defined measurement will also help manage the analytics adoption. Don't start any analytics project without setting clear measurements and metrics to track the performance and the success of the project.

INTEGRATED PROCESSES

Successful analytics implementation should be based on an integrated process. In other words, your analytics implementation should be integrated across your organization, without silos, competing functional team agendas, or disconnected work flows. Processes related to analytics should be integrated as much as possible, either formally or informally. For example, the technology required to implement analytics must be integrated into your business analytics function, through either a direct reporting relationship or a close and trusted collaboration. The goal of integrated processes related to analytics is to optimize the overall success of your analytics initiatives and ultimately deliver for the organization, with the highest impact at the lowest cost. If time is wasted in trying to track down disparate technology resources, data, or corporate knowledge, your ability to execute analytics effectively will suffer. Analytics needs to be delivered via an integrated process: a one-stop shop.

An integrated process could include but is not limited to

- Getting 360-degree consistent and credible views of customer information across departments.
- Integrating customer information from multiple sources (internal and external data) with cross-departmental access to ensure that it is properly leveraged.
- Connecting all recent corporate customer analytics history via the organizational touch points into one central repository.
- Making technology resources aligned and accountable for analytic success.

All four of these integrated processes are keys to effective analytics implementation and will put your team on its way to becoming a full-fledged analytical competitor.

CUSTOMER EXPERIENCE

As with any manufacturer, companies such as Apple are successful because of their ability to anticipate customer needs and create a positive end-user experience. Likewise, to implement a successful business analytics solution, your team must always keep the focus on the end-user experience. How the end user will interact with the solution, gain access to it, and use it are key factors of success. To this end, convenience and ease of use are central to the value proposition of a new analytics solution implementation. As a result, the feedback gathered from the experience of end users and consumers of these systems must be constantly reviewed and the solution refined. Also, for an analytics culture to develop, end users must be involved at the beginning of the analytics project. People's need to feel part of the team and the decision-making process is vital to the success of the analytics endeavor. Many projects have failed due to the rejection of the solution from the end users. End user buy-in can make or break the project and ultimately affect the overall success of the organization in its quest to become a full-fledged analytical competitor.

TECHNOLOGY AND TOOLS

Most organizations are surrounded by an overwhelming amount of data, contained within various technologies and tools. Selecting the right technology and tools for your analytics implementation can be a daunting and overwhelming task, because there are so many options, and you are sometimes limited by what your company has used in the past. A comprehensive process for selecting the right type of data tools and technologies is beyond the scope of this book. However, following are some key principles to consider:

- **Easy to use**. Ease of use should be considered. As you bring on new staff in the future, you want a tool that can be learned and adopted by different user types.

- **Business relevant**. Is each tool or technology business relevant, and does it help you achieve your business objectives more rapidly? Stay away from tools that appeal only to your team's intellectual curiosity.

- **Increase your team's impact**. Does the tool or the technology make your team more efficient and have greater impact on the organization?

- **Data integrity**. Does the technology or the tool place a high priority on data quality?

- **Extensible**. A tool should be capable of growing with you and the changing needs of your organization. You don't want to find yourself forced to migrate to a different tool because your business requirements have outgrown it.

We also encourage you to consult expert reviews from companies such as Gartner, GigaOM, and Forrester, as well as to consider peer reviews on analytics community sites. Just remember, the selection of an analytical tool can be a big commitment in time and resources, so it should be considered thoughtfully. Too often, tools are selected based on the reputation of a vendor, rather than on the business goals that need to be met or the quality of the tool itself.

CHANGE MANAGEMENT

Great business analytics initiatives can fail when change management processes do not reinforce the importance and the proper use of the analytics solutions. Change management processes for your analytics solutions must incorporate end-user needs and input. This not only enables "buy in" from different levels of the organization, but it improves the probability of success for the solution. Internal communication strategies are essential for effective change management and must involve the executive sponsors, as well as the analytics project leaders, reaching into all project touch points. The change management communication must also provide a process to support the change and help those affected understand its impact on the organization. In addition, as part of the change management process, every end user, such as sales and services representatives, should be trained and rewarded for leveraging the power of the analytics solution. Following are some key change management principles to keep in mind for your analytics implementation:

- Change management must ensure that every stakeholder understand and support the change.
- When the anticipated benefits are communicated before the change takes place, they become incentives and a measure to assess progress.
- Collecting staff input early in the change process creates an opportunity for the development of "best practices," leadership development, and team development.
- Employee performance will benefit from the support received throughout the change process, which leads to an understanding of the changes being implemented

As a general guiding principle, we recommend that you take a baby-steps approach for your analytics implementation. Start with a small pilot group on which to test and learn. This will help quickly address potential implementation issues and minimize the impact on the business. Also, assuming the pilot is successful, it will reinforce commitment from stakeholders involved in the proof of concept or pilot phase.

We leave you with some questions to ask of your team when developing an analytics implementation plan for a project. The ability to thoughtfully answer these questions can mean the difference between success and failure.

- What is your goal (or business question) for the project?
- What are the risks of not addressing that goal/question?
- When will you meet that goal or answer the business question?
- What is the analytics strategy to do so?
- What technology and tools will implement the strategy most effectively?
- Who should be involved, from top executives, senior management, and customer-facing employees?
- What impact (benefits) will the solution have on customer experience?

- What impact (benefits) will the solution have on our customer-facing employees?

- How will end users be trained to use the solution?

- What resources are required to achieve your plan?

- Who will be involved in executing your plan, internally or externally?

- Is your analytics solution integrated with current customer-facing insight tools?

- What metrics will help you track/measure the performance (progress) and success of the analytics solution?

Answering these questions will provide you with a blueprint for building a foundation of success for any business analytics implementation.

 KEY TAKEAWAYS

- Putting analytics to work in any organization requires a comprehensive and well-thought-out implementation model for each analytics project.

- Transform your business challenge into an analytics implementation that will improve your customers' and clients' experience and have a positive impact on your organization.

- Your implementation model should be:

  - Specific: Define a clear scope (vision) and mandate.

  - Measurable: Track your progress and success.

  - Attainable: Ensure the change is realistic.

  - Results oriented: Set clear operational measures and report progress on them frequently.

  - Time bounded: Avoid a long schedule that exhausts the interest and energy of everyone in the business; instead, deliver sizable components in 3-month milestones. The overall project time frame should not exceed 6 to 9 months.

- Consider all 10 factors in implementing your business analytics projects: vision, strategy, organizational collaboration, change management, metrics, integrated processes, customer experience, information, technology and tools, human capital.

- Don't start to implement any analytics project if you don't have executive sponsorship.

- Don't start to implement any analytics without the involvement of key functional groups.
- Whether they're in sales, marketing, or customer service, the end-users' experience should be a focus of your solution.
- A baby-steps approach for successful analytics implementation is best. Start small, test and learn, adjust, then expand.

NOTES

1. Bill Goodwin, "Poor Communication to Blame for Business Intelligence Failure, Says Gartner," ComputerWeekly.com, January 10, 2011, http://www.computerweekly.com/news/1280094776/Poor-communication-to-blame-for-business-intelligence-failure-says-Gartner.

2. Thomas H. Davenport and Jeanne G. Harris, *Competing on Analytics: The New Science of Winning* (Cambridge, MA: Harvard Business School Press, 2007).

3. Goodwin, "Poor Communication to Blame for Business Intelligence Failure, Says Gartner."

4. David Kiron, Rebecca Shockley, Nina Kruschwitz, Glenn Finch, and Michael Haydock, *Analytics: The Widening Divide*, MIT/IBM Study, Fall 2011, http://c805803.r3.cf2.rackcdn.com/MIT-SMR-IBM-Analytics-The-Widening-Divide-Fall-2011.pdf?utm_source=WhatCounts+Publicaster+Edition&utm_medium=email&utm_campaign=TNIE+2011+Report+Download&utm_content=http%3a%2f%2fc805803.r3.cf2.rackcdn.com%2fMIT-SMR-IBM-Analytics-The-Widening-Divide-Fall-2011.pdf.

CHAPTER **8**

Voice-of-the-Customer Analytics and Insights

By Abhilasha Mehta, PhD

"The customer is always right."

—Marshall Fields and Harry Gordon Selfridges, early twentieth century

---

Abhilasha (Abby) Mehta is the director of global customer insights for Staples, the world's largest office products and solutions company operating in 26 countries. Abby conducts both qualitative and quantitative research among Staples' business (B2B) and personal (B2C) customers to guide customer-centric decisions across all business units. She was the head of marketing research and customer insights at Monster Worldwide, the leading Internet career website, and the director of research at Gallup & Robinson, a marketing research company. She has been published widely and speaks at various industry and academic venues. Abby has twice been the recipient of the Advertising Research Foundation's David Ogilvy Award for Excellence in Research.

———————

The epigraph at the beginning of this chapter was coined almost 100 years ago, but the emotion behind it, which showed a company's keenness to put the customer first, is still just as relevant. Today, almost a century later, the customer is more in charge than ever before. Whether "right" or not, customers today are certainly much more sophisticated, analytical, demanding, savvy at comparative shopping, and also talking openly and loudly about the products and the services they use. Businesses that are not listening hard to what customers are saying and are not appropriately leveraging this input into their daily business decisions do so at their own peril.

CUSTOMER FEEDBACK IS INVALUABLE

Customers today—and by "customers," I mean *current* customers, as well as *future* customers—have choices. They will come back to do business with you only if you are responsive to them in fulfilling their needs. Getting feedback from your customers and turning the feedback into action that satisfies and delivers value to them is essential for your business success. Without doing this, you will typically be playing catch-up to your competitors and will spend time simply stomping fires to help customers get what they are looking for. Done right, putting the voice of the customer (VOC) in the business decision-making loop can provide a huge opportunity for an organization to be proactive, on target, and responsive to customers, ultimately improving loyalty, retention, and new customer acquisition. For example, Netflix had a brilliant idea and can be truly acknowledged as the pioneer that changed how entertainment is distributed. It saw major success, but down the road, a lack of understanding and respect for the customer, in the form of an almost haughty price increase in 2011, boomeranged badly on the company. From then on, it has been a slide downhill. Short-term profitability is certainly great, but you need the continued enthusiasm and patronage from customers for the profitability to last.

Technology has changed the way businesses work today—the long tail of the Internet means competition has increased multiple-fold as customers are shopping far and wide, not just down the street or within driving distance. With a click on the keypad, products and services from thousands of miles away can be compared and obtained conveniently and easily. Even people shopping at bricks-and-mortar facilities are typically checking out what they want to buy before going to the store, or even at the store via smartphones and tablets, to make the purchase. Easy access to information, such as peer reviews, user testimonials, expert advice, consumer reports, price comparison data, and shared comments on social media, are a few of the sources that have made it extremely easy to comparison shop and find the best options, a perfect fit.

It is a complex business environment today, and you need to be relevant to your customers. This can be achieved only if you clearly understand who they are and their needs, attitudes, perceptions, and behaviors toward your own, as well as your competitors' products and services. You need to sift through your customers' "voices" to identify where you are not meeting their expectations and find out what they like about you, then plan appropriate actions. Make sure to stay focused on your strengths as you pay attention to what needs fixing and the areas of opportunity. VOC insights support the strategic, as well as the tactical, decisions and help fine-tune operational processes. For example, recently at Monster Worldwide, the leading online recruitment site, this chapter's author, Abhilasha (Abby) Mehta, was monitoring the customer satisfaction for a newly launched high-cost flagship product six months after its release. The post-purchase satisfaction results showed some high ratings and also some opportunities for improvement among a small group of customers. The reason customers gave for these ratings was that the product not supplying the results they expected—which was surprising, given that the new product was designed to provide better results than previously! With further analysis and deeper dives with customers via one-on-one in-depth interviews, Abby found that lack of knowledge about *how to use* some of the specific features in the new product was the critical issue behind the problem for this group. As a result, products, sales materials, and sales operations were evaluated and improved, and customer training programs, including training documents, were reviewed, revised, and enhanced in several ways to assure optimum product function use. By the following year, customer satisfaction ratings for the product improved by a wide margin. Listening to the customers and then implementing the VOC insights were key steps in resolving this issue.

Substantial evidence shows that there is a strong relationship between customer experience and loyalty to a company. Recently, Megan Burns from Forrester Research confirmed their previous findings and concluded, "Years of Forrester data confirm the strong relationship between the quality of a firm's customer experience. . . . and loyalty measures like willingness to consider the company for another purchase, likelihood to switch business, and likelihood to recommend."[1] Burns further noted that "better customer experience can be worth millions in annual revenue." The increased revenue calculations are based on existing customers' incremental purchases, savings made possible by lower churn levels and the net sales driven by word of mouth. These results are not surprising—in fact, they are quite intuitive, and each of us can relate to this quite easily. Can you remember when you had a bad experience with a product or with customer service and still went back to do business with the company?

PUTNAM INVESTMENTS

CASE STUDY

Putnam Investments, the 75-year-old firm that manages money for individual and institutional investors, has been recognized for its world-class customer service as the winner of the prestigious DALBAR service award for the last 22 consecutive years. During this time, Putnam, like many other asset management firms, has endured challenges, including turbulent market conditions—but one of the constants during this period has been the firm's well-recognized commitment to service. Steve Krichmar, the chief of operations at Putnam Investments, explains the secret behind this heritage: "This has been possible regardless of every conceivable market condition over the last two decades because excellent customer service is very important to us as a firm, it differentiates us in the marketplace—and the key to our success is that the voice of our customer is a critical input in everything that we do."

Steve notes that staying responsive to the investment service needs of customers as the business and economic environment changes is critical, and to that end, Putnam is constantly trying to listen to its customers: "We don't work in a vacuum, but rather in the context of the evolving financial needs of customers, changes in the stock market and in the rules and regulations of the industry, as well as the emergence of new technologies and ways of doing business today. In adapting to a constantly evolving landscape, we want to fully understand what our customers want and how changes to our approach will be received *before* we even make the changes." In a recent example, Putnam Investments realized there was added convenience for customers in moving from paper statements to digital options, as well as cost savings in making the transition—a win-win proposition overall. Customers were fully engaged as this development moved from concept to execution. Currently, Putnam offers paper, CD, and online statements—allowing customers to choose whatever delivery method they prefer, with some customers continuing to want and receive paper statements. Steve says, "We want customers to always consider us easy and accessible to do business with. Listening to customers is what we do every day, it is a continuous process, and we always try to work seamlessly across the firm for their benefit, whether it be incorporating customer feedback into our daily approach or spearheading new, far-reaching innovation."

Customer feedback is also very valuable in explaining trends in your *behavioral* data. For example, let's assume you notice a decline in your purchase data among a specific segment of your target, but you can't really know *why* this is happening from the sales data you have available. Customer feedback is needed to provide answers. Talking with lapsed customers within the declining segment will help you understand why they have stopped buying, and combining this with current customer needs and satisfaction will help you identify actions that are needed to stem this declining sales trend. Connecting customer feedback with behavioral data provides comprehensive insights about not only *what's* going on, but also *why* it's going on. Decisions based on such a panoramic view are powerful.

KRAFT FOODS

CASE STUDY

Integrating analytics with customer feedback and making sure business partners can implement the insights is key for Kraft Foods, the leading packaged foods company. Sudeep Haldar, the senior director of Strategic Insights at Kraft, notes, "Consumer insights plays a key role in our business and brand strategy, as well as tactics. There are three major pillars around which we are organized: consumer insight, shopper insights, and analytics. We leverage each of these areas individually, as well as holistically, to drive business decisions. We build intuition around our brands, as well as have hard measurement on ROIs on our marketing programs. It is both an art and science."

The processes of go-to-market strategy heavily depend on understanding the consumer in the competitive market context, which includes learning how consumers shop the category and choose brands, testing product quality and benchmarking against the competition, and testing alternative merchandising plans and pricing and promotion tactics, as well assessing how consumers react to the marketing campaigns in real time. "The analytics brings it all together by measuring our ROIs on marketing drivers and the impacting of future plans. It helps create a win-win strategy for the customer and the manufacturer," says Sudeep.

For example, Kraft found that 15 biscuit brands were growing in one of their priority markets. Qualitative and quantitative consumer insights helped determine how these brands competed for share of the consumer's wallet. Based on this, Kraft was able to develop a strong portfolio plan for future growth that went over and above the plan by 7%. "The consumer insights and analytics helped us with key decisions, such as determining different price strategies for some key brands, identifying the investment needed for a full range of products, including better-for-you options, planning joint brand promotions because individual promotions were cannibalizing sales, and optimizing media spend offline versus online. We delivered insights that were integrated and timely to the brand managers. It required an investment—which more than paid off."

That there is value in customer feedback is not a new concept. What is new, however, is the sophistication of the business environment and the multiple channels of interaction and purchase options that customers now have with an organization. The challenge today is how to systematically capture the customer voices across these various touch points, integrate them with one another and with the other sources of behavioral data within the organization, effectively sift through all of this to find the key insights, and make sure these insights are socialized within the enterprise so that appropriate actions are identified and implemented. There are several potential roadblocks in getting this process done right. Among the companies Abby Mehta talked to, the reasons mentioned that can impede an effective VOC and customer feedback program include:

- Lack of resources to fund such a program.
- Lack of knowledge and skills needed within the enterprise to go about it correctly.
- Lack of priority and value placed by top management for setting up such a program.
- Lack of value placed on using customer feedback by line managers, who either feel they already know the answers well enough or are afraid to confront reality.
- Lack of a process to effectively take action and implement the insights gained from such a program.

THE MAKINGS OF AN EFFECTIVE VOICE-OF-THE-CUSTOMER PROGRAM

Many customer-centric companies have overcome the roadblocks and established effective voice-of-the-customer programs. They have installed centers of research and insight to manage these programs and encouraged a culture of information-based, customer-centric business decision making across the enterprise. A systematic VOC program, in its simplest form, is about being proactive in constantly capturing the customer input and incorporating this input into the key functions of the organization at the strategic, tactical, and operational levels (see Exhibit 8.1).

Listen, Monitor

Obtaining relevant, timely, and objective customer feedback is the first step to a successful VOC program. Irrelevant information distracts the

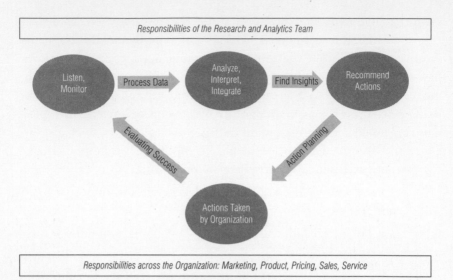

Exhibit 8.1 Voice-of-the-Customer Program Paradigm

business manager, and insights that come too late cannot effectively have a positive impact on the business. In addition, biased opinions obtained from a handful of selected customers can be more harmful than no information at all, because such quick-and-dirty research can give the false impression of an information-based decision-making process, when in fact it is not. You need to avoid at all costs decisions based on insights obtained by unreliable research methods and poor-quality data, because these insights will be misleading and will push the wrong business decisions.

There are several systematic methodologies to obtain high-quality customer feedback. Some listening mechanisms need to be continuous, constantly monitoring customers in real time with ongoing data collection, while others may be administered periodically, such as on a quarterly, biannual, or annual basis. The most appropriate method for you depends on your situation and market environment. There are a number of factors to consider, such as what are the specific goals for this feedback, how will the data be used, what decisions will be made with it, how often and when are the results needed, what resources can be allocated to the process, and, most important, who are the customers you need to obtain feedback from, and what mechanisms will be most effective in getting their feedback? In addition, you may solicit feedback in formal ways, such as inviting customers to provide their reactions by means of structured surveys administered online or by telephone, via in-depth personal interviewing, in focus groups and mini group discussions, or informally through suggestion boxes in business locations, on feedback links on websites, or by observational listening to what is being said externally, such as comments in social media. Furthermore, you will also want to gather feedback from front-line employees and mine the customer service contact database where complaints/kudos are stored, because these are also effective ways to supplement the directly obtained customer feedback data. The most commonly used customer feedback—gathering mechanisms are discussed further on, with advantages and caveats about when each may be most appropriate.

Online, Telephone, and Web Surveys

Well-designed survey questionnaires can be very useful in gathering customer and prospect feedback about a variety of issues that can guide business decisions. Formal surveys are typically designed to obtain feedback from large numbers of respondents that can provide quantitative results and also be used for high-level analytics to help companies fully understand the issues of interest. Well-designed, quantitative surveys based on a representative sample of respondents can provide a clear and accurate snapshot of the audience's base and can also be predictive about what is to come in the near future.

Online surveys are getting more and more popular, because they allow respondents to think through the questions and respond at their own pace and at their convenience and are relatively inexpensive, compared to phone surveys. Internet penetration rates are now high, which has allowed online surveys to become more reliable and valid than they were several years ago. Telephone surveys, on the other hand, may be more appropriate when trying to reach audiences that may not be online or hard-to-reach targets, such as lapsed customers, who typically may not respond to your online survey. Telephone surveys are conducted by trained interviewers and allow for more flexibility in the branching out of questions, because interviewers can gauge the response pattern and guide the questioning in the appropriate manner, as well as probe for reasons for the ratings and responses provided previously. Surveys could also be "popped" up on your company website to gauge the site experience and manage the user experience.

In-Depth Interviews

In situations where a deep diagnosis of the issues of interest is needed or when the topic of interest is in its early, exploratory stages, so that you are still trying to gauge the exact nature of the issues of interest, in-depth telephone interviews are appropriate to gather relevant feedback. Such interviews are designed to allow the respondents to discuss the issues in detail and pontificate on their responses. The key to success with this type of research is having well-trained interviewers who are flexible and can channel the interview in the direction that is most suited to the respondent to obtain maximum input.

You can use in-depth interviews in conjunction with quantitative surveys to provide deeper insights and understand the reasons for results obtained in the surveys and in the behavioral data you may have, such as those related to sales, traffic, purchase volume, purchase channels used, market share, customer satisfaction ratings, and so on, to fully understand customer preferences and shopping behavior. In-depth interviews can also be very helpful as early exploratory research to guide future quantitative research and can help hone in on the questions and issues of interest.

Focus Groups

Focus groups are among the most commonly used qualitative research methods today. Focus groups are cost-effective and offer good insights and feedback about what the target audience is thinking. The appeal of focus groups is further enhanced by the fact that the business sponsors of the research are able to sit behind a one-way mirror and observe the participants, which allows the sponsors to feel involved in the issues of interest and observe customers and prospects directly. With new technologies, online focus groups are also gaining traction.

Focus groups, however, should be used with care and caution, because there are some caveats to being effective with focus groups. One of the main disadvantages of this methodology is the group dynamics that can often occur. Sometimes these are obvious, such as when selected participants try to force their views on the group and are loud and assertive, taking up too much "voice time." More subtle, but equally damaging, is when this happens quietly because there are a charismatic participant in the room who speaks eloquently, and others are persuaded to agree with this person, rather than voice their own differing opinions. Another caution about using this methodology relates to the fact that only a small group of respondents can participate in the research, and they must be located within limited geographic areas where the focus groups are being conducted. As a result, generalizing results from such research to the full, wider target population of interest can be an issue. Focus groups should be used as exploratory in nature, providing some direction for future research, or to gain good insights when one needs to dive deeper into issues uncovered by other quantitative research, rather than being relied on as conclusive research.

Customer Service Contact and Interaction

One of the most valuable sources of customer feedback is the communication directed by customers to your customer service team within the organization. This could be kudos for what you may have done well or a complaint that needs attention; in the case of the latter, you probably have a system in place about how to address the issue, and, most likely, the issue will be resolved in a timely and appropriate fashion. To what extent, however, are you using this information from a strategic perspective? These "episodes" of your customers' direct and proactive contact with your organization are an immensely rich source of data from the larger perspective of gathering customer feedback for strategic use. Whether it is the kudos or the complaints, both inform you about how you are doing.

A systematic process of capturing and analyzing this service contact database can provide deep insights into what is working best and where there is critical need for improvement. One of the first steps in using these data effectively is to catalogue these customer issues with a high level of granularity to yield quantitative results that can be tracked over time. Periodic, possibly weekly or monthly, reporting and analysis may be installed to help you identify the most common issues and track them as you make changes to address these issues. You should also conduct root-cause analyses for frequently recurring issues and identify where within the enterprise a change is needed, so that the issue ceases to be a concern going forward.

TIME WARNER CABLE

CASE STUDY

At Time Warner Cable, a leading cable telecommunications company, customer service support metrics are closely integrated with customer satisfaction metrics to improve customer loyalty, as well as service cost efficiencies. Joseph Arsenault, the senior manager of metrics and reporting, notes: "Key customer service metrics and customer satisfaction surveys have often been used independent of each other to measure a company's service goals. Linking the two provides a true 360-degree view. We use the six 'S's in this approach—Symptom, Support, Survey, Summarize, Savings, and Spherical—to provide successful and efficient customer service within the enterprise."

When a customer has an issue, this "symptom" is resolved by providing appropriate "support" to the customer. This is followed by sending a "survey" to the customer, which measures the customer's satisfaction with the provided service. Once the survey response is obtained, a "summary" of the episode is developed, which includes a review of the specific customer's issue and the service provided in context of how it was received by the customer. The next phase, termed *spherical*, involves having the life-cycle team analyze each episode summary and revise future response actions to the same issue, based on how well the response worked. This loop continues, and, depending on the whether the customer satisfaction value improves or declines, appropriate further changes are made going forward. Joe notes that "By using this approach, companies like AOL and Time Warner Cable have shown significantly lowered service support costs, up to $100,000, on a specific issue. The overall savings, by applying this method to numerous support issues, has resulted in savings in the millions of dollars. By optimizing the service cost savings against customer satisfaction improvement, a model of efficient and effective service can be created."

Front-Line Employee Listening Systems

In addition to directly asking customers about what they are thinking, learning what they tell your employees who interact with them is another source of customer feedback that you will want to integrate in your VOC program. Your sales associates, customer service agents, call center employees, training staff, front-desk personnel, and others in similar roles are well-trained to provide information about the organization to customers in a consistent and clearly defined manner, ensuring standard customer experience. The flow of information, however, is two-way. These employees are the recipients of customers' concerns when things don't go well, as well as praise when things do go well. This indirect intelligence should be tapped into systematically and brought back to the rest of the organization to be leveraged in your business decisions—not only to improve specific operational issues but to improve overall enterprise processes and also potentially offer ideas for innovation as well. Obtaining customer-related feedback from employees is best done in real time as the issues surface, for authenticity and reliability in reporting the interaction. Some companies have set up employee listening systems that are directly accessible to all employees on the intranet, where they are encouraged to note any new information gained from customers. Alternatively, you may conduct employee surveys periodically to gather such information.

Word of Mouth and Social Media

In this super-wired world, the Internet has considerably accelerated and widened the reach of word-of mouth communication that traditionally occurred among relatively smaller groups of friends and family. In the past, it was hard to reliably and comprehensively gather what was being said about you, your organization, your brand, and your products among your customer network and use in it a systematic way. That has changed tremendously with the digitizing of information. Social networking, blogs and micro-blogs, direct comments on company websites, and company pages on social networks have not only encouraged customers to openly talk about products and services and create their own content about these products and services, the digital nature of these comments has created the unprecedented opportunity to capture this information systematically. You have probably already recognized the need to listen to this chatter and respond to it appropriately, often immediately. This scattered information, however, is precious customer feedback and needs to be integrated and channeled into your organization's VOC mechanism on a regular and systematic way, to be leveraged appropriately in planning the business strategy. This has just about begun, and systems are being built around this need—there is certainly much more to come in this area.

Customer Communities, Crowd Sourcing, Ethnography, and Diary Keeping

The new digital world offers some novel and interesting ways to engage with customers and listen to them efficiently and easily or transform older tedious methods into a much more accessible and convenient format. Customer communities are online groups of passionate customers who are typically invited by an organization to be part of the community because they want to talk to you and to one another on an ongoing basis to exchange ideas for your business. These have been successfully created and used by some companies. Crowd sourcing refers to an open online network of customers who post their thoughts and interact with one another to offer ideas and react to other members' ideas. Ethnographies and diaries are traditional methods that have received a makeover; previously, they were done manually, which took huge amounts of time and expense, but now respondents keep online diaries, and ethnographies are conducted using video cameras, making it much easier not only to collect the data but to process the data as well. These methods can supplement the ongoing VOC efforts, as and when needed.

Analyze, Interpret, Integrate

You may have put in place many of the processes listed previously to effectively collect and capture the voices of the customers, but are you *truly listening* to what is being said?

Turning the raw data collected from the various customer listening tools into meaningful insights is a key step in making the VOC program successful so that it can affect business decisions. In today's world, there seems to be no dearth of data within an enterprise—but managers note that there aren't enough insights. You need to make sure that you are leveraging the right tools and put in place the right talent and skills to transform the raw data into usable insights that can guide your actions.

It is a good idea to analyze the VOC data in quantitative ways whenever possible and to design the customer feedback data collection to allow such quantification as much as possible. Such quantification allows for reliably measuring customer perceptions, attitudes, and behaviors and for these to be systematically tracked over time and compared across groups. Whether the feedback is in terms of a rating scale (brand perceptions or satisfaction ratings on a 0 to 10 scale) or verbatim comments made by customers to explain their concerns or delights, you should plan to provide the results in quantified metrics. For example, the customer satisfaction metric based on a rating scale could be analyzed for the proportion of respondents who are satisfied (in other words, those giving top ratings on this scale), which can then be compared across time (did the level of satisfaction improve or not, as compared to last quarter or last year or since a new product was introduced, and so on) and across different groups and segments (for example, are older customers more or less satisfied than younger ones, or how does satisfaction differ among those purchasing online versus those buying in the store, and so forth) and across competitors (how much better or worse are you performing versus others in the space, how they are changing over time versus you, and so on).

Along the same lines, verbatim comments provided by customers should also be processed and quantified to provide a clear report of what the top issues are and how these may have changed over time or may differ across segments. These are quantified by coding each comment into a category and counting how often each was mentioned. You will need to develop an appropriate classification scheme to categorize the open responses into relevant topics and then compute the frequency of occurrence for each topic. Traditionally, the coding process has been done manually, which requires substantial resources in manpower and time to complete; presently, excellent text-mining solutions have been developed to help quantify open-ended comments far more quickly and cost-effectively. At Monster, we conceived of and developed an effective text-mining solution to quantify the ongoing survey comments regarding website satisfaction. A custom classification scheme was put in place to quantify the suggestions that job seekers who visited the website made, to improve each task they performed on the site. An analysis was undertaken each month, and we provided the product team with a clear picture of the top issues that month, as voiced by our site visitors; in addition, this allowed the effective tracking of the monitored issues when the site changes were made. Similar text-mining solutions are valid for open-ended questions in surveys or feedback comments in stores, on websites, or sent via e-mail.

Advanced statistics and modeling may also be used as appropriate to analyze the VOC data. This book has already outlined various statistical methods, such as multivariate modeling, conjoint analyses, segmentation, and market mix modeling, to name a few, to mine customer behavioral data; the same can be used with VOC data that is collected via appropriately designed quantitative surveys, asking customers what they want, feel, think. Questions such as the following can be answered using such advanced statistical techniques:

- What drives your customer loyalty, and how should the enterprise prioritize strategy?
- What product features are most likely to provide you with competitive advantage?
- What mix of products is most wanted by customers in your product portfolio?
- What is your best pricing strategy for each segment of interest?
- How does your brand health and brand equity compare to that of your competitors?
- Which parts of your marketing spend are providing the largest return on investment?
- Which target segments are most likely to purchase your products?
- What is your customer lifetime value for each segment of interest?

Finally, as noted previously, an important aspect to keep in mind as you analyze and interpret your VOC data are to integrate the various pieces of data across the enterprise. In other words, do not simply integrate the various VOC elements that are related to one another, which certainly needs to be done, but also connect the customer feedback data to the behavioral data you are collecting and to the analytics you are undertaking within your enterprise. For example, integrate click-stream data with customer perceptions and reactions about the website, segment customer satisfaction by product usage patterns, and by how people buy (for example, in-store versus online), evaluate customer needs and product value proposition by the product sales trends, and so on. Such an integration of behavioral and customer attitudinal data provides a comprehensive picture and offers much more powerful insights than either VOC data or behavioral data analytics can provide in isolation.

MARKET RESEARCH AND CUSTOMER ANALYTICS

CASE STUDY

Jim Tincher, a customer experience consultant and blogger, combined analytics with market research interviews to gain deep customer insights for his client, one of the nation's largest health savings account banks.[2] This bank works with thousands of companies who offer these HSAs to their employees. Jim notes, "Unfortunately, a review of the data showed that even when employers offered to contribute hundreds of dollars into the HSA, 1 out of 7 employees failed to open the account, forfeiting the money. The first step was to conduct an analytics review. We found no impact of demographics of the participant on this behavior. The single factor that drove the issue was the participant's employer. Simply put, at some companies nearly everybody followed through to open the HSA, but at others, there were thousands of employees who missed out on up to $1,000 of the employer's money, all because they did not take the time to open the HSA."

To learn why some companies' introductions were so much more effective than others, the bank conducted interviews with its most successful

(continued)

customers to learn what they did differently. "What we found was that these companies used completely different approaches to rolling out the health-care program. Rather than treating it as an HR issue, successful companies used a comprehensive approach, providing full information and benefits." The bank used these results to develop a formal change management model to help new companies implement HSA plans, rather than leaving each company to its own devices. It led to the development of a suite of education tools that employers could use within their company and could involve senior management to communicate the messages. "As a result, two years after we began this program, we redid the analytics and found that the percentage of eligible consumers opening the account had increased by +7 percentage points, from 86% to 93%. Working directly with our customers helped us develop a customer-centric strategy we could never create on our own."

Recommend Actions

So, you have effectively gathered customer feedback, applied the appropriate analysis, and obtained insights about what's going on in your business. What now? The next step in the effective VOC program is to take the identified insights and make recommendations to the business about what needs to be done, whether it is to continue moving along the same path or change what is currently being doing. One of the common challenges that VOC researchers have faced is communicating the results effectively and making sure there is actionability at the end of the road.

As noted earlier, the company culture is an important factor in how your VOC insights and recommendations will get used. To that end, maintaining a culture of information-based decision making is important. Make sure not to perpetuate a culture where inconvenient research results are questioned and dismissed because they make managers uncomfortable and unwilling to change course. Senior leadership can play an important role in this. Rather than using the customer feedback results as a means to point fingers and assign blame for things that may not have gone well, make your VOC program proactive and solutions-oriented. It is important to note that promot-ing effective collaboration among the research/VOC professionals with business teams will go a long way in making your VOC-based recommendations realistic and actionable. Although the data will provide insights and understanding about what customers think and want, effective actions can be developed only when researchers work closely with functional business teams to understand the enterprise's priorities and focus and get a good handle on the feasibility of proposed actions.

Communicating results and recommendations effectively is another key factor in a successful VOC program. Make sure they are accessible and easy to understand, relevant, objective, strategically aligned, and timely. VOC professionals need to be great storytellers— and, at the same time, well-grounded in facts and unbiased toward the outcomes, making sure they support the organization's strategy and vision.

THE FUNDVISUALIZER

CASE STUDY

Engaging with customers and obtaining and incorporating their feedback throughout the process has helped Putnam Investments successfully design and market its patent-pending FundVisualizer, a first-of-its-kind financial services analytical tool that enables investment advisers to conduct in-depth real-time evaluations of thousands of investment choices. It brought home the MITX 15th Annual Interactive Award for Putnam Investments, quite an achievement for a financial company among the many cutting-edge digital companies competing for the same. Mark McKenna, the head of marketing at Putnam Investments, a 75-year-old financial asset management company, notes, "Many were slow to understand how the brand interactions on the Internet would pan out. We wanted to embrace Web 2.0. The Internet is very open, and we can't be myopic about it. This tool allows us to help our customers in ways that they would like. As we developed its mobile and desktop user experience and created appropriate marketing materials, we said, 'Let's put ourselves in the shoes of our customers.'"

The FundVisualizer tool offers free access to all investment advisers, regardless of their relationship to Putnam, and allows them to create scenarios in real time with iPad applications, substituting the printed, dated, hypothetical comparisons of mutual funds that advisers would develop ahead of client meetings. The Putnam team listened to the customers via focus groups and conducted periodic meetings to discuss the progress of the product. The team also created an advocate group of passionate customers

(continued)

who constantly provided feedback to help refine and enhance the product and to guide the value proposition and the creation of marketing materials. Mark says, "We listened to what our customers wanted. That was very valuable in being so successful with this tool."

Actions Taken by Organization

Acting on the VOC insights is an organization-wide responsibility. For your VOC program to be successful, develop processes that help take the VOC recommendations to the appropriate business teams and senior executives. A customer-centric culture makes managers at all levels hungry for data and insights, and they will then use the information to plan actions.

VOC insights help in guiding strategy across marketing, product, pricing, sales, and service teams in their daily business decisions. The types of business actions that your VOC program can assist with are discussed in great length in the following sections. Use the VOC data and customer feedback to identify breakdowns in the system on an ongoing basis and plan actions where they are needed to repair the breakdowns. Ask whether the issues that have surfaced are isolated or systemic, and conduct root-cause analysis to go beyond metrics and diagnose the issues to develop actionable recommendations. Don't simply use VOC to trouble-shoot customer issues, however; make it an integral and proactive part of the business strategy across the company. Make it a habit to use customer information when making decisions.

In addition, once an action is taken, the role of your VOC program should not stop there—keep the evaluation loop in place, continue to talk to the customers to find out how well the new strategy worked, how things have changed for your customers and whether there is need for further improvements. This applies to all functional areas; for example, marketing will want to evaluate how well its recent campaign performed, while product may want to know if the new features or flavors it introduced are working well, and service will want to make sure the changes in the service protocol are working effectively, and so on.

Both happy and unhappy customers share their experiences with others; however, the unhappy ones do so at higher rates. The Temkin

Group Customer Experience Survey found that 63% of those who had a very good experience with company shared this with someone, whereas 77% of those who had a very bad experience did so.[3] Make sure to take action on issues your customers have brought in front of you and communicate with them about how you are resolving their issues, because there is a clear ripple effect that you will want to manage. Within the service organization, Abby Mehta found that how a customer issue was handled was more important than whether the issue was resolved, in terms of overall satisfaction with the service provided.

AT&T

CASE STUDY

Tim Ruth, the director of consumer insights at AT&T Mobility, comments about the effective use of voice of the customer: "Sophisticated research techniques and analysis have their place, but what's more important is objectivity, timeliness, and consultative ability—being able to think with the business managers about the 'what ifs' that go beyond the research results."

As an example, Tim outlines the research that helped AT&T introduce its capped data plans in a timely and effective manner. It was becoming clear by the beginning of 2009 that the era of "unlimited" data plans in the wireless market was coming to an end. As smartphone penetration increased, data usage was skyrocketing on a per-subscriber basis. In addition, wireless networks have finite capacity, and a small number of users were taking up a lot of it. Tim notes, "We needed to do something to help consumers to manage their usage and also to compensate the company for heavy usage, since there is a variable cost to data consumption. That would make the system work better for everyone."

Ending these programs was potentially a huge headache for the carriers, because consumers didn't understand how much data they were using and didn't want a plan that potentially could push them into costly overage. Managers were slow to realize the issue. "We conducted a series of focus groups, turning them around in a week, to understand the issue and what we could do about it. The results forced management to accept that there was a problem—a number of them were in what I'll call 'willful denial'—and quickly shift to problem-solving mode. The research results stressed the need for explaining the situation to the public, as well as providing our customers with tools that let them avoid overage situations. This definitely worked its way into what we ultimately did in June 2010."

STRATEGY AND ELEMENTS OF THE VOC SYSTEM

As a leader in your organization, you will need to develop a strategic plan about what your VOC program looks like and how to incorporate this VOC system into the enterprise so that it can be effective. Customer research in some companies is very tactical and simply means going from one research project to another. In such a scenario, the results obtained from a specific effort will get used by the team that sponsored the research in helping with the particular decision it was designed to address and then will be put away and forgotten. There is no sharing of the findings among other groups across the company, and no accumulated learning was being managed. This is not effective from a strategic perspective, because there is tremendous waste in such an approach; learning is not leveraged across the organization, duplication of efforts may occur, and no collective knowledge base gets built.

One way that many organizations have approached the concept of an efficient and effective VOC program is by creating a central customer research and insights team that serves the enterprise as a center of excellence. This team is responsible for, and manages, all customer experience and customer feedback efforts across the company. VOC professionals design the strategy for VOC, in collaboration with other functional team members. Ideally, learning is integrated across the various research studies and shared across functional teams, regardless of where the need originated from. What strategic framework for the VOC program works best for any particular organization depends on the company's needs, structure, and culture. Some options that could work are outlined in the following sections.

VOC Strategy by Organizational Areas

What do your marketing, product, pricing, product marketing, sales, and service teams need to know about their customers and prospects to set strategic priorities for their teams, as well as to make business decisions on a daily basis? One way to organize your VOC strategy is to identify the needs of each of your functional units and incorpo-

Marketing	Product, Pricing	Product Marketing	Sales	Service
-Brand Awareness	-Needs and Wants	-Perceived Benefits	-Value Proposition	-Satisfaction, Loyalty
-Brand Image	-Product	-Value Proposition	-Needs Fulfillment	-Complaint Issues
-Messaging and	Development	-Competitive	-Competitive	-Issue Resolution
Communication	-Innovation,	Positioning	Positioning	-Root Cause
-Ad Reactions	Enhancements	-Value Proposition	-Win/Loss	-Quality, Speed, Ease
-Media Habits	-Pricing Strategy	-Advertising Strategy	-Lapsed Customer	-Agent Quality
-Social Media	-Packaging, Naming	and Execution	-Agent Quality	-Knowledgeability
-Shopper Insights	-Satisfaction, Loyalty	-Shoppers Insights	-Satisfaction, Loyalty	

Actions Taken by Functional Teams Based on VOC Insights

Exhibit 8.2 VOC Strategy and Elements by Organizational Functional Areas

rate these various needs into the VOC program. The following (see Exhibit 8.2) outlines a VOC strategy that is defined by the needs of each of an organization's key functional areas.

A VOC strategy based on functional area needs can be an easy and simple way to organize the customer feedback. It helps identify the needs of the specific business teams, and the feedback processes are well aligned to the team's need. Managers understand what their particular needs are, and the VOC elements are designed to specifically fulfill these needs, so that business strategy can be well informed. The needs are well thought out and planned ahead, collaboration across departments is undertaken when there are overlapping needs, and a library of research is accumulated for all to use as needed.

There are, however, some cautions that need to be kept in mind if such a strategy is to be used.

A functional team–based VOC system runs the danger of becoming siloed in its approach, and unless this is carefully and deliberately avoided, it could lead to a lack of cross-functional collaboration. This is clearly detrimental to the one-company goal and, more important, results in a chopped customer experience, due to a lack of synergy across departments. In addition, given the overlap in some of the needs of the functional departments, there is bound to be a duplication of efforts—which at best means a wastage of resources and at worst results in inconsistency in making strategic business decisions across functional areas.

VOC Strategy Based on Customer's Experience Stage

An alternative approach is to build the VOC strategy around what Abby Mehta calls the *customer's experience stage*, rather than one that is focused on the organization and its structure. This is an approach that is recommended, because it unifies the organization's business teams, is collaborative in nature, provides consistency in the use of results and follow-up of business actions, and promotes a customer-centric approach in the enterprise.

Customers experience your organization and brand in many ways. The most direct experience they have with you is through your products and services that they try or use and through the interactions with your sales and service employees during the pre-purchase, purchase, and post-purchase process. These interactions are based on what you have defined as the process in your organization within your product, sales, and service teams. Your customers also hear about your company from your organizational communications and marketing efforts, in the form of advertising, e-mails, newsletters, company blogs, and social media pages. In addition, they also learn about you from external sources, both formally and informally, via news channels, independent bloggers, friends and family, and other current and lapsed customers.

These direct and indirect experiences do not happen in a vacuum; rather, it is within the larger environment of the marketplace, where similar experiences that your customers have with your brand and organization are occurring at the same time as their experiences with your competitors' brands and organizations—all of which are contextualized within the economy and other current events happening locally, nationally, and globally. Each of these types of input interacts with the others and produces a unique customer experience for each individual. Your VOC program is designed to capture this experience and help you be most responsive to the largest number of, and most profitable, customers.

An effective way to design a successful VOC program is to try to capture the customer feedback in each stage of the customer experience: start with understanding of who your customers are and what their needs are, and then evaluate how you fulfill these needs and how

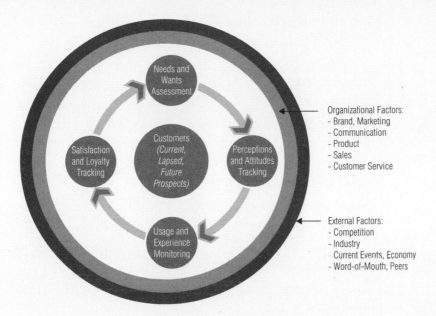

Exhibit 8.3 VOC Strategy Based on the Customer's Experience Stage

they feel about you and your brand, products, and services in relation to your competitors' Next, you must gain insight about their usage of your products and services as compared to your competition's, and finally, you will learn how they feel coming out of this usage experience, in terms of being fulfilled and wanting to come back to do business with you and wanting to recommend you to others (see Exhibit 8.3).

■ **Customer needs and wants assessment.** This is a first step in understanding your customers. Who are they? What core needs do they have that you want to address with your products and services? What problems are you solving? How do these differ by segments, such as demographics, psychographics, beliefs and attitudes, location, usage patterns, and so on, and what segment or segments are you best positioned to sell to? The landscape is changing constantly, and need assessments should be done periodically so that you do not run the risk of falling out of style as competitors improve and new products and technologies come along. The answers to these needs and need fulfillment types of VOC-based questions help the enterprise with the following:

- Product innovation, new product development, product enhancements, and innovative merchandising to effectively fulfill needs.

- Value proposition, needs, and benefit identification to establish appropriate brand positioning.

- Marketing materials development to build awareness and communicate product and value benefits.

- Facilitating the shopping process at every step of the way by gaining shopper insights.

- Sales materials development and sales personnel training to directly address the customer's needs and relevant questions.

- Service readiness and training for effective and relevant problem solving.

CASE STUDY

UNDERSTANDING WHAT CUSTOMERS WANT

In an effort to better understand her company's customers, Amy Quigley, the VP of global marketing at a strategic consultancy firm, notes, "There was not a good alignment in the company about who our core customer was. It was generally felt that everybody was." Amy conducted Persona research among the firm's customers to identify the key customer set and came up with five Personas. Personas are profiles developed to represent behavior patterns, goals, skills, attitudes, and the environment of the customer, going beyond simple segmentation.

The firm decided that four of these five Personas were of interest, while the fifth was not a profitable target, and one of the four was identified as having the highest worth. By fully understanding their customer groups—in terms of who they are, how they think, what their needs and goals are, how skilled they are at the issues at hand, what drives their decision-making process with respect to choosing a strategic partner company, and who in these customers' minds is a partner they want to work with—the firm made big changes in its strategic marketing plans and sales approach to target its most profitable groups. One of the key takeaways for the group was that a customer's physical visit to the consulting firm's offices to see the technology and the space made a big difference in the customer signing off on the deal. This was incorporated into the sales process. "Developing client Personas in our organization was pivotal in building alignment with our executives and arming our sales team with the information it needed to have more targeted conversations. Not only did it make a huge difference in sales and marketing, but it helped drive our growth strategy."

- **Tracking customers' perceptions and attitudes.** What customers know about you and how they perceive you affects whether they want to buy from you or use your products and services. Are your products and services the first that comes to mind when they have a need that you can solve? What is your "mind share" and how do you stack up against your competitors? How are your products and services perceived? How is the health of your brand versus others in the field? What exactly do your customers think of you? Does this image match what you set out to tell them about yourself? Are new players coming into the field to upset your balance and your position in the marketplace? Some of the business decisions that are supported by tracking customers' perceptions and attitudes about you and your competitors are:
  - Development of marketing, advertising, social media, and sales materials to build awareness about your brand, product, and services.
  - Business strategy and planning across all functional areas, based on competitive benchmarking via a SWOT (strengths, weaknesses, opportunities, threats) analysis.
  - Product innovations, product marketing, and pricing strategy, by evaluating perceptions of your value versus your competitors'.
  - Message architecture and communications development to enhance your image across all relevant channels.
  - Media planning to assure effective return on your marketing investment and optimal reach and frequency for your offline/ online advertising efforts.
  - Evaluating a change in image and perceptions as a result of actions taken by the organization.

■ **Monitoring Customer Usage and Experience.** You need to be on top of what your customers are doing with respect to you. Who are your most important customers, and how are they interacting with you? What is the shopping process, and are you facilitating each aspect of this process? What about the post-purchase process, how is it working for your customers? Do you have a clear understanding of how your products and services are getting used? Are you keeping up-to-date with your company portfolio and making sure you continue to be the preferred place of business? Are there any areas within the enterprise where things are breaking down? More specifically, these questions help in

■ Devising product strategy, including product enhancements and innovations based on usage and efficacy feedback.

■ Creating product marketing strategy, based on target customer identification and usage segmentation.

■ Developing marketing materials to align with customers' perceptions and needs.

■ Planning marketing campaigns, based on evaluating the success of past marketing efforts.

■ Planning product distribution, based on shopping behaviors and shopper insights.

■ Managing sales operations, developing sales materials, and instituting sales training for support customer needs.

■ Enhancing service readiness and service training for your products to be in line with what customers need help with.

■ Identifying areas of improvement across the enterprise, based on systematic root-cause analysis of high-volume customer complaints.

■ Understanding your sales, revenue, and other behavioral data trends.

■ **Tracking customer satisfaction and loyalty.** As you are well aware, retaining a customer is a lot easier and less expensive than acquiring a new one. Thus, one of the key objectives of your VOC program should be to monitor your performance among your current customers, assess their satisfaction and loyalty levels, and use the insights gained from this to make decisions that promote customer retention. In addition, it should be recognized that insights gained from these types of customer-focused studies are also extremely useful in planning acquisition strategies.

Satisfaction measurement efforts need to be ongoing at the micro-level across all touch points for your customers to ensure that there are no problematic issues in any part of the customer experience. For example, you will want to evaluate customers' satisfaction with your products and services, your customer service, your store that a customer visited, your website, your sales staff or other front-line staff, your billing team, and so on. These studies should be supplemented with periodic, broader satisfaction and loyalty research that evaluates your entire organization, your company, and your specific functional areas. There have been significant advances in the measurement of customer satisfaction, and advanced statistical modeling should be undertaken to fully understand what drives customer loyalty at your organization. Results from these types of analyses help set priorities for the business, identify the areas that need attention, and guide resource allocation to maximize business benefit. More recently, the Net Promoter Score (NPS), an index of how likely your brand would be recommended by your customers (computed as a percentage of "promoters" who would recommend you minus "detractors" who would not), has gained popularity and has worked well for some companies in predicting revenue trends, even as there are challenging claims from other sources.[4] Abby Mehta believes this is one of the several important measures that you should be looking at to obtain a full understanding of customer loyalty.

You will also want to understand why some customers leave you, and you should take the appropriate actions to stem this as much as possible. In addition, it is a good idea to obtain competitive information related to satisfaction and loyalty to benchmark your own performance and get a better understanding of your category and leverage this in competing against specific competitors.

Satisfaction and loyalty studies will help you understand customer issues, and insights gained from these efforts are crucial for the strategic planning of each of the functional areas within your organization, such as product, pricing, sales, service, marketing, billing, and training. Some specific studies within this stage that you will want to conduct are

- Ongoing satisfaction studies to monitor operational issues that are designed to continuously collect data on a daily basis from customers who visit your store or your website or interact with your sales, service, front-desk, training, or other staff.

- Periodic satisfaction studies to evaluate customer satisfaction with the company as a whole, as well as with each of the functional areas and specific products.

- Competitive satisfaction studies to benchmark your performance against your competitors' and help you understand your strengths and weaknesses in each of the functional areas.

- Lapsed customer analysis to improve customer retention by understanding the reasons for lapsing.

- Win/loss studies to diagnose winning sales strategies and improve marketing and sales as appropriate against the competitors.

- Driver analysis to help you understand what drives your customer loyalty and set priorities to focus on areas that are key drivers in your organization.

INTEGRATED VOC APPROACH

CASE STUDY

Abby Mehta supported the launch of a high-value, premium B2B online product for an Internet company via a complete program of research to advise the product, pricing, marketing, sales, service, and training teams and continued the research into the post-purchase time frame to evaluate customer satisfaction and loyalty with the product, identify improvements and feature priorities, and improve product support activities. This is an excellent example of an integrated VOC program approach (see Exhibit 8.4).

The new product was an innovation, a first for this industry, and many questions arose as the company readied itself for the launch, such as who would be the best target prospect, what would be the competitive impact on market share, how to price the product for each target segment, what

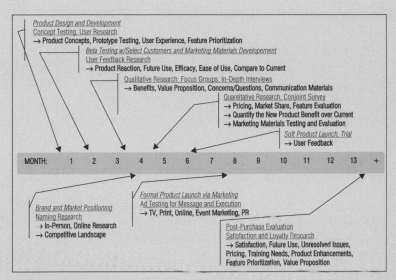

Exhibit 8.4 New Product Launch Research Program for Innovative Online B2B Product

product features are most desired, how to brand it, what is the value proposition, how to position it in the market, what sales and service support are needed, and so on.

The program of research was planned to illuminate and guide the many aspects of the product launch. Several research studies were conducted at various stages of this launch, as outlined in Exhibit 8.4. What made it extremely effective was using a customer-centric, cross-functional approach, rather than an organizational-focused, siloed approach. Each piece of research was designed to illuminate the issue at hand from a customer's perceptive, and input was deliberately obtained during the research planning and implementation process from a collaborative, cross-functional team that was set up to work closely with Abby's research team. As results came in from each of the various research efforts, they were integrated with the prior learning to provide a comprehensive picture, and this was shared and presented effectively to the various functional teams, as well as to senior executives, to guide the decisions about the product launch. The launch was a huge success, with substantial press articles touting the product and recognition from industry leaders, as well as customers. Within a year, more than two-thirds of the existing customers had switched to the new, higher-priced product. Research and customer insights supported this successful launch every step of the way, and post-purchase satisfaction studies continued to help improve and finesse the product over time.

COMMON VOC PROGRAM PITFALLS

Over the years, Abby Mehta has come across many excuses that business managers offer for not using the VOC insights in their decision making. Here is a sampling that should show you what *not to do* as you design, plan, and execute your VOC program—and some thoughts on what you *can do* to make it work!

"Why didn't I use your VOC insights?"	What can you do?
"I did not see them in time for my decisions."	Be timely.
"I did not know you had any that could help me."	Be proactive.
"I did not understand what you were saying."	Be clear.
"I am not sure why you sent them to me."	Be relevant.
"I was not sure what I should to do with them."	Be actionable.
"I didn't believe in your data and methods."	Be credible.
"I did not get approval to action it."	Be strategic.

VOC professionals need to take responsibility for providing the senior leaders and business managers with insights that support and guide customer-centric decisions as they plan their strategy. VOC researchers should be well aligned with the organizational priorities and work closely with their business partners to help them truly listen to and understand what the customers are saying and act on the basis of these customer insights.

KEY TAKEAWAYS

- In this chapter, I outlined the need for organizations to be customer-centric and to infuse customer feedback into their business decisions across the enterprise, in order to be successful and stay ahead of the competition. A systematic VOC program can help you realize these goals and show strategic, tactical, and operational benefits.
- A VOC program involves understanding who your current, future, and past customers are and establishing their needs, perceptions, attitudes, and behaviors toward you, your brand, your products, and your services in the context of the competitive landscape and applying these insights in making business decisions

across the organization within your product, merchandising, pricing, marketing, sales, service, and other functions.

- Customers experience your brand in many ways: directly through your products, services, website, and front-line employees, as well as through your marketing efforts. All of these touch-points are important, and gathering customer feedback about each of these is the goal for an effective VOC program. In addition, your customers also experience your brand via external sources, such as peer reviews, word of mouth, news media, and so on. These are equally important to monitor within the VOC program.

- Various methodologies have been outlined that can direct the planning of a relevant and effective VOC program. The key steps are listening to and monitoring what customers are saying, analyzing and interpreting what is being said, integrating and recommending appropriate future actions based on this, and, finally, taking action. Continue the loop.

- VOC research professionals and business managers across functional areas need to work in collaboration to make the VOC program effective. A culture of customer-centricity and information-based decision making in the organization is key to making the VOC program valuable.

- VOC also needs to be integrated with other forms of behavioral data and analytics in the organization; to the extent that companies do this, they are more successful with their VOC measurement programs than are those that do not. Integrating what customers are saying with other data points, such as purchase data, competitive preference, online or in-store behavior, and so on, provides a comprehensive picture that is very powerful.

- Put a process in place that can take the insights and the recommendations and turn them into actual actions. It is not enough to gather customer feedback and identify issues; make sure to *truly listen* to what is being said. Insights and recommendations don't create success; actions do.

FURTHER READING

Kai Yang. *Voice of the Customer: Capture and Analysis Design* (Six Sigma Operational Methods). New York: McGraw-Hill, 2008.

Ranjay Gulati. *Reorganize for Resilience: Putting Customers at the Center of Your Organization*. Cambridge, MA: Harvard Business School Press, 2010.

Tony Hsieh. *Delivering Happiness: A Path to Profit, Passion and Purpose*. New York: Grand Central Publishing, 2010.

NOTES

1. Megan Burns, "The Business Impact of Customer Experience, 2011," Forrester Research, July 7, 2011.

2. Jim Tincher, "Heart of the Customer," www.heartofthecustomer.com.

3. Temkin Group, *Q1 2012 Customer Experience Survey*.

4. The Net Promoter question is, "How likely is it that you would recommend our company to a friend or colleague?" Customers answer by awarding a score from 0 ("not at all likely") to 10 ("extremely likely"). Net Promoter, Net Promoter Score, and NPS are registered trademarks of Bain & Company, Inc., Satmetrix, Inc., and Fred Reichheld, www.satmetrix.com. Timothy L. Keiningham, Terry G. Vavra, Lerzan Aksoy, and Henri Wallard, *Loyalty Myths: Hyped Strategies That Will Put You Out of Business—and Proven Tactics That Really Work* (Hoboken, NJ: John Wiley & Sons, 2005.

CHAPTER 9

Leveraging Digital Analytics Effectively

By Judah Phillips

"Data is a Divine gift to humanity, yet it rarely impacts our lives as positively as one might expect. The problem it turns out is not the gift, it is our ability to do something with it. So read, learn, internalize AND act! Carpe Diem!!"

—Author interview with Avinash Kaushik, digital marketing evangelist, Google

---

Judah Phllips creates economic value by helping businesses increase revenue or reduce costs by using data, analytics, and research. He has worked globally, managing business and digital analytics teams in the Internet and software industries since the 1990s, including Sun Microsystems (now Oracle), Reed Elsevier, and Monster Worldwide. Judah created and launched Analytics Research Organization and founded and globalized Digital Analytics Thursdays. He guest lectures at graduate business schools, including the Stern School of Business at New York University, Olin School of Business at Babson College, Baruch College, and Boston College. Judah advises start-up companies through SMARTCURRENT, his advisory and management firm. He serves or has served on the boards of advisors of several Internet and technology companies, including YieldBot, Localytics, and glib.ly, and has served on the strategic advisory boards for Webtrends, Observepoint, Online Marketing Institute (OMI), and Rubinson Partners. Judah is also an adjunct professor at the University of San Francisco.

———————

D igital analytics is a newer name for what is commonly known as "Web analytics" or "site analytics" and includes niche digital analytics activities, such as online advertising, organic search (SEO), paid search (SEM), social media, mobile analytics, and multi-channel analytics across other digital methods, devices, platforms, and experiences that are not yet being actively measured and may not yet have been invented. The key point is that digital analytics comes from multiple channels.

Effective digital analytics should focus on using data, research, and analytical techniques to create economic value for your organization by helping a business generate new or incremental profitable revenue or reduce cost. *Digital analytics* is also a term that refers to the upstream activities that are critical and necessary in order to analyze related data, such as technical and process work (for example, data collection and tool configuration). Digital analytics brings together data from different systems to create cohesive and relevant analyses that answer business questions. The best digital analysts can do two things. First, they know how to convincingly articulate business-relevant insights about digital behavior to executive leaders, which includes providing recommendations that will help make their company money. In my interview with Jonathan Mendex, the CEO of Yieldbot and a blogger at www.optimizeandprophesize.com, he said this about digital analytics: "The first step to achieving value with data is shaping in ways that provide meaningful correlations to your customers and their experience with your business." Second, the best digital analytics can also execute effectively within the organization, both on the upstream technical aspects of digital analytics and on the downstream social and organizational processes.

Digital analytics collects data related to how people use digital experiences, such as websites, mobile sites, social media, advertising, and any other Internet-enabled experiences—from interactive TV and billboards to set-top boxes to video game consoles to Internet-enabled appliances to the world of "Apps." The ubiquity of digital data collection and the usage of the data are more common now than ever before. IBM estimates that 90% of all of the world's data ever created was created during just the last two years.[1] All of this largely digital data can be thought of as "clickstreams"—a legacy "Web analytics" term referring to the trail of information a user leaves when interacting with a digital device.

Clickstream refers to the discrete series of actions (often clicks) during a visit to a digital experience (such as a website or a mobile device) and the pages/experience viewed on the device (such as a browser). While the clickstream may contain an abstraction of the visitor's behavior, the Internet's underlying infrastructure enables other information, such as:

- Discrete series of clicks and page views during a visit to a website.
- The visitor's IP address, browser, and operating system.
- The referrer (where the user came from—such as a search engine).
- Keyword types written by the user.
- The duration of the interaction.
- What was purchased and how much was spent.
- The number of views and visits in a given time period.

For example, when you go to Facebook, Facebook knows whether you visited the site from another site, such as Google. You are then "cookied" and become a unique visitor. Facebook knows an IP address associated with you, when you first requested a page. If you came to Facebook from Google and entered a keyword on Google, then

Facebook knows the keyword you used. Facebook knows the events you "Join" and to which you are "Going." It has graphed your social connections on Cartesian coordinate 3d grid associated with other metadata (just as you learned to do in high school, $y = mx + b$) and is using all of these data to target advertisements to you (and help you stay connected with your "Friends"). Facebook knows much of these data because it collects the data itself in its data center—and dedicates massive servers and technical infrastructure to analytics. Facebook also spends capital on people to analyze the data. Other companies, with less deep pockets, may use third-party tools to collect digital analytics data, such as IBM Unica/CoreMetrics, WebTrends, Adobe Omniture, or any of the hundreds of tag-based, SaaS tools that are released daily. Facebook even uses third-party tracking tags (or at least allows them) in order to collect data Facebook may not easily have access to.

Digital analytics also involves integrating data together from multiple data sources and channels—both from internal databases (such as CRM) and from external, third-party data sources. Thus, it is possible to use modern software and proprietary technology to enhance clickstream data. All of these clickstream and related data, regardless of source, are stored in one or more databases and made available at the detailed (raw) or aggregate (summary) levels for querying, reporting, integrating, and analyzing.

Digital analytics, however, is not a technical discipline. Do not be confused; technology is crucial and necessary for digital analytics, but it is insufficient for business value generation. Creating business value from your analytics requires, most important, people who have technical and business skills (see the section in this chapter titled "Digital Analytics Team").

Exhibit 9.1 shows how data can move from being only informational (the upper left quadrant) to taking action into the future (the lower right quadrant). Each cell identifies the questions and potential business activities for digital analytics. The labels in first two rows of the following grid were created by Tom Davenport (the Information and Action rows).[2] The third row was created by the author of this chapter, Judah Phillips (the Action row and parenthetical activities). The grid shows the idea of using analytics to understand what happened, to learn what is happening now, and to predict what will

	Past	Present	Future
INFORMATION	What happened? (Data mining and reporting)	What is happening now? (Alerts)	What will happen? (Trending, extrapolation)
INSIGHT	How and why did it happen? (Data modeling and experimental design)	What's the next best action? (Recommendation)	What's the best and worst that can happen? (Prediction, simulation)
ACTION	How do we leverage what we already know? (Dynamic interaction/profiling)	How do we dynamically modify the site in real time? (Detection)	How can we apply data to the future? (Ongoing optimization)

Exhibit 9.1   Effective Digital Analytics

happen in the future. In addition, the idea of understanding "Insights" of why things happened, what may happen, and whether what happened is positive can be gleaned from the data. Finally, the idea of taking action, of using the "What" and the "Why" of data to apply it in a timely way to ensure a profitable business future, is a core underpinning of effective digital analytics.

Digital analytics creates value in your organization by informing work activities and ensuring that your data are considered across the decision-making process from the very beginning. Exhibit 9.2 shows in vertical columns ways that analytics can help different functional teams—and is by no means meant to be exhaustive, only to provide you with examples.

As mentioned previously, *digital analytics* is the current name in 2012 for what was formerly titled "Web analytics" or "site analytics." When we say "digital analytics," we are referring to analytics from digital sources such as Web, mobile, social, and other Internet-enabled devices (such as set-top boxes, video consoles, and interactive billboards), regardless of the device or screen-size. *Web analytics* is an archaic term that refers to "site analytics" when the Internet was not pervasive and ubiquitous across human life in first-world countries.

Marketing	Product	Sales	Executive	IT
Landing page optimization	Behavioral analysis	Customer value	Dashboarding	Performance monitoring
Lifetime value/ RFM/customer segmentation	Search engine optimization	Sales readiness	Scorecarding	Site usage for capacity planning
Search engine marketing	Demo/GEO/ firmagraphic analysis	Sales collateral	Custom research	Disaster recovery
Ad and media plan optimization	Funnel and flow optimization	RFP and RFI	Financial performance	Infrastructure enhancements
Social media optimization	Application and product performance	Customer usage information	Competitive intelligence	Tagging and QA

Exhibit 9.2 The Ways Digital Analytics Can Help Functional Teams

When Web analytics was invented and commercialized in the 1990s, the primary vehicle with which to access the "World Wide Web" was the browser. A popular browser was Marc Andreessen's Netscape. In this past world, which was not highly mobilized, Web analytics was created. Today, the Internet is everywhere—in our household appliances, in our pockets on our mobile phones, in our automobiles, in stores, and almost everywhere we go, we are hyperconnected. Hence, the new identity for the analysis of Internet behavior: digital analytics.

As you read previously, digital analytics refers to helping businesses use analytics, research, and data collected from digital sources to create new or incremental profitable revenue and or reduce cost. It is subtle but important to note the difference between "digital analytics" and "Web analytics," regardless of the tool that is used to access the digital experience. In fact, it is important to understand that difference. Web analytics is about the "site" as accessed, primarily but not exclusively, through the Web browser (such as Google Chrome, Mozilla Firefox, Opera, or Internet Explorer). Digital analytics does not regard the tool that is used to access the Internet as critical to the measurement of behavior. This difference will become clear in this chapter as I now explain and review what Web analytics is—in the context of evolving conceptually into the idea (and ideal) of digital analytics.

The highest goal of any business analytics, including digital analytics, is to create measurable value for the organization. Amazingly easy to say, the creation of business value from analytics requires an entire reframing of how businesses think about using digital data in what the author of this chapter calls the "analytical economy." All business analytics exists within the "analytical economy," which is defined as

> How data, research, and analytics are being used in traditional, new, and differentiated ways by combining Insights derived from multiple-channels (or sources) and using those unified Insights to create, evolve, and optimize global commerce.

As a result, the goal of this chapter is to elevate the conversation about "Web analytics," not only to help you understand it as "digital analytics," but so that you can grasp how digital analytics operates within a larger global economic, social, cultural, and societal construct that is newly developing, due to the emergence of Big Data. If you would like to help elevate the conversation about digital analytics, please considering joining ARO—Analytics Research Organization (pronounced "Arrow"). Sign up for free at ARO website: http://www.the aro.org This organization, the world's first digital analytics group, was created in 2011 by the author of this chapter.

Within this larger macro context and goal, this chapter will review the following:

- **Digital analytics concepts.** A high-level business overview of what is distinctly important to understand when you are an executive, a senior business leader, or even a middle manager working in either "the business" or "IT" in a company, regardless of size, location, sector, or industry and whether B2B, B2C, or both. This chapter should also prove fruitful for the student and the entrepreneur who seek to understand a practical and common-sense approach for understanding "digital analytics" in our modern society and economy.

- **People.** Without a doubt, the key to any successful digital analytics program is the people who work in the analytical function—at all levels. It *does not matter* what technology you use or how smart you think you are or know your company to be. Nor does it matter what school you or your employees went to or what degrees they have earned. In digital analytics, none of it matters because the people who *truly* understand digital analytics did not learn it in school. They learned it by watching the world and the Internet evolve over time—and were keen and savvy enough to take the time to test and experiment with whether the field of digital analytics would appeal to them.

A lot of people claim to "do digital analytics," but I profess that many of these professionals are not analysts at all but rather technologists who know how to configure software tools and use programming skills to work with *clean* data. The skill set for success in digital analysis depends on the person and the company.

- **Process.** After hiring people to do digital analytics, a manager needs processes to manage them. It's simple to say that—but a very difficult concept to satisfy against the rigor of analytical requirements. In other words, creating a process that bridges multiple functions to support a complex digital analytics function is not easy. It is one filled with landmines of politics, annual budgets, road maps, egos, bonuses, and sometimes even customers and shareholders. Read this section for the real deal on the creation, establishment, management, and optimization process to support analytical success.

- **Web analytics tools.** Although counterintuitive, one of the least important factors in digital analytics is the tools you use. Vendors would have you believe otherwise—and the vendors are also correct. Tools and technology are critical and necessary, but alone, they are insufficient for doing digital analytics. I dedicate several mini sections to what an executive running or supervising an analytics program must understand about the selection, deployment, and maintenance of digital analytics tools. These sections are by no means exhaustive or the last word but are learned from considerable experience.

- **Reporting.** Many digital analytics teams are merely reporting teams. The team from top to bottom churns out reports based on some process and uses some technology to do it. Reporting is not analytics and never will be. In this section, you will learn about what matters when you're doing digital analytics reporting and how to cut through the red tape to get the reporting you need to the people who need it when they need it.

- **Goals, funnels, and conversions.** These three concepts are key to success when doing digital analytics. In this section, we will discuss these concepts in the framework of a cross-domain digital experience.

- **Advanced digital analysis.** Traditional media in the twenty-first century demands the lion's share of ad spend. Although advertising spend on digital media is growing, gaps exist between the time spent on digital media and the advertising dollars spent on that digital time, when compared to the ad spend per time spent on traditional media, such as billboards, radio, and television. In this section we will highlight how traditional and digital research can be used together to create value. Examples of techniques to apply at a high level will be discussed.

- **Site optimization and landing page optimization.** At the forefront of digital analytics are automated engines that detect and interact with visitors in nonspooky ways. An example where marketing technology meets user experience meets IT meets revenue is in a niche part of the technology industry: site optimization and landing page optimization—where computers dynamically generate the best possible customer experience to increase sales.

STRATEGIC AND TACTICAL USE OF DIGITAL ANALYTICS

Digital analytics can be used to do many things in business, but the two goals for the highest and best usage of digital analytics is to create value for your organization by either (1) generating profitable revenue or (2) reducing cost. When I sat down with Alex Yoder, the CEO of WebTrends, a leading global digital analytics company, he had this to say about digital analytics: "Analytics is powering the future of marketing. Real time analytics that allow instant engagement. Deep, cross-channel analytics that enhance understanding of customers and drive relevant content and tactics. And next, predictive analytics. Data is the fuel for the modern marketing machine." Not all businesses are ready, however, to execute at full throttle with maximum success as they execute analytics at work. In fact, I highly recommend reading Tom Davenport's books *Competing on Analytics* and *Analytics at Work*. Much of this section's content was inspired by Tom but also references his work.

Digital analytics or, in fact, any analytical method, as has been discussed through this book, can be applied only when you have data that addresses your critical business goals. It sounds obvious, right? Yet many business people will bend data to fit their own conclusions when the data do not fit them. It is sometimes incorrect or just plain irresponsible to exploit the data. First and foremost, data must be given to someone who can take action or do something useful with it. Data, in and of itself, is not "actionable," but the people who consider and use the analytical deliverables can take action based on recommendations that result from the data. In that context, do not waste time building reporting or providing analysis to people or teams who can't do anything with it. Sometimes people "just want to look at it." Other times, the business has no clear data to help, and cobbling data together without standard definitions from disparate systems usually does not work. Still other times, the business questions are not clear or adequately stated, or there is no alignment on business goals or the expected business outcome of the project.

When you are considering using your analytics team or handling data requests as an analytics practitioner, remember that there are times when data can help and other times when, for reasons outside of your or the data's control, the analytics team is not the right team to help. Consider the previous paragraphs to be helpful. Finally, I have always found it useful to ask stakeholders, analysts, my managers, and myself the following question about any analytical request: if you had the data in your hands right now, what business decision would you make?

UNDERSTANDING DIGITAL ANALYTICS CONCEPTS

It is often such a baffling and confusing topic because little formal education exists for digital analytics, and people have learned their skills through hard work, determination, and real-world effort. This section is by no means an attempt to be exhaustive but will give you a simple framework with which to understand conceptually the common vocabulary of digital analytics:

■ **Visitor (or unique visitor).** Critical and confusing, the unique visitor is among the most often cited metrics related to how many "people" visit a site. The term *traffic* or *site traffic* is often used to refer to visitors. The following table shows what you need to know.

Tool	How a Unique Visitor Is Defined	Example of Tool
Digital Analytics	A count of deduplicated cookies during the time period. In other words, if you stay at the beach house for all 30 days during an entire month. Then you are 1 "monthly unique visitor." If the owner of the rental property was asked by his accountant, "How many people stayed at the house?" the correct answer is 1. In that same scenario, you stayed every day, correct? If the manager asks how many "people stayed at the house each day, you could say "30 daily visitors" stayed during the month—because you did stay 30 times, once per day. You were "30 daily unique visitors" but only "1 monthly unique visitor." This scenario illustrates the potential for confusion between "monthly unique visitors" and "daily unique visitors."	Google Analytics, Omniture/Adobe, Webtrends
Audience Measurement	Audience measurement uses black box data collection methods that are not transparent, but a few companies are in the process of being partially audited by the MRC. Similar to the algorithms within analytical software, audience measurement tools often combine data collected directly from sites with data collected from a panel of people who choose to have their digital behavior (such as Web surfing) monitored in exchange for some incentive, such as free software. Some audience measurement firms refer to the joining of site analytics data and audience measurement data as "unifying" the data. Audience measurement companies take these data collected about digital behavior, such as website visitation	comScore, Nielsen, Compete, Quantcast, Google

(*Continued*)

Tool	How a Unique Visitor Is Defined	Example of Tool
	(and much more) and use proprietary statistical methods to estimate the size of an audience to a website or another digital asset. Since audience measurement companies have changed their core methodology at the most fundamental level around 2010 to bring together panel data with site data, then I question entirely whether the panel-based estimates were ever actually accurate historically for unique visitors. In fact, the disdain for audience measurement data from the most vocal critics and savvy analysts points at dramatic changes in unique visitor totals as direct proof historic panel only—based estimates site traffic were not only wrong for years, but also based on an inherently dated and archaic model. If combining panel data with site data gives better estimates, then it is logical to conclude that the previous estimate was inaccurate.	

If multiple vendors exist using multiple data collection and measurement methods—few of which are transparent and standardized—and if those same vendors use the same name for different things, such as *unique visitors*, then the potential for confusion will exist across the industry. As of 2011, industry initiatives from the IAB, AAAA, MRC, DAA, OWA, AGOF, ICOM, and several other non-U.S. organizations have attempted to get together to standardize the global definition for "unique visitors." At this point, however, no standard really exists. Everyone has great ideas—and a bunch of different definitions (sometimes called standards) for which various entities advocate. The digital analytics industry also has many recommendations on what the standards should be and the names of metrics should be, yet digital analytics standards applied in technology and adopted by practitioners have yet to exist widely.

Let us all not forget what the goal of the unique visitors metric is: to accurately count people who are exposed to and engage with a digital asset. In that context, you might hear "people," "unique cookies, "unique browsers, "unique people," "absolute unique visitors," "absolute visitors," or just plain "visitors." These are all an attempt to quantify mostly the same concept. What can an executive do to cut through the noise and confusion?

- **Ask for the definition.** Make no mistake that definitions are not standards. There are few standards—and a discussion of them (or a rant on the lack thereof) is beyond the scope of this book.

- **Ask for time-series trends for your site.** Ask the vendor to show you a time-series trend of the last two years of your site. This will not be possible for a software vendor, but may be possible for an audience measurement firm. Then compare all of the data sources together. Don't freak out! Relax.

- **Ask questions until you understand.** Any vendor who is worth your budget should easily and accurately be able to express his or her data definition for "unique visitors" (or unique whatever) clearly and simply. If the vendor can't, then move on.

Following are high-level definitions for other concepts that are important in digital analytics:

- **Visit.** If visitors visit a site, then a visit is the number of times a visitor goes to a site. If you go to your house five times a day in between shopping, taking the kids to sports, going to get take-out, and doing other errands, then you had five visits to your house but were just one visitor to your house. Get it? If you have one monthly unique visitor to your website, and that unique visitor visits the site five times during the month, then your analytics tool would show one visitor and five visits— assuming the definitions for these data supported my assertions in this use case.

- **Page (screen) views.** A visitor has visits during which pages are viewed (or not). If you go to coffee shop once per day every day during a month and read a 10-page newspaper during every visit, then you did this in digital analytics logic: 1 monthly unique visitor, 30 visits, 300 page views. In the same sense, when you go to a website (or a mobile site or another Web-enabled experience, such as an in-store kiosk) and you view content, it is generally said that you "viewed a page," hence the metric "page views." Page views are simply the number of pages that were viewed during a visit by a visitor (or summed cumulatively during a certain time period). It is important to note that the modern post-2008 Web is full of dynamic content that does not create or render traditional page views. For the more advanced reader, I am talking about Rich Internet Applications (RIA) and Asynchronous JavaScript over eXtensible Markup Language (AJAX), which have resulted in a decoupling of the client and the server that traditionally held together in HTML 1.0. With HTML5, FLEX, AIR, FLASH, AJAX, RUBY, and other technologies; the traditional "Web analytics" concept of the page view sometimes no longer exists. Yes, you can fake it with various calls to imitate a page view (see the definition of any "event" further on). In mobile experiences or interactive experiences that are Web-enabled (such as set-top TV boxes and interactive billboards), the construct of a page view is insufficient to express the object around which the behavior is centered. For certain digital experiences, I call the viewing of content to be agnostic of device or browser and thus a "screen view." Or, as described next, the "event."

■ **Events.** In 2006, I had lunch with Frank Faubert, who created one of the first "Web analytics" companies, Sane Solutions. During our lunch, Frank and I discussed much of what I explained toward the end of my description of page views. We shared a philosophy that page views had subordinate elements and that those elements could be called "events." The event model describes conceptually that things happen within the page that do not necessarily create a communication back to the Web server. To many industry practitioners, this event model seems almost obvious. It did to Frank and me back in 2006 as well. In essence, you can do things within a page such as fill out a form, click a button, start and stop a video, select from a list, or click on this or that. All of these things that occur on the page are considered "events." Anything you click, swipe, pick, select, rub, push, and touch with your finger, pad, point, mouse, or any other input device to any Web-enabled or programmed interactive digital environment is an "event."

- **Cookies.** Cookies are very important to understand because they are key to the mechanics and technicalities of how unique visitors and visits are counted by Web analytics tools. A "cookie" is simply a piece of digital code that a website provides to a visitor's computer that lets it know when a computer comes back again. A cookie may also record information specific to that visiting computer, such as location and data entered when on the website. People delete cookies. Therefore, the count of unique visitors derived from cookies may be overstated. This overstatement due to cookie deletion is thought to be a general weakness of Web analytics tools.

- **Conversion (and conversion rate).** A conversion is a value-generating activity within a digital experience. For example, a conversion might be when someone places an order for a product on an e-commerce site. The conversion rate in this case would just be a percentage expression of how many people ordered. For example, if 10,000 people came to a site and 200 bought a product (that is, converted), the conversion rate is 2%. See the section on "Goals, Conversions, and Benchmarks" in this chapter for more details.

- **Deduplication.** Specific to cookies and the measurement of visitors and visits, deduplication expresses how multiple cookies are reduced to a single count in order not to overstate the number of visits or unique visitors. For example, if a cookie is set every day during a month for a logged-in user on a website, then it is possible to know that those 30 cookies (each set during one day of the month) are tied to one known visitor. *Deduplication* is the term referring to the method by which, in this case, 30 cookies are understood to be just one visitor (who has more than 1 cookie). Thus, instead of counting those 30 cookies as 30 "unique visitors," deduplication occurs to say, "These 30 cookies are duplicated to just one visitor." Deduplication reduces to one and allows for more accurate aggregate counts of visitors.

- **Uniqueness.** Similar to deduplication, the ideal of reducing to one visitor across multiple sites/domains or across multiple devices (such as exposure to mobile, TV, radio, site, and QR code) exposed to one or more messages (generally advertising-based) is called *uniqueness*. If you have one visitor to Facebook on mobile and the same visitor also using the site, to express uniqueness you would deduplicate the visitor on Facebook across both mobile and site usage to accurately count (or estimate) deduplicated visitors and their visits. In other words, if you use your computer to check Twitter and then use your mobile phone, you are one unique person on two devices using Twitter. The concept to express this singularity across digital devices is named *uniqueness*.

■ **Attribution.** Entire books have been written about attribution—and entire companies exist to do attribution modeling. Attribution refers to understanding the source of visitors and visits to your digital experience. Attribution is most often cited in the context of marketing budgets (and justifying them). Traditional analytics does attribution modeling and calls it many different names. In digital analytics, attribution can take many approaches: first click, last click, appropriate, equal, weighted, and so on. Attribution can refer to understanding the impact of paid, owned, and earned media and on the digital experience. For example, how many sales did we have from Google? Or did e-mail or social media cost us more for customer acquisition? What is the return on media spend for every dollar we spent? Attribution can help answer these business questions.

In digital analytics, one can segment site traffic into the following categories. Note that the following list is not exhaustive and contains only the most important categories. Also, the labels and definitions used to define the segments may shift over time. Digital analytics helps you understand the direct (and even indirect) response from these channels and in some cases even the impact on brand.

■ **Paid.** Paid media is just what it sounds like. You or your company pay to advertise in order to drive behavior toward various consumer and shopping goals.

  ■ **Display advertising.** Banners ads and other ad units of all sizes are served on Internet-enabled devices, primarily the

Web and mobile devices, but increasingly on interactive billboards and mobile and television applications. The ads you see on the Web are display ads.

■ **Affiliate marketing.** This is marketing resulting from relationships where some form of capital is exchanged. For example, affiliate marketing generally occurs after you purchase or even abandon a purchase on the Internet. For example, you buy flowers and are offered, after checkout, the opportunity to also buy chocolates from a different company.

■ **Paid search.** The purchases of keywords on search engines in order to display a relevant link/offer to a current or new customer. Paid search is complicated, and it is easy to go bust if you don't know what you are doing. When an agency buys the word *diapers* or *crib* from Google on behalf of Walmart .com, and a person clicks on the paid search ad and then visits Walmart.com, paid search appears to have worked (or did it? . . . remember conversions!).

■ **Owned.** If you have ever "built it because they will come," then you know about "owned media." It's what happens when you spend your capital to create something fully or partially owned by you or your company.

■ **Sites.** Web "traffic" used to be only from websites. Much traffic is still from websites that you access with http://www and various TLDs (top-level domains).

■ **Ad networks.** I use the term *ad networks* loosely to identify every technology that in some way, whether automated or done manually, is used to buy, sell, match, target, exchange, bid, target by X and Y, or automate Internet-enabled advertising in some way for serving and targeting ads.

■ **CRM e-mails.** Customer relationship management e-mails are the communications sent to lists that are maintained by your company. These lists are most often customer or prospect lists from opt-ins, but not always. When you e-mail your customers with offers to which you know (and hope) they will respond (or so your CRM team has told their boss), it is the analytics team that can identify performance.

- **Automated agents.** It is entirely possible and not uncommon to receive automated offers for products or content that result from simple customer activities, such as opt-ins, or from complex machine-learned, algorithm processes, which some customers may even consider spooky or annoying.

- **Earned.** Earned media are the content, branding, perception, mind-set, awareness, and favorability that result from your business activities in the minds of people. These perceptions are formed by the brand, customer experience and word-of-mouth that come from your business activities. As a result, earned media (and thus the analytics supporting them) is as much about how people feel and perceive your brand, beyond that which the brand controls, as it is about how people behave within constructs the brand does control or influence, such as your products, your PR, and even your marketing, both online and offline. Earned media is also social media. See Chapter 12 on "Social Media Analytics" for more information. Following are some examples of earned media.

  - **Organic search (i.e., search engine optimization [SEO]).** Although some may argue that this is a paid activity, the ranking of your site and pages will happen whether you hire people to improve your search rankings or not. Google, Yahoo, Bing, and the other engines all crawl the Web and will find you. The best SEO is always relevant content. Digital analytics lets you know how you are doing at SEO.

  - **Social media.** Facebook, Twitter, YouTube, Slide Share, Pinterest, Foursquare, Gowalla, Groupon, and LinkedIn— much of the online world lurks or participates at levels in social media from highly engaged to barely listening. Social media analytics is covered in a deeper way in Chapter 12.

  - **Blogs.** Blogs are social media, but I think it is important to call them out as a separate segment because blogs often exist outside of corporate products that provide an online user experience. Blogs populate the Internet at all scales across all countries.

- **Other sites.** Any site linking to your site can be measured by digital analytics. However, in some cases, technical externalities that are entirely outside of your control can prevent measurement of traffic from other sites that link into your sites—even the sites on which you spend money to advertise.

- **Direct.** Direct traffic refers to a visitor who comes directly to your site through activities such as typing your Web address directly or from a bookmarked page. In digital analytics, when traffic is from an "unknown source" it is frequently labeled *direct traffic*; however, analytics tools cannot always measure this with 100% certainty, and some traffic that is considered direct may actually come from an unknown source. Therefore, use caution when reviewing traffic labeled "direct." In other words, there are a lot of reasons traffic shows up as "direct" traffic.

Regardless of which source you attribute your visitors as coming from, you must also consider the following concepts when analyzing your digital data:

- **Recency.** When examining digital data, it is important to ask, "When was the last time my customers came to my site (or another digital experience)?" This time period is called *recency*. Depending on your goals, recency may vary. Watch key customer segments for volatility in recency. Jim Novo, the author of *Drilling Down*, calls recency "time since."

- **Frequency.** When examining digital data, it is important to ask "How often do my customers came to my site (or other digital experience)"? This time period is called *frequency*. Depending on your goals, frequency may vary. Watch key customer segments for volatility in frequency. Jim Novo, the excellent author of *Drilling Down*, calls frequency "time between."

By understanding the concepts presented in the previous lists, you will soon have a firm grasp, if you do not already, of the core concepts you need to understand to begin to create business value using digital analytics data.

DIGITAL ANALYTICS TEAM: PEOPLE ARE MOST IMPORTANT FOR ANALYTICAL SUCCESS

The right people and leadership are absolutely key to the success of any analytics team—traditional or digital or unified. A full-force, world-class digital analytics team should be out talking and interacting with people, not only working with data. Your team will also need to handle most of the technical work to produce the data, then will need to analyze the data, and next present the data. Without analytical narratives, the face-to-face telling of stories using data, an analytics program will never run at full power. World-class analytics teams hire and do whatever it takes to retain multidimensional, intellectually curious people who are able to understand the technical, comprehend the mathematical, and succeed at the social components of analytics.

In the many years I have been running analytics programs in large, globally distributed multinational companies or consulting with them, I found the wrong mix of people to always be a recipe for disaster and stress for all involved. Any analytics managers taking on roles where they must manage people *must* carefully consider the business requirements for the job and quickly determine whether the current team or the team you will build is based on skill sets and personalities that fit business goals for the team.

Digital analytics professionals with real experience in managing and/or executing across the analytical value chain are uncommon, even rare, to find. The key to a successful digital analyst is multidimensionality and intellectual curiosity. Although people run the gamut from linear to quadratic, it is possible to find the right mix of skills to execute with wild success in digital analytics—it simply takes time and money to find these people.

Companies that derive revenue from multiple channels sometimes have two analyst teams: the "database marketing team" and the "digital analysis team." These groups may not communicate or be connected formally within the organization. In some companies, however, these teams are merging to form the "multichannel analytics team." This specialized team analyzes, reports, and evaluates both digital data and offline data—often in coordination with a "business intelligence team." The emergence of this new team structure makes sense for companies that are shifting their offline business models to become more online-centric and that want to understand value-generating connections among channels.

Several macro-level catalysts are necessitating the shift to a multichannel approach for data collection and analysis. The ongoing mainstreaming of the Internet channel for enabling commerce, conversation, and relationship and acquisition marketing is certainly pushing this movement. The burgeoning set of analytics tools that integrates with other technologies to enable event detection and trigger a customer-specific response is also promoting a change in the way companies think about connecting offline and online data to improve overall business performance.

If database marketers and digital analysts are evolving into a new type of team, then what roles are necessary on this new multichannel team? Here are a few:

- **Digital analyst.** The overall Web analytics professional has a deep understanding of digital channels, most often focused on site or Web analytics. This person uses a digital analytics tool, both internal and external, proprietary and third party, to understand the performance of site traffic and online marketing campaigns and to segment digital data, in order to understand how people referred from various channels are generating business value. Digital analysts do many things, including collecting, tracking, measuring, understanding, reporting, analyzing, communicating, and socializing analysis related to the success of digital business. Digital analysts can measure whether the site, paid search, online advertising, and other business programs (online and offline) are fulfilling their business and behavioral goals for conversion, task completion, and other KPIs when compared to past, current, and predicted performance.

- **Site optimizer.** A niche type of digital analytics professional (see the discussion in this chapter on site optimization and landing pages), the site optimizer is in charge of determining the right approach for configuring and reporting the results for AB (champion/challenger) and multivariate tests. This person is all about testing components of site and page design to yield the best combination of elements that provides a lift in a particular metric against a goal, such as conversion rate. Content targeting may also fall under this person.

- **Social metrician.** Another niche type of digital analytics professional, this person is concerned with the performance of customer touch points outside of the main website. He or she collects, monitors, and analyzes data related to things that happen in other channels, such as syndicated video, mobile, widgets, blogs, social networks, and other social media.

- **Database analyst.** This is the traditional offline analyst and database miner. He or she analyzes data from channels that are not online but may reference and promote online interaction, such as television, radio, print, catalogs, and direct mail. Of course, these analytics skills can be applied to online data as well.

- **Search analyst.** The analytics professional in charge of keyword identification/selection, keyword management, bidding, and analyzing the outcomes of searches and their impact on site conversion. He or she may be in charge of analyzing site performance against known SEO goals, too, not only SEM.

- **Researcher.** Part market researcher and part analyst, this individual is in charge of online customer and visitor surveying, relating customer feedback and visitor opinions to the context of on-site behavior to help deduce "why" people did something on your site. This person must bring together offline survey data with data from digital channels.

- **Ad analyst.** Solely dedicated to assessing the performance of advertising campaigns, the ad analyst assesses and educates clients on ad campaign performance, both online and offline. He or she determines the impact of advertising after click-through and ad exposure, which includes creating an analysis of ad effectiveness based on narrative, creative positioning, and other details of serving online ads.

- **Audience analyst.** The wielder of an audience measurement tool informs competitive decisions, influences media plans, and provides benchmarking and competitive data to give context to other data analysis activities, such as keyword bidding or media buying.

How would these professionals all work together? The researcher's data are used to help craft a customer-focused and competitively differentiated campaign strategy. The audience measurer provides data that focuses the strategy on the right online demographics and sites, while the database analyst mines historic data to figure out the best-performing offline tactics for the identified demographics.

Let's say a mix of search, social media, and online and offline display ads are selected as part of the campaign. The search analyst concentrates on search engine optimization and marketing, while the ad analyst tracks the performance of display ads to the site. The social metrician examines the social media ecosystem's response to the campaign. The digital analyst analyzes how campaign-referred visitors behave and navigate through the site, taking into account the context of the researcher's voice-of-customer data. Meanwhile, the site optimizer tests landing pages and funnels to ensure that they effectively convert visitors and fulfill business goals.

For many companies, it would be unrealistic and perhaps impossible find and hire people to fill each of the roles I've presented here. In fact, in some companies these roles and activities are completed by only a few people, if at all. That said, companies that are unable to bridge together online and offline analytics teams will miss important data points. In the digital future, we'll see different types of analytics professionals working together across channels to yield profitable insights that support campaign and business goals—and create value for the organization.

DIGITAL ANALYTICS TOOLS

Digital analytics tools are obviously very important to any digital analytics program. Tools, technology, the IT resources, the administrators, and the configures of tools are all essential to digital analytics. Yet alone, all of these things are insufficient for value generation with digital analytics. People, process, and leadership are all as important as the tools and technology supporting them. Tools are various, and the options for digital data collection, reporting, and even analysis are all advancing daily, release after release. The landscape from digital analytics vendors is all about multichannel—whether providing software that is run by IT teams on premises or "in the cloud" as SaaS (software as a service) or from third-party data vendors (such as audience measurement or risk-management firms).

The idea of multichannel means that data exists across more than one channel. In traditional media, a channel would be TV, radio, billboard, and magazines. In digital media, a channel would be paid search (SEM), organic search (SEO), display advertising, QR codes, or hyper local mobile campaign or social media campaign. The best tool vendors aspire to be able to bring together all of these data, organize it, and allow for querying and reporting and the application of advanced statistical techniques that can predict the future (indeed, see Chapter 10 on "Winning with Predictive Analytics"). By moving all of these data from where they exist to databases, we expect that the data can be mined for relationships that help us understand how to create new or incremental business opportunities.

I propose the following guidelines for analytics tool and vendor selection to consider when you select a digital analytics tool. In these guidelines, the key questions you should answer before considering the purchase of a new tool or extending your existing analytics tool are

- How much money can I spend?
- What resources do I have?
- Do I have the organizational capability and maturity to run an in-house software solution?
- Do I prefer to eliminate overhead and technology expense by delegating control of my Web analytics technology and infrastructure to a hosted solution that is run out of a vendor's data center (i.e., SaaS or in the cloud)?
- Do I want to bring together analytical data from multiple channels (cross-channel data integration)—either within my own systems or outside of my company? If so, what systems have the data I need (CRM, Ad Server, and so on)? And what method for extracting, transferring, and loading the data can my IT team support (i.e., Web services, API calls, flat files)?

After discussing and agreeing on the answers to these questions, you will find it entirely possible to identify a set of vendors to consider.

The guidelines for analytics tool and vendor selection evaluates products across key attributes of the product and the vendor selling it. The following list of criteria are not exhaustive, and these criteria must be discussed in the context of how they are relevant to your business needs and goals. A tool and vendor evaluation must include relevant facts and data about the vendor's company, technology, services, products, organization, strategy, and cost.

To synthesize and work with these criteria, I find it helpful to create a matrix with the criteria on the left axis and the companies you are selecting on the top axis. Fill in the cells with your custom information and more, when evaluating a vendor according to these guidelines.

- **Company description.** Describe the company that is using publicly available sources. How long has the company existed? How solvent is it? What do customers say about the company?

- **General technology description.** Explain the technology and how it works. For example, if the technology uses online analytical processing, what happens to the confidence level and the confidence interval (i.e., the margin of error) when drilling down on the data? Can I report on every dimension and attribute of available data about a segment or is the reporting limited? How about when exporting?

- **Product and service capabilities.** Assess the overall ability of the vendor's technology and services organization when compared to the industry. What percentage of the company's customers successfully deploy tags and get complete tag coverage across every page from day one? Or successfully transfer and correctly parse customized log files from day one?

- **Product(s) required for the solution.** List the product or products required to support the full solution. Can I run identical queries and get identical answers across all company technologies?

- **Ease of use.** Indicate the complexity of interacting with and navigating through the interface and the reports. Assess the user experience of the graphical user interface from usability and information architecture perspectives. Can I simply find the data I need to gain analytic momentum?

- **Product updates and difficulty.** Indicate the difficulty of product updates and the general migration path for upgrades. Does taking advantage of new functionality in a release usually require upgrading the code throughout my website?

- **Real-time reporting latency.** Identify the delay or lag in availability of the data within the technology. Continuous processing? Batch?

- **Time to implementation.** Indicate the time to deploy the baseline, out-of-the-box solution. What percentage of the company's customers have successfully tagged all site pages and/or processed logs within one month after beginning? Three months? Six months?

- **Ease of implementation.** Indicate the difficulty level of implementing the technology. What percentage of the company's application can I use if no changes are made to the JavaScript page tag?

- **Data collection model.** Identify data collection methods. Does the company's data schema simply roll up and report "unique" counts across time periods and delete the underlying data (even if I don't buy an additional product)? Does it cost more money to retain full, unsummarized visitor data for 12 months? For 24 months? Longer?

- **Data retention and ownership.** Indicate whether I retain ownership of my data. If so, for how long and at what level of granularity? For what duration does the company retain visitor data? Is that the same across all applications (not just a data warehousing component)?

- **Integration.** Identify features and methods for integration with external systems. API? Web services? Summary extracts? Only Excel?

- **Innovation.** Indicate the level of innovation perceived by looking into the company when compared to industry competitors. What do the analysts say? How large is the company's engineering organization? What percentage of overall expense does the company spend on R&D? Partnerships?

- **Security.** Identify the security model. Does the tool support integration with active directory or lightweight directory access protocol? What is the cost per seat or license?

- **Segmentation.** Identify the flexibility and ease of segmenting the data. What is the total maximum number of segments available for use "out of the box"? How much more does it cost if I want to increase segments or filters?

More attributes exist. More questions should be asked. Truly understanding a digital analytics technology means asking hard questions and assessing the way a company answers those questions to frame your subsequent analysis and guide your selection.

ADVANCED DIGITAL ANALYTICS

Digital analytics and traditional marketing analytics (such as media mix modeling) are well-suited and highly compatible disciplines—in the same way that machine learning and statistical analytics are complementary and symbiotic with each other. In the digital age, analysis is both an input and an output of research. Several macro tactics exist for the advanced analysis of digital data:

- Longitudinal analysis, where the business examines data during a number of time periods and compares the variables (the input) in each of those time periods to one another.

- Cross-sectional or segmented analysis, where the same data are compared side-by-side against the same or different input and evaluated against each other.

Each of these tactics is useful and applicable for advanced digital analysis—and a combination of both methods, in the context of statistical and machine learning and exploratory data analysis (EDA), is applicable to digital analytics.

Analytics, when functioning to generate revenue or reduce cost, is symbiotic with traditional research methods as well. Digital analytics and traditional analytics, when integrated together, can inform business, brand, product, and marketing strategy in a grounded way that is based on empirical, observed, and direct evidence, which can be used to generate analytics insights that answer the following questions—according to Joel Rubinson, the leading global researcher and founder of Rubinson Partners:

- How do I grow brand sales effectively and efficiently?
- How do I create brand loyalty?
- How do people use my brand?
- How do people shop?
- How do target consumers consume and respond to media?[4]

As has been emphasized throughout this book, analysts and researchers should not work in silos but rather should work tightly together across disciplines on your organization's critical business issues. For some companies, this will mean all of them working in the same team, with no departmental, organizational, or political silos. One way to ensure that digital analysts and traditional analysts are collaborating positively is via the integration of quantitative analytical data—such as digital behavioral data—with qualitative data from surveys' verbatim answers, focus groups, and other written research responses.

DIGITAL ANALYTICS AND VOICE OF THE CUSTOMER

Digital behavioral data are commonly believed to answer the "what" about customer behavior, such as what revenue was generated by customer segment N from marketing channel X? The answer to "why," such as "Why did the customer respond favorably to that marketing campaign?" involves the integration of voice of the customer analytics. In other words, digital behavioral data are very effective for improving and optimizing the digital experience but less effective for measuring, understanding, and being able to draw conclusions about site satisfaction and brand awareness. Higher-order marketing concepts, such as awareness and favorability, are not easily measured using only digital behavioral data. Voice of the customer analytics were discussed in detail in Chapter 8; however, here we revisit the importance of digital analytics and voice of the customer analytics working together to paint a full picture of the digital experience.

With social media (see Chapter 12), combining quantitative data and qualitative data can help a business understand new insights that were not previously known. However, combining quantitative data with quantitative data requires, as with all analytical projects, a considerable amount of careful preplanning. Although the full details for successfully integrating VOC and digital data together are beyond the scope of this book, here are some proposed guidelines for digital and VOC integration, which should help you determine how to execute on this digital analytics integration goal.

- Create a control group of visitors who viewed similar amounts or types of content.

- Compare critical voice of the customer metrics (for example, site satisfaction or brand favorability) of those who used social/ feedback components with those who did not. Determine, with a higher degree of confidence, the real impact of satisfaction.

- Attempt to control and ensure consistency of issues such as those who used certain features/components in the past, demographic profiles, attitudes, psychographic profile, and user intent. In doing so, it will help minimize any potential bias in the analysis of your results. At this point, behavioral impact can be better understood and integrated with categorical and discrete variables attained by having people answer questions (often in pop-up surveys). Here are useful questions to ask—several can be reviewed on Avinash Kaushik's worthwhile and excellent blog *Occam's Razor*, as well as within his 4Q survey tool:

- Did you complete your task?

- Were you satisfied?

- Why were or why weren't you satisfied?

- What could we do better?

- Will you come back to the site?[5]

As the data collection layer is being determined, designed, coded, and tested, it will be necessary to have a "primary key" that you can use to join the voice of the customer and digital behavior data together to understand the opinions of people who complete certain behaviors on your site. Once this hard work is accomplished, your analytics team can apply rigorous and valid analytical methods to the unified data.

ANALYTICS OF SITE AND LANDING PAGE OPTIMIZATION

The buzzword *optimization* is thrown around loosely in digital analytics culture. The goal of digital analytics? Optimization. What are you going to do to the site? Optimize. How are you going to do it? With optimization technology. With no tongue in cheek, site optimization software is important and helpful for digital analytics. Site optimization companies are studied by leading analyst firms, such as Forrester, Gartner, Altimeter, and IDC, as a small but growing niche brand of bleeding-edge software. These companies, such as Sitespect, Adobe, and Monetate, provide tools for testing how a site looks and appears to a defined audience, in order to increase the site's business performance for that target audience. For example, software exists that can serve every single combination of the elements of user experience, such as the color of buttons, the text on the page, pictures, and so on. Testing software for site optimization aspires to determine the correct combination of user experience to reduce "friction" and ensure that the site is "persuasive" enough to fulfill site goals (such as selling products).

I had a chance to sit down with Eric Hansen, the CEO of Sitespect. He summarized the importance of optimization this way:

> Success with analytics requires taking action from insights derived from analysis. Traditionally, analytical recommendation delivered by analysts can take months to go live on the site. Such delays in implementation impact the relevancy and currency of the analysis when executed some months later. Site optimization technology removes the delay from analytical realization to implementation. By using optimization technology for creating customized dynamic experiences delivered to visitors, in real time, based on behavioral data, the business impact of analysis may be more quickly understood and payback more quickly achieved.

As an example of optimization, consider that your site may have a page or an experience that contains an image, a button, a text-based promotional offer, and some advertising. All of these elements are static and locked and rarely change. Site optimization and testing software allows you to have 10 different images, 10 different buttons, 10 different promotional offers, and 10 different places to insert ads. The software would then automatically test some or all of the possible different combinations of these elements to determine which combination worked best for your business goals. In this sense, site optimization may require overhead to generate the elements of user experience to test, while proving the technology can dramatically increase revenues to cover the costs.

Landing page optimization applies a similar technique as site optimization, where a combination of landing page elements (often called a "recipe") is tested to determine the best site experience for the targeted audience. Online advertising campaigns and other programs send people to a page on the destination site. This site is called the landing page. It is known that if the landing page has "scent" and a strong "call to action," then "friction" is reduced and "conversion" is more likely to occur.

For more information about site and landing page optimization and for solid guidance on how to use data to drive your business and enhance performance, please review the work from the Austin-based Eisenberg Brothers. Both Brian and Jeffrey Eisenberg are the world's leading thinkers, authors, and speakers on the subject of digital optimization and in their books coined the following terms in the context used in this section: *persuasion, friction, scent, and call to action.*[6]

CALL TO ACTION: UNIFY TRADITIONAL AND DIGITAL ANALYTICS

As we progress even further into the Internet age, digital and traditional analytics must work more closely together and learn from each other. Symbiosis exists, and the evolution of global commerce in the twenty-first century demands that organizations leverage analytics more effectively going forward. Traditional analytical techniques can be used by research to benefit digital analytics. Understanding the possibilities and the potential of digital analytics will benefit research analytics as well. For example, the following tools and methods can be unified and applied across both traditional and digital analytics:

- Loyalty modeling can be used to compare the digital usage of non-loyal versus loyal customers.

- Game theory statistics can be applied to attribution analysis.
- Conjoint analytics can help digital experimental design and the impact of an attribute on choice.

Traditional brand marketing is missing the input to media mix models from digital data because such modeling is usually done at the market level—where owned media are undervalued, earned media are larger than social media, and paid media include paid search (SEO) and banner ads. Thus, it is absolutely essential that traditional research analytics work with digital data.

Use traditional research models on digital data to understand pricing and price sensitivity and the impact of packaging during product development, and apply experimental design methods for testing display advertising (for example, image/no-image, RIA/No RIA, ad unit size/format, targeting approach). The possibilities are endless, if traditional and digital analysts continue to evolve to work effectively together to drive global commerce using unified data, research, and analytics, regardless of collection method, source, technology, or channel. The rallying cry for merging traditional and digital analytics is discussed, in greater detail, in Akin Arikan's excellent *Multichannel Marketing Analytics* book.[7] We exist in a multichannel world where content has been loosened and abstracted from presentation and device, democratized through social participation across cultural, national, and geographic boundaries. Multichannel digital experiences are constrained only by screensize, bandwidth, and the limitations of current technology; thus, analytics must analyze this complex world by bringing together digital and traditional analytics in a centralized way that helps create economic value for the organization.

KEY TAKEAWAYS

- Digital analytics is entirely about using data, analytics, and research to create economic value for your business by either generating new or incremental profitable revenue or reducing cost. It is about collecting and integrating, reporting and analyzing data in statistically rigorous ways, using scientific and artful methods from multiple channels, such as the website, social media, mobile media, online advertising, and paid/organic search, as well as offline and non-line channels, such as television, radio, and qualitative survey data.

■ Digital analytics requires people, process, and technology. Multidimensional and intellectually curious people who have strong analytical skills, crossing the technical, managerial, mathematical, social, strategic, and business fields, are necessary. People require process in order for analytical teams to function, execute an analysis, and provide outcomes-based analytical deliverables that recommend one or more business actions.

■ Investment in digital analytics is necessary to stay competitive going forward. The companies that create centralized analytical teams that exist on the "business-side" and not in "IT" or "technology" are crucial to staff appropriately and empower effectively. All technical functions and resources should have documented roles and responsibilities for support of the analytics team—both within standard corporate processes (such as road mapping, project management, engineering, and QA testing), and also outside of standard processes when the business and the customer require analytical agility.

■ Digital analytics requires cross-functional teamwork and learning and applying new technology in a business context with business justification. Analytical teams should be expected to work socially and to articulate the analysis to stakeholders, internally and externally, at all levels. Reporting is not analysis—and any team that simply provides "reports" should be made accountable for analyzing the report and producing an analysis with business value.

■ Concentrate on business questions and the needs of internal business people, such as sales, marketing, PR, analyst relations, and executive management, instead of getting caught up in the technology and nuances of digital data collection. Realize that digital analytics tools and the resources that support them are simply overhead if the team is not producing an analysis and providing the best possible answers to prioritized business questions that help generate projected (and thus provable) business value.

■ Apply advanced analytical techniques, but do so judiciously and after you have clean data, have established analytics processes, and have a solid, high-performing analytical team. Although it is certainly possible to do predictive modeling after you collect digital data, make sure that you do not put the cart before the horse. Ensure that you have the foundation of your analytics house in order before you take on new projects, such as data mining, machine learning, predictive analytics, and automated site optimization. Yet don't be too cautious. Keep experimenting and pushing forward the grand analytical agenda, but be realistic and judicious to the analysis projects you approve.

■ Digital analysts can learn from traditional analysts and vice versa. Digital analytics requires integrating data from multiple sources, including sources from which traditional analytical data are derived (such as TV). Many models, methods, and procedures already exist in direct marketing and offline advertising that not only are relevant conceptually but are directly applicable to digital analytics. Traditional advertising and the impact of it on brand, as well as on direct response, can be measured by digital analytics—and digital analytics data can be brought into media mix models and be used to inform media buying, planning, selling, and trafficking on both the buy and sell sides by vendors, brands, and agencies.

ADDITIONAL RESOURCES

Analytics Resource Organization, http://www.thearo.org

Digital Analytics Thursdays, http://www.digitalanalyticsthursdays.org

Digital Analytics Association, http://www.digitalanalyticsassociation.org

Interactive Advertising Bureau, http://www.iab.org

Brian and Jeffrey Eisenberg, http://www.bryaneisenberg.com/

Avinash Kaushik's blog, http://www.kaushik.com/avinash

Justin Cutroni's blog, http://cutroni.com/blog/

NOTES

1. "Bringing Big Data to the Enterprise," 2012, http://www-01.ibm.com/software/data/bigdata/.

2. Tom Davenport, *Analytics at Work: Smarter Decisions, Better Results* (Cambridge, MA: Harvard Business Review Press, 2010).

3. Eric Peterson, *Web Analytics Demystified: A Marketer's Guide to Understanding How Your Web Site Affects Your Business* (Portland, OR: Celilo Group Media, 2004).

4. Joel Rubinson, "Exciting Announcement from Rubinson Partners, Inc." *Joel Rubinson on Market Research*, blog post, April 25, 2012, http://blog.joelrubinson.net/2012/04/exciting-announcement-from-rubinson-partners-inc/.

5. Avinash Kaushik, "Web Analytics Tool Selection: Three Questions to Ask Yourself." *Occam's Razor*, blog post, January 30, 2007, http://www.kaushik.net/avinash/web-analytics-tool-selection-three-questions-to-ask-yourself/.

6. Brian Eisenberg and Jeffrey Eisenberg, *Call to Action: Secret Formulas to Improve Online Results* (New York: Wizard Academy Press, 2005); Brian Eisenberg and Jeffrey Eisenberg, *Waiting for Your Cat to Bark: Persuading Customers When They Ignore Marketing* (New York: Wizard Academy Press, 2005).

7. Akin Arikan, *Multichannel Marketing: Metrics and Methods for On and Offline Success* (Sebastopol, CA: Sybex Publishing, 2008).

CHAPTER 10

Effective Predictive Analytics

What Works and What Does Not

"If we can keep our competitors focused on us while we stay focused on the customer, ultimately we'll turn out all right."

—Jeff Bezos

In today's era of overwhelming data and with the explosion of new digital information, companies are facing new business challenges and opportunities from all directions. Customers are more technology savvy and are using social media, the Web, mobile apps, and other new media to compare products and services and to get and provide feedback regarding their purchases. They are digitally connected and can get information about your product, services, and brand without reaching out to your organization directly.

According to an article published in the *Economist*, the world contains an unimaginably vast amount of digital information that is increasing at an ever more rapid pace.[1] This makes it possible to do many things that previously could not be done: spot business trends, prevent diseases, combat crime, and so on. Managed well, the data can be used to unlock new sources of economic value, provide fresh insights into science, and hold governments to account. However, data are also creating a host of new problems. Despite the abundance of tools to capture, process, and share all of this information—sensors, computers, mobile phones, and the like—it already exceeds the available storage space. Moreover, ensuring data security and protecting privacy are becoming harder as the information multiplies and is shared ever more widely around the world.

In this new environment where companies are inundated with astronomical amounts of data, some don't even know where to start, whereas others are leveraging analytics to get a competitive advantage. As the torrent of information increases, it is not surprising that companies feel overwhelmed. "There is an immense risk of cognitive overload," explains Carl Pabo, a molecular biologist who studies cognition.[2] The mind can handle seven pieces of information in its short-term memory and can generally deal with only four concepts or relationships at once. If there is more information to process, or it is especially complex, people become confused.

Forward-looking companies have increased their investment to reorganize their information technology infrastructure to effectively capture, process, analyze, and manage their big data. However, capturing and storing customer information is not alone sufficient. What will differentiate a company from its competition is its ability to transform data from the information stage into actionable intelligence. It is the ability to detect and uncover patterns from the multiple sources of data that leads to smarter decisions. Successful companies are those equipped with skilled people, technologies, and processes to leverage advanced business analytics, in order to create value from their data assets. Most important, successful companies are those that will leverage the power of predictive analytics to forecast outcomes and plan scenarios that will lead to achieving their organization's business objectives.

In the following sections, we present a nontechnical review of some fundamentals for predictive analytics, as well as provide examples and case studies of organizations that are using predictive analytics to maintain their competitive edge. We provide examples from a variety of industries facing today's business problems. You will learn from companies that have leveraged predictive analytic insights to keep, protect, and grow their customer base, as well as engage and interact with their prospects. Winning with analytics today is much about whether your organization can put predictive analytics into action.

WHAT IS PREDICTIVE ANALYTICS?

In the age of big data, demanding customer expectations, and increasingly aggressive competitors, organizations are moving from traditional analytics/reporting solutions that provide a snapshot of the past (hindsight) to solutions that provide an accurate picture of the present and a prediction of future trends (foresight). As a result, predictive analytics is one of the most powerful approaches that companies can use to compete with analytics.

During the last few years, there have been a lot of discussions around predictive analytics. For example, Forrester's paper "Predictive Analytics and Data Mining Solutions" provided the following definition of advanced predictive analytics: "Any solution that supports the identification of meaningful patterns and correlations among variables in complex, structured and unstructured, historical, and potential future data sets for the purposes of predicting future events and assessing the attractiveness of various courses of action. Advanced business analytics typically incorporate such functionality as data mining, descriptive modeling, econometrics, forecasting, operations research, optimization, predictive modeling, and simulation, statistics, and text analytics."[3]

From a business perspective, the most important aspect of predictive analytics is its ability to provide an accurate, forward-looking perspective to your organization. Supported by traditional analytics, research, and business intelligence, advanced predictive analytics is a combination of sophisticated analytics solutions (such as data mining, text analytics, segmentation, predictive modeling, forecasting, and optimization) that helps discover trends and complex patterns from structured and unstructured data, identify the relationships between multiple data elements, create meaningful insights, and predict the future for a variety of outcomes and events. Some of the events predictive analytics may address include

- Customer attrition (churn)
- Customer conversion
- Online purchase patterns
- Product adoption (customer cross-selling and up-selling)
- Preventing youth smoking behavior
- Predisposition to commit a crime (such as fraud)
- Susceptibility to a disease
- Susceptibility to an adverse event
- Customer online behavior (website visit behavior)

As you can imagine, the business applications for predictive analytics are broad. They include predicting sales and marketing customer behavior, predicting unhealthy lifestyle behaviors and their outcomes, predicting fraudulent insurance claims, predicting military supply chain problems, predicting customer attrition, and predicting the spread of the infections, such as the H1N1 flu.

Predictive analytics can even be used in the most critical of situations. For example, in 2002 America's Defense Advanced Research Projects Agency, best known for developing the Internet four decades ago, embarked on a futuristic initiative called Augmented Cognition, or AugCog. Commander Dylan Schmorrow, a cognitive scientist with the navy, devised a crown of sensors to monitor and predict activity in the body, such as blood flow and oxygen levels. The idea was that virtual modern warfare requires soldiers to think like never before, whether managing drones, overseeing a patrol from a remote location, or monitoring advanced communications channels. Soldiers must perform multiple simultaneous tasks that require the processing of large amounts of information. The AugCog system was designed to help soldiers make sense of the flood of streaming information. If the AugCog sensors predict that the wearer's spatial memory will soon become saturated, new information will be sent in a different form, maybe via an audio alert,

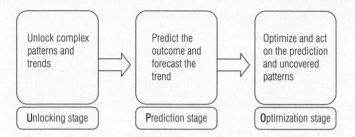

Exhibit 10.1 Advanced Predictive Business Analytics

instead of in text. During trials, the device achieved a 100% improvement in recall and a 500% increase in working memory.[2]

Although there are many ways to frame the notion of advanced predictive business analytics, we believe the most business-relevant definition is one that classifies predictive analytics as an umbrella with three main components, as seen in Exhibit 10.1.

- Unlocking stage
- Prediction stage
- Optimization stage

From our perspective, all three stages are required for effective predictive analytics.

UNLOCKING STAGE

The unlocking stage is the point at which data are cultivated to provide information on what has happened, who was involved, how often it happened, and where it happened. This discovery phase helps identify complex patterns and trends from structured and unstructured data. It helps discover and quantify important relationships that you may have been unaware of, thus providing insight to better define customer segments to target for an acquisition or an up-sell campaign; to detect fraudulent insurance claims; to assess product affinity and analyze online shopping carts; and to identify high-value customers to keep and protect. Uncovering patterns and trends enables benefits that include

- Effective segment targeting
- Marketing CRM campaign optimization

- Merchandise strategies optimization
- Fraud reduction and cost reduction
- Risk reduction
- Increases in customer profitability
- Keeping and protecting your high-value customer segments

These patterns and trends are usually discovered via statistical analyses, complexes queries, and descriptive analytics that include the following four points:

1. **Data mining.** Data mining refers to a collection of techniques that aims to uncover complex patterns in data (big or little) to support the decision-making process.

2. **Segmentation.** Segmentation is an associative technique by which similar customers/companies are put together in groups called segments. It is based on the premise that similar behavior or characteristics are derive from similar needs and helps to provide insight regarding what's happening in the market. Segmentation can be based on one variable or multiple variables. The more discriminating variables we have, the more specific and personalized our segmentation will be. In today's connected world, customers expect service from companies that implies some type of segmentation. They expect companies to remember them, know what they like and don't like, and keep track of personal connections, such as where they went on their last vacation or what book they last read. Segmentation is typically used to define the go-to-market strategy and better allocate resources to cover a market opportunity or territory.

Exhibit 10.2 illustrates how data mining and segmentation have been used to build market opportunity size for all companies in United States. The market opportunity has been obtained by unlocking the potential of companies according to number of employees using multiple types of data intelligence: internal data, external data, and macroeconomic indicators throughout predictive models. The most important insight of this business visualization is the well-known

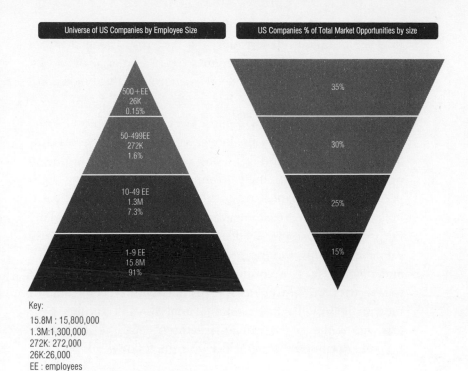

Key:
15.8M : 15,800,000
1.3M:1,300,000
272K: 272,000
26K:26,000
EE : employees

Exhibit 10.2 Business Opportunity Visualization

20/80 rule that is perfectly showcased via the two pyramids. On the left pyramid we can see that companies with a large employee population (more than 500 employees) account for only .15% of the universe in terms of number of companies, but they posted the largest market potential: 35%.

The left pyramid represents the breakdown of companies into four groups by number of employees:

- 1 to 9 employees
- 10 to 49 employees
- 50 to 499 employees
- 500+ (500 employees and more)

The inverse pyramid (the right pyramid) represents the market opportunity for each employee size segment group.

3. **Artificial intelligence.** Artificial intelligence is the ability to uncover complex relationships and patterns among the data using machine-learning techniques, such as neural networks. Artificial intelligence helps detect patterns, make predictions, and learn over time.

4. **Text analytics.** With the explosion of the Internet and social media, text analytics is no longer a choice for any forward-looking company wanting to stay current and to continue to operate in this extremely competitive marketplace. High-performance companies are turning to text analytics for path-breaking insights on customers and market knowledge building. For example, customer feedback can be harnessed from voice e-mail comments, forums, message boards, blogs, social media, and opinion sites. According to Gartner, more than 80% of today's data are unstructured.[4] This unstructured data contains meaningful insights that traditional analysis can't uncover. Text analytics is the analysis of unstructured data, the analysis of text and documents; it helps perform the following:

- Content categorization
- Sentiment analysis
- Semantic search matching
- Customer feedback (e-mail text analysis and categorization)

Text analytics will continue to become a primary analytical challenge for organizations to address in the future.

PREDICTION STAGE

Predicting the future is the centerpiece of predictive analytics and the heart of this chapter. Prediction is about providing information on what will happen, what could happen, and what actions are needed. Predicting the future is based on analytics that include predictive models and forecasting.

Predictive Models

Predictive models aim to address the who, when, and why questions for business issues, such as those related to customer behavior, product usage, and likelihood to purchase. Questions we can answer with predictive models include

- Which of my existing customers will turn to the competition?
- Why will my existing customers leave?
- When will my customers leave?
- Whom can we retain?
- Why would a new prospect convert to being a customer?
- When will a prospect convert to being a customer?
- Who will buy?
- What will they buy?
- Whom can we acquire?
- Which product and services will a customer buy next?
- Who is more likely to default on a payment?
- What are our probable costs?
- What are our liabilities?
- What are our future revenues?

Predictive models help executives make informed strategic, operational, and tactical decisions, to prevent and predict transactions or risks or improve the insight into your customers'/members' behavior.

Forecasting

Forecasting will generally provide answers to questions such as: How many customers will you lose in the next 6 months to competition? How many people will be affected with a certain pandemic disease in the next 12 months in a given country? What are the forecasted liabilities from incurred, but not reported, insurance claims? Predictive modeling is different from forecasting. Forecasting will help you predict how many customers you will lose to your competitor, while predictive modeling will answer why you are losing them and under what conditions.

PALO ALTO MEDICAL FOUNDATION ZEROS IN ON DISEASE

CASE STUDY

With its diverse Asian population, the San Francisco Bay Area provides medical researchers with a unique setting in which to study disease trends among an ethnic group for which few studies exist. Using SAS Visual Data Discovery, the research institute of a local health-care organization analyzes medical data from the local Asian American population—often with life-saving results.

The Palo Alto Medical Foundation Research Institute's Department of Health Policy Research conducts studies in the areas of cardiovascular disease and epidemiology. Focused on 660,000 active patients throughout the San Francisco Bay Area, the team's research is aimed at disease trends among the Asian population in particular.

"There haven't been many studies on the Asian American population," says Eric Wong, the senior statistician in the Department of Health Policy Research. "And those that have been done did not look at specific Asian subgroups. We have a unique opportunity in the San Francisco Bay Area to study the six largest subgroups, comprising Asian Indian, Chinese, Filipino, Japanese, Korean, and Vietnamese—in one geographic setting and in one health-care organization."

Not-for-Profit Leader in Cardiac Care

The Palo Alto Medical Foundation for Health Care, Research, and Education is a not-for-profit health-care organization and a leader in the multispecialty group practice of medicine. Part of the Sutter Health family of not-for-profit hospitals and physician organizations, it serves more than 100 communities in Northern California. The organization is also a regional leader in cardiac care and a pioneer in advanced patient safety technology and the use of electronic health records.

Under the leadership of researcher Dr. Latha Palaniappan, Wong's team conducts a variety of studies, such as research into the trends and risk factors for diabetes and whether they vary among racial/ethnic subgroups. Findings inform internal policies that lead to improvements in patient care, Wong explains.

"If we find that one population is at a higher risk than other racial/ethnic groups, we can develop culturally relevant content on risk factors, suggestions on nutrition, or recommend lifestyle changes," Wong says. "We also disseminate our findings back to clinical staff so they can implement changes and policies that result in higher-quality patient care. We share everything we learn with the medical community at large, and we make it a priority to publish our findings."

Wong points to a number of interesting studies that clearly illustrate how disease trends are different among Asian ethnic subgroups. One found that Asian Americans have a greater prevalence of metabolic syndrome—a cluster of conditions that increases the risk of heart disease, stroke, and diabetes—even though they present at lower levels of traditional risk factors.

In 2004, Wong says, the World Health Organization published a research article suggesting that Asian populations should be examined at body mass index (BMI) cut points lower than traditional values. So Dr. Palaniappan, Wong, and their collaborators studied the association of BMI to the risk of metabolic syndrome in Asian Americans, compared to non-Hispanic whites. For every Asian subgroup, the researchers learned that the risk of metabolic syndrome was higher than in non-Hispanic whites across all BMI values.

"We also looked at the burden of cardiovascular disease in Asian Americans, specifically focused on stroke and coronary heart disease," he explains. "What we found was a similar discovery. Compared to non-Hispanic whites, we found that stroke rates were elevated in some subgroups, though not statistically significant. We also found that coronary heart disease rates were higher in Asian Indian and Filipino men, compared to non-Hispanic whites, which was statistically significant."

In yet another interesting study, Wong describes how his team analyzed the effectiveness of shared medical visits versus one-to-one patient and provider appointments.

"One of our physicians was conducting shared appointments as a way of promoting weight loss in a clinical setting," Wong says. "In a shared medical appointment, one physician meets with a group of patients for a longer period of time, for example, 6 to 12 patients for 90 minutes. The approach borrows from forums that involve a group of individuals facing similar circumstances, where there's group camaraderie—they learn together and share information. The question we had was whether the approach affected health outcomes. Did it really promote greater weight loss, compared to

(*continued*)

individual medical appointments? What we found was that it did. On average, patients in the group setting lost two pounds during the observation period, compared to one-to-one patients who actually gained weight on average. And while a decrease of a pound or two might not be that dramatic, if we can at least use shared medical appointments to maintain weight, then that is a victory as well."

Proactive Intervention

According to Wong, analytics from SAS also support proactive medical intervention practices and policies throughout the health network.

"When there's an observation of a trend, we try to figure out the immutable risk factors associated with the probability of having the disease," he explains. "Based on that, we can think about whether there's something we can do about it, like education, screenings, or preventative measures. If we identify a specific population at a higher risk, it's natural to design specific intervention or screening methods that target that group, as well as design communication methods to reach the at-risk population."

To perform the myriad studies it conducts each year, the research team derives its de-identified data from a variety of sources, including electronic administration, registration, and billing data; electronic medical records; and Census, state, and national health surveys.

"We are striving to be leaders in multispecialty care and at providing the full spectrum of primary care services. Having a better understanding of the patient population and disease risk factors is integral to becoming a real pioneer and leader in the industry."

OPTIMIZATION STAGE

The optimization stage is about deriving and refining the best business action by taking into account multiple factors and business goals against business constraints. The goal of the optimization stage is to single out the best possible action that will lead to the desired outcome from a variety of possible options. As an example, one of the coauthors, JP Isson, worked with a company recently on an optimization challenge. The optimization goal was to increase the acquisition team by 20 people, in order to maximize the sales coverage in the United States. However, the following constraints had to be factored in:

- Create 20 equal basket portfolios to be assigned to new sales representatives.
- Each portfolio should have the same number of companies.
- Each portfolio should have an equal distribution of employee size (high, medium, low).
- Each portfolio should have an equal distribution of company potential (high, medium, low).
- Weighing in time zone and company location (Eastern Time Central Time); companies should be equally distributed across location and zone for each portfolio.
- Service representatives should be equally distributed to support the portfolio.
- Each portfolio should have an equal distribution of industries.

Factoring in and weighing all of the aforementioned constraints and criteria require more than human intuition and experience. Optimization is a technique that leverages mathematics to maximize the results in helping to answer complex business questions.

There were several rounds of analysis and optimization required for this project, with the resulting solution proving successful and accomplishing all of the desired outcomes under the aforementioned constraints.

We will conclude this nontechnical review of predictive analytics fundamentals by recalling the IMPACT cycle stages we introduced in Chapter 5. As a reminder, the IMPACT cycle is designed to ensure that all of your team's analytical deliverables are business focused and will have the optimal return on investment to your organization. This is especially important when undertaking predictive analytics. The IMPACT cycle (Exhibit 10.3, previously shown in Chapter 5) includes six stages, outlined here:

- **Stage 1: Identify the question.** In a nonintrusive way, help your business partner identify the critical business question(s) he or she needs help in answering. Then set a clear expectation of the time and the work involved to get an answer.

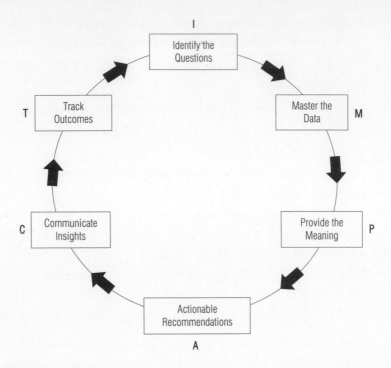

Exhibit 10.3   IMPACT Cycle: Analyst Guide for Creating for High-Impact Analytics

- **Stage 2: Master the data.** This is the analyst's sweet spot—assemble, analyze, and synthesize all available information that will help in answering the critical business question. Create simple and clear visual presentations (charts, graphs, tables, interactive data environments, and so on) of that data that are easy to comprehend.

- **Stage 3: Provide the meaning.** Articulate clear and concise interpretations of the data and the visuals in the context of the critical business questions identified.

- **Stage 4: Make actionable recommendations.** Provide thoughtful business recommendations based on your interpretation of the data. Even if they are off base, it's easier to react to a suggestion than to generate one. Where possible, tie a rough dollar figure to any revenue improvements or cost savings associated with your recommendations.

- **Stage 5: Communicate insights.** Focus on a multipronged communication strategy that will get your insights as far and as wide into the organization as possible. Maybe it's in the form of an interactive tool others can use, a recorded Webex of your insights, a lunch and learn, or even just a thoughtful executive memo that can be passed around.

- **Stage 6: Track outcomes.** Set up a way to track the impact of your insights. Make sure there is future follow-up with your business partners on the outcome of any actions. What was done, what was the impact, and what are the new critical questions that need your help as a result?

DIVERSE APPLICATIONS FOR DIVERSE BUSINESS PROBLEMS

Whether analyzing insurance claims, creating attrition models, implementing a segmentation model for a wireless service provider, building global acquisition and retention scoring models for a global online retailer, predicting the spread of the H1N1 flu, or simply predicting the behavioral indicators of Canadian high school smokers, predictive analytics can help. The use of predictive analytics is pervasive in many aspects of today's life. From aspects such as suggesting a new book to buy on Amazon to selecting advertisements to display on your mobile device, modern-day companies are leveraging data, coupled with predictive analytics, to uncover insights about their customers, business environment, and important product features.

Predictive analytics even lends itself to matters of government and public policy. For example, Bruce Bueno de Mesquita, an academic at New York University, has made some impressively accurate political forecasts. In May 2010, he predicted that Egypt's president, Hosni Mubarak, would fall from power within a year. Nine months later, Mr. Mubarak fled Cairo amid massive street protests. Since then, de Mesquita has made hundreds of prescient forecasts as a consultant both to foreign governments and to the U.S. State Department, Pentagon, and intelligence agencies. What is the secret of his success? "I don't have insights—the game does," he says, referring to the analytics that enables his predictions.[5]

In this section, we review a few examples of how companies have put predictive analytics to work and the business outcomes they have achieved.

FINANCIAL SERVICE INDUSTRIES AS PIONEERS*

The insurance and financial service industries have been pioneers in the collection, management, and predictive analytics of data. Given their mandatory reporting environment and that their revenue relies on being accurate with data, financial institutions and insurance companies started using simple analytics in the 1800s to price life insurance and underwrite marine insurance. They have since kept on innovating and have undergone many waves of improvement, including the use of neural networks to optimize premiums, the introduction of credit scores in evaluating a customer's financial position, and the use of various behavioral and financial third-party datasets and social media data to supplement their future predictions. The success stories are numerous, and a financial institution that is not using predictive analytics today in product pricing and underwriting would be seen as obsolete and doomed to failure.

We see these companies now expanding their analytics into newer business units and newer applications being born. For example, safety analytics is the science of using information about a company's current state and other geo-demographic data to prevent accidents from happening in the first place and avoid the associated insurance costs through a safer workplace. Claims analytics is a discipline where claims severity is scrutinized for drivers of high dollar claims by injury type. It aims at understanding what causes a particular claim type from being settled at a reasonable cost vs. escalated to five times its reasonable threshold (including behavioral drivers, litigation involvement, and so on). Fraud analytics is also a hot topic. It is estimated that fraud claims are costing the insurance industry $5 to $7 billion every year. Complex predictive models that look to find intricate patterns of unusual behavior to uncover fraudulent schemes are being used by various insurance

---

* The authors would like to thank Amel Arhab, manager at Deloitte Consulting, FCAS, MAAA, for her assistance and guidance in writing this section.

organizations and state agencies throughout the country. Models involving machine-learning techniques to adapt to new schemes are being built and put into production to pinpoint which of the incoming claims are likely to be fraudulent so that investigation can take place.

One of the authors, JP Isson, conceived, developed, and implemented the Customer Lifetime Value (CLTV) Model, Customer Attrition Model, Conjoint Analysis and Product Adoption models at Fido, a Canadian wireless company. We will share how predictive analytics was put to work, helping Fido compete with other wireless providers and win.

CASE STUDY

TELECOMMUNICATIONS: COMBINING DIFFERENT TYPES OF INTELLIGENCE

- **Business challenge**: Identify the most profitable customers and products; serve customers based on their value and retain the most profitable in a competitive growing marketplace.

- **Solutions**: Advanced Analytics, Attrition Model CLTV Conjoint Analysis models.

- **Benefit**: Increase customer acquisition, increase retention, increase profitability, and reduce low and very low value customers from 25 to 12%.

Founded in 1996, Fido (now a Rogers Wireless company) was a pioneer in providing state-of-the-art wireless products and services. Fido was the first Canadian carrier to deploy Global System for Mobile (GSM) communications technology, the most widely deployed wireless standard in the world. And Fido was the first wireless service provider in North America with a General Packet Radio Service (GPRS) data network, ensuring fast, always-on wireless connectivity to the Internet and corporate intranets.

As mentioned in Chapter 2, when JP Isson joined Fido, one of the most pressing needs for the company was to reduce customer attrition. To do so, JP worked with cross-functional teams to develop and implement a customer attrition predictive model. Why build a customer attrition predictive model? Well, as we all know, it is always much easier to retain an existing customer than to acquire a brand-new one. Some studies estimate that the cost of acquiring a new customer (marketing and promotion and so on) is about $300 to $500. So being proactive by keeping and protecting existing customers

(continued)

should be the number one priority. Therefore, at Fido, we developed a model that analyzes the behavior of customers and assigns a "likelihood to attrite" score to each of them. Once in place, on a monthly basis every customer was assigned a "likelihood to churn" score. The churn score was available to all customer touch points and to the marketing CRM team. This was to ensure that they could proactively contact customers before it was too late.

After implementing the churn model, we went to the next level, seeking to service customers based on their lifetime value, thereby managing Fido's call center based on customer profitability, not only on call volumes. To do so, we built a customer lifetime value (CLTV) model against Fido customer's base. As its name implies, the CLTV model refers to the value of a customer over his or her lifetime of being a customer. Often, people will confuse customer spend with CLTV. This is a common mistake; however, CLTV is not only customer spend, but also includes a factor for how much it costs to serve the customer, called cost of servicing (COS). At Fido, we teamed up with marketing and, more important, with finance to get the COS. A CLTV score was built for every customer in our database. After we built the CLTV model, every customer was assigned to a segment.

By using the CLTV score, marketing was now able to send e-mail campaigns to the most valuable customers for proactive retention activities. Furthermore, the customer service team had critical information on its screen and was able to service customers based on their value and could make sure that the cream-of-the-crop customers received the service they deserved (premium service reps, with less waiting time). In addition, the retention team reshuffled its activities to increase the focus on the most valuable customers, and for those customers who were destroying the margins, less investment and effort were deployed. This telecommunications example underscores how putting predictive analytics to work can provide a cutting-edge competitive advantage when managed and implemented properly.

Exhibit 10.4 illustrates how customer attrition was addressed at Fido by leveraging the business analytics successful pillars discussed in this book. This could be applied to other industries and business challenges as discussed. Within each pillar we provide major actions that support the pillar. Actions are mapped to each of the seven pillars showing how the BASP could be summarized throughout a business goal. By using this framework, Fido increase its retention by 13%.

Business Challenge	Analytics Implementation Vision	Data	Insights	Distribute Knowledge	Execution Measurement	Innovation
• Reduce customer attrition	• Senior management sponsor • Skilled analytical resources • Collaboration from other groups • Customer experience • Change management and training • Metrics	• Internal and external data sources • Transactional data • Usage • Service • Plan • Socio-demographic • Credit bureau • Macroeconomic data	Customer Attrition Predictive Model to proactively target at-risk customers. The attrition model provides likelihood to attrite score to every existing customer	• The attrition model's insights are distributed by roles and responsibilities: PowerPoint presentation to the executive team and managers. Meeting and Web demo to the customer touch points • Point of sales via Web application available to customer	• Proactive retention activities based on customer attrition score segment Measurement: • % decrease in customer attrition • % increase in low-value segment	• Integration of different types of intelligences to harness customer acquisition, retention, and up-sell • Launch of the first price plan with free incoming calls in Canada • Visualization of the combined intelligence at every point of sales

Exhibit 10.4 BASP Application in Telecoms: Customer Attrition, Fido Case Study

In the following example, we will discuss how Monster Worldwide has been leveraging advanced analytics (segmentation and scoring) globally to stay on top of the competition.

MONSTER WORLDWIDE CASE

Monster Worldwide is the global online recruitment solutions company, with presence in more than 55 countries, including Europe, North America (NA), Latin America, and Asia Pacific.

Business Objectives

Segment and conquer the B2B market in every country where it operates, in order to

- Deepen customer knowledge
- Increase sales productivity
- Increase customer retention
- Increase marketing productivity
- Increase customer retention

Solutions and Benefits: Segmentation and Predictive Analytics

Monster Worldwide has been using segmentation and predictive analytics as a tool to better understand and target both its customers and prospects. The segmentation work has helped Monster Worldwide achieve its desired results, getting high potential customers to advertise on its site. This has a huge impact on customer intimacy, improved retention, and up-sell and cross-sell, to name just a few of the tangible benefits.

At Monster Worldwide, we tackled the data challenge by looking for data in innovative places. We augmented our internal databases with information from third parties, including information on the entire business universe and macroeconomic data (such as gross domestic product, unemployment, turnover rates, payroll, and cost per hire). To achieve success with predictive analytics, you often have to marry external and internal data to get the full picture, as outlined in Exhibit 10.5.

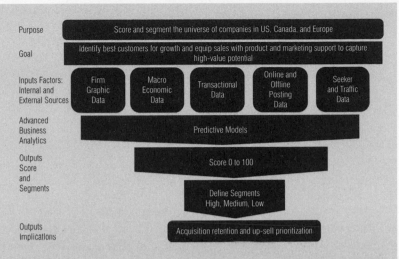

Exhibit 10.5 Business-to-Business Scoring and Segmentation Using Different Types of Data

We used third-party data to segment the NA and Europe business universe into three prospect segments, based on their propensity to buy and potential value. This allowed the sales force to spend time where it expects to get the best return.

Using segmentation and optimization techniques and the Innovative Execution Segment grid, shown in chapter 16 in Exhibits 16.4 and 16.5, we were able to calibrate the sales rep portfolios to give everyone the same chance to reach high-value prospects. This approach allowed Monster Worldwide to understand sales performance and increase sales productivity by 40%. In addition, this type of success helped fuel the acceptance of advanced predictive analytics by the sales force, leading to buy-in for further initiatives.

The segmentation and optimization also helped Monster Worldwide use resources more effectively to proactively retain high-value customers. After the first year of implementation, retention was up 17%.

The segments were not only used in sales; Monster Worldwide also leveraged them when serving high-value customers and synchronized its efforts with customer service. Monster also leveraged what it had learned to adjust advertising efforts. For example, banner advertising was adjusted to reflect where high-value segments could be found online. After the first year of adopting predictive analytics, marketing efficiency improved by 30%.

KEY TAKEAWAYS

- Predictive analytics is predominant in many aspects of today's life. From predicting the next book to recommend on Amazon to identifying at-risk customers for a telecommunications company.

- Predictive analytics will become more and more ubiquitous as the volume of data is becoming ever bigger.

- Organizations seeking to harness their customer intimacy, customer retention, customer acquisition, and customer up-sell must use predictive analytics.

- Merely capturing customer information is not sufficient; what will differentiate a company from its competition is its ability to transform data from information into actionable predictive analytics. Successful companies are those that will leverage the power of advanced analytics to predict outcomes and scenarios for their business objectives to drive sales marketing and services activities.

- Predictive analytics is made up of three major stages: unlocking, prediction, optimization. Predictive analytics is about unlocking patterns and trends from big data, predicting the future of an outcome or an event, and optimizing business actions.

- We also introduced examples of how predictive analytics are applied, including an example from telecommunications using customer lifetime value.

FURTHER READING

Lindoff, Gordon, and Michael J. A. Berry. *Data Mining Techniques: For Marketing, Sales, and Customer Relationship* (Indianapolis, IN: Wiley Publishing, 2011).

Olivia Par Rud. *Data Mining Cook Book: Modeling Data for Marketing, Risk and Customer Relationship Management* (New York: John Wiley & Sons, 2000).

NOTES

1. "Data, Data Everywhere," *Economist,* February 2010, http://www.econo mist.com/node/15557443.
2. "Handling the Cornucopia," *Economist,* February 2010, http://www .economist.com/node/15557507.

3. James Kobielus, The Forrester Wave™: Predictive Analytics and Data Mining Solutions, 2010," Business Process & Applications Professionals, February 4, 2010.)

4. Raymond Paquet, "Technology Trends You Can't Afford to Ignore," Gartner, January 2010, http://www.gartner.com/it/content/1258400/1258425/january_6_techtrends_rpaquet.pdf.

5. "Modelling Behaviour: Game Theory in Practice," *Economist*, September 3, 2011, http://www.economist.com/node/21527025.

CHAPTER 11

Predictive Analytics Applied to Human Resources

By Jac Fitz-enz, PhD

"There is an almost universal quest for easy answers and half-baked solutions. Nothing pains some people more than having to think."

—Martin Luther King Jr.

Dr. Fitz-enz Jac is known as the father of human capital strategic analysis and measurement. He published the first HR metrics in 1978 and introduced benchmarking to HR in 1985. His many honors include: HR World's claim that he is one the top five "HR management gurus"; cited by the Society for Human Resources Management as one who has "significantly changed what HR does and how it does it"; and recipient of the Chairman's Award for Innovative Excellence in Information Management by the International Association for Human Resources Information Management _____

G lobal competition, market volatility, and declining labor pools make investing in people a high-risk gamble. Still, future success is dependent primarily on your ability to attract, retain, and productively manage a shrinking pool of talented, motivated people. However, only since about 2010 has predictive analytics appeared on most HR agendas. Nevertheless, it is becoming more popular, even though fewer than 25% of HR departments have more than a passing experience with it.

Who makes the big decisions in your organization? Who has the last word? Final decisions are typically the province of a person who has the most formal organizational power. If the decision maker is a C-level executive, he or she asks for input on the decision process. Yet decisions are not always based on data. Fear, bias, greed, ignorance, arrogance, and other human foibles sometimes carry the day. If one person is very eloquent, he or she may influence the decision. Occasionally, I have seen decisions made at the highest level with little hard data because of the selling skill of one person. In one company, the senior vice president of sales and marketing convinced the CEO to acquire another company, without presenting valid evidence for the commitment. It was pure salesmanship.

Despite these obstructions, more often than not decisions are based on objective data. It is the responsibility of the C-level executives, the people at the Table, to optimize the assets of the organization. They have a fiduciary duty to allocate resources in a manner that will achieve the goals of the business. In profit-making companies, the goal is to deliver a good rate of return on the stockholders' investments. In not-for-profit institutions, the mission is to serve the needs of its constituents. There is a proven way for HR not only to win a seat at the Table but to effectively own it with data that amounts to human capital business intelligence as well.

The question is often asked, "Why don't CEOs recognize and invest in people as they do in other initiatives and functions? The answer is twofold. First, often a C-level executive can make an investment in a nonhuman arena, such as sales, production, or technology, and feel confident that a reasonable return on that investment will ensue. That is not the case with people. Investing in complex human beings is a high-risk decision. In the second case, human resources managers have done a poor job of teaching the C-level executives how to achieve high rates of return on employee investments. Quite often, HR will report something and not talk about the implications of it. A good example is turnover. We report that turnover has risen 2% this year. What we don't tell is what difference it makes in terms of productivity decline, customer losses, or operating cost. Does turnover make any difference? Who would care if turnover doubled, if it did not affect the business? We act as though our executive audience should know the effects of some employee factor. That is an unreasonable assumption. Most executives have had little, if any, experience in managing a human resources function during their careers. Typically, their background is in finance, engineering, or sales and marketing. They are not HR professionals. We are, so we must educate them about human capital forces and factors.

STAFF RULES

Staff functions exist to apply professional skill, knowledge, and budgeted resources in support of the organization's goals. Finance manages cash flow. Marketing and advertising attract prospective customers. Sales turn prospects into customers. Customer services retain customers. Information technology provides data and communication systems. Human resources acquire and grow talent to carry out the organization's operations.

To fulfill its responsibility, HR needs not only personal and professional human capital management capabilities; it also needs resources. A well-run human resources function starts with a strategy, an operating model, and a business plan. Then it must acquire equipment and supplies to support its operating processes and systems. Here is the rub. These tools come through budgeted funds that are the result of proposals made to a C-level executive. If HR wants to earn a share of the funds pie, it has to operate like a business with a profit-and-loss mentality. The following is a business management model that can lead the human resources director to owning the table.

ASSESSMENT: BEYOND PEOPLE

HR deals with the impact of market forces, doesn't it? When the economy rises or falls, the labor market is affected. When educational institutions emphasize finance over engineering or marketing over production, the number of qualified applicants shifts accordingly. Advances in technology, actions of competitors, new government regulations, and markets going global all affect how HR can carry out its responsibility. Too often, HR people look only at the current crop of applicants or employees and fail to recognize those other driving forces. In fact, the pool of applicants is a result of many nonhuman forces acting throughout the world. HR must also pay attention to internal factors that are affecting the company's ability to be competitive. Issues of CEO vision, the state of corporate finances, culture, leadership capabilities, and even brand affect HR operations.

Often overlooked is the interaction of vision, culture, and brand. If they are not in sync, the organization is suboptimized. If the CEO claims that the organization is to be a model of cooperation, the brand and the culture must show that. A brand is a function of cooperation when a customer has a need or a problem. A cooperative organization does not shove the customer from silo to silo. Rather, whoever fields the call sees to it that the customer is connected with the unit that can and will solve the problem. In a cooperative culture, information and learning are shared, not hoarded. HR has the responsibility to monitor the corporate culture. Thereby, it also has an effect on brand management and actively supports the CEO's vision.

At Human Capital Source, we lead HR departments through a situational assessment, where the external forces and the internal factors can be considered in terms of their effect on organizational capital. Every organization has three forms of capital. These are human capital, which are the employees and the contingent workers who are *on loan* to the company. Structural capital consists of the things that the organization owns. This includes everything from facilities and equipment through codified processes such as software

ORGANIZATIONAL CAPITAL	HUMAN	STRUCTURAL	RELATIONAL
EXTERNAL STATE Labor Supply Changes			
Economy Slowing			
Globalization			
Technology Advances			
Competitor Actions			
New Regulations			
INTERNAL STATE CEO Vision			
Leadership Quality			
Culture			
Brand			
Capabilities			
Finances			

Exhibit 11.1 Situational Assessment

and patents. Relational capital is the people outside who have a stake in the organization. This includes suppliers, customers, communities in which we do business, government regulators, and even competitors.

Exhibit 11.1 shows how changes in human capital should be tracked for effects on the structural and relational capital of an organization. This is implied by the fact that the column dividing lines are broken, rather than solid.

For example, if the emerging labor force has different values than many of the people currently employed and if they will be using new technology, this might affect the way in which we house them: structural capital. Such is the case today. The latest generation to join the workforce wants a balance between work and personal life. That was not so prevalent 20 years ago. In addition, social networking and networking tools are changing the way employees communicate and what types of information they are willing to share. The clear result is that we need to rethink putting them in cubicles and requiring that they work on site every day. These are HR management issues that affect our strategy and operating models. Situational assessment is the most important aspect of the human capital management model.

CASE STUDY

ANALYTICS AND HUMAN CAPITAL

In a recent global Deloitte survey, 68% of surveyed executives expressed high or very high concern about losing essential and high-potential talent.[1] In today's aggressive business environment and tight talent market, organizations are viewing their human capital as their most valuable asset and a top business challenge. It is no wonder that retention of current talent preoccupies the minds of many business leaders.

Whether it is for a better professional opportunity or for personal reasons, organizations are eager to understand what drives their top performers to leave the firms. Traditional tools included exit interviews, employee surveys, and other types of market research to anticipate voluntary attrition. Yet many companies are now turning to analytics to uncover drivers of attrition and forecast which of their current workforce is at high risk.

The advantage of analytics is to process a large amount of information, including hundreds of variables at a time, to uncover what drives a business problem. In human capital, companies are looking at human resource information (for example, tenure and performance), geo-demographic data (such as age and gender), workload metrics (hours worked and vacation days taken), peer interaction (e-mail traffic and project team composition), travel schedules (frequency and distance from home), and other behavioral data (surveys and sentiment analysis) to determine the profiles of high-attrition risk. In addition, we find that interactions play a large role in attrition analysis (for example, travels for a younger age segment is not as important as for an older age segment). Other econometric and third-party data describing the economic state of the market (such as unemployment and gross domestic product levels), as well as the social environment (for example social media posts/Tweets), is used to paint a more complete picture of circumstances leading to a departure.

We have seen companies scoring their workforce at consecutive periods and focusing their retention efforts on top performers with high risk. Specific actions are then taken to avoid such departures, including a focused HR discussion, a reorientation of workload and career focus, and interaction and compensation adjustments. With attrition costs representing anywhere from one to five times the annual salary, the ROI can represent millions of dollars for a medium-size salary. Intangible costs (such as employee productivity and company brand) can also add to the balance.

Source: Amel Arhab, manager and claims analytics leader, Deloitte Consulting, LLP, *Talent Edge 2020: Blueprints for the New Normal*, December 2010, Deloitte.

PLANNING SHIFT

Once our operating model is spinning out business-related data, one of our first tasks is workforce planning. This topic has been given a great deal of attention in the last couple of years. The brighter minds in the business see that there are two fundamental changes taking place in planning. The first is recognition that strategic workforce planning is basically risk management. Some now call it human capital risk management (HCR). As such, it is part of enterprise risk management (ERM). Therefore, HR should have a voice in corporate planning. After all, very few corporate plans do not to some extent depend on human capabilities to carry them through.

The good news is that surveys are showing an increased appreciation for human capital risk (HCR). Yet when assessed against other forms of risk management, the people issues fall far down the urgency list. Typically, risk surveys show that HCR is effectively assessed in less than one-third of the responding companies. Effective HCR requires that factors such as labor availability, incoming skill levels, willingness to engage, and attrition rates must be translated into various types of business impact. The application of predictive analytics can be extremely useful in managing HCR.

My observations and experiences tell me that the industrial era, supply-demand, gap-filling model of planning is rapidly becoming obsolescent. Until recently, HR planners would be handed the business plan for the coming year and told to fill the expected job openings. This worked for decades when businesses and markets were relatively stable. Certainly, stability is not a hallmark of the current or future marketplace. As a result, attempting to fill jobs in July for a staffing plan developed the previous November is a fool's errand. Obviously, due to continual organizational realignment, project teams, and changes in product development, the third-quarter and fourth-quarter workforce will look very little like the one envisioned late the previous year.

COMPETENCY VERSUS CAPABILITY

The definition of competency is the possession of the skills, knowledge, and capacity to fulfill current needs. The definition of capability is the qualities, abilities, capacity, and potential to be developed. Note the

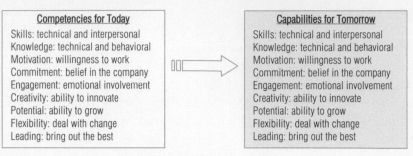

How will they differ if change comes from...
Technology vs. Regulations vs. Economics vs. Labor Demographics or Other Forces?

Exhibit 11.2 Current Competencies to Future Capabilities

word *potential*. While competence deals with the current state, capability focuses on the ability to develop and flex to meet future needs. In the market of the twenty-first century, the potential for growth is an absolute necessity.

When we think about the future and the changes that it will bring, we need to ask ourselves, What types of changes are likely to occur and from whence will they emanate? Exhibit 11.2 shows a list of common skills, abilities, knowledge, motivation, commitment, engagement, creativity, and so on. Those traits exist currently and will exist in the future. The point is, how will they differ in the emerging market? Certainly, skills and knowledge will be somewhat different, but what about motivation or engagement? Most likely, they will change as well. What will drive that change? Will it be from within the person? Will it be induced by new technology or regulations? It is up to the planner to consider this dynamic. Look at Exhibit 11.2 again. What do you think will happen in your situation?

PRODUCTION

Sooner or later, we have to stop planning and begin to produce. All of our plans and resources need to be brought to bear on the job. Some people like to talk about new titles for HR professionals, such as caregiver, casting director, deal maker, systems integrator. That is fine and somewhat titillating, but as a top executive at a major bank once said to a group of branch managers I was training, "There are lots of questions we could ask and criticisms we could make, but eventually we have to put our heads down and go to work." Talk is cheap. Performance is mandatory.

Daily, we face performance issues such as these:

- What should we do to improve the quality of our hires?
- How can we use incentive pay to stimulate performance?
- What types of training would be most effective for this group?
- How do we encourage people be more engaged?
- How can we improve the level of leadership?
- What can we do to manage the retention of mission-critical people?

The third step in our model deals with how to analyze and improve processes.

HR PROCESS MANAGEMENT

Recently, I was asked by a staffing manager what she could do to improve the efficiency and effectiveness of her staffing program. My answer was, first assess the situation. Look at the factors that can be affecting your staffing strategy. When that is clear, and you believe it to be appropriate for the current job market, then review your hiring process.

Almost everything in life is the result of a process. It starts with getting ourselves ready for work in the morning and doesn't end until we turn out the lights and shut down the house at night. At work, the basics are the source of inputs and the three steps of process are inputs, throughputs, and outputs. Apply this model to staffing, training program development, pay program design, or anything else you do. The following list is an example of the hiring process.

Job Group	Sourcing	Selection	Results
Applicants	Newspaper advertising	Personal interviews	Performance
	Job boards, referrals,	Group interviews	Potential rating
	Professional journal ads	Tests, assessment	Pay progression
		On-boarding	Retention

In staffing process management, we make a list of hires during the last two years for mission-critical job groups. We look at the medium that we used to source applicants. For example, within the job group being studied (programmers, nurses, actuaries, technicians, and so on), where did Allen, Barbara, and Charlie come from: ads, job boards, and so forth? Next, which selection processes were used for each of them: interviews, tests, and so on, and did they go through a formal on-boarding experience? Finally, what was the result you wanted to study? Basic questions are, How did they perform? What is their potential rating? And are they still here? In the course of this exercise, you will have looked at every aspect of your staffing process.

This very short example should give you an idea, collectively, of what is the best method for attracting, selecting, and managing people from a given job group. When you have a small number of applicants to study, you don't need statistics. You can eyeball the data and see rather quickly which are the driving forces. Conversely, if you are hiring hundreds or even thousands of people, you will need to run a regression analysis to pick out the drivers. Sampling is a good way to reduce the size of the population. Finally, this method speaks to the need to collect process data as part of your staffing program.

HR ANALYSIS AND PREDICTABILITY

HR analysis comes in three flavors: descriptive, predictive, and prescriptive. The latter two are tightly interwoven, yet distinct.

1. Descriptive analysis tells us what happened.
2. Predictive analysis tells us what will happen.
3. Prescriptive analysis tells us how to make it happen.

Consider how this works in a medical model. Jack is not feeling well, so he schedules an appointment with an internist. On arrival, the doctor asks what the problem is. Jack says he has a headache, a runny nose, a sore throat, chest congestion, a bit of fever, and no energy. This is description.

Additional questions are asked by the doctor, along with his performing checks of vital signs, palpitations, chest soundings, and an eyes, ears, and throat examination. After this, the doctor tells Jack he has a bronchial infection, along with a few related minor inflammations. Then she says to Jack that if he will take the medicine she is recommending, azithromycin, he will be cured within a week. This is prediction.

The third phase comes in when Jack picks up his medicine at the pharmacy that afternoon and reads the dosage: take two tablets on day one, followed by one tablet each day for five days. This is prescription.

ELEVATE HR WITH ANALYTICS

We have reached a point in the development of computer technology and predictive analytics where HR can truly influence the highest levels of the organization using analytics. The first step of using analytics HR effectively with senior executives is to ask yourself the following questions:

- What do you need to know about future human capital investments and how they will affect your organization? This process reveals what you must know and how to get it.
- Why do you want to know it? With this information (actually intelligence), you can plan and manage talent in a way that leads to greater efficiency and profitability.
- How much value could you create with this intelligence? The value will be many times the expense, in terms of cost reduction, customer delight, and revenue generation.
- If we showed you how to produce these leading indicator reports, would you know how to use them in discussions with the C-level? Not sure? We'll teach you how to sell it.

After you clearly articulate answers to the previous questions, the result will include a list of relevant metrics that HR needs to show the impact of people to the bottom line. Those metrics may include

- Workforce productivity
- Revenue per FTE
- Cost per FTE
- Profit (EBITDA) per FTE

- Total cost of workforce
- Compensation and benefits
- HR service costs
- Talent management impact
- Recruiting quality and cost differentials
- Mobility—Internal and external impact
- Leadership and management: costs and impact
- Training effectiveness—performance differentials
- Engagement—revenue linkage
- Turnover and retention analysis

Some HR professionals may feel overwhelmed with the thought of sourcing, calculating, and tracking metrics such as those listed previously. They may react with skepticism, "We could never get the data." At Human Capital Source, when working with clients, we point out to them that they already collect a lot of it in various HR activities, but it is simply not pulled together in one place. Much of the data will also be available in corporate accounting statements. If you really want to elevate the stature of HR in your company, use some of the approaches discussed in this book and in this chapter. Give it a try. The concepts we are presenting have been thoroughly tested in practice, both in industry and government.

What Is More Useful?

If you plan a trip far from home, you need to know what the weather will be like so you can pack the proper clothes. You can look up the past weather pattern for this time of year in an encyclopedia, or you can go online to the weather channel and get the prediction for the week you will be there. It is obvious which would be more useful.

The same thing applies to all business data. Knowing what happened last period is useful, in that it is an evaluation of past investments. Hopefully, we learn from that and take it into consideration for our next decision. Even more useful would be to know with a high level of confidence what is most likely to happen in the future.

Most HR departments today are engaged in some type of measurement. However, until recently, almost all HR reporting has been about the past. This is also true of accounting, sales, and most other departments across the organization. Planning is the only function whose primary responsibility is to forecast the future. As the market has become so volatile, all functions have turned to predictive analytics to improve their forecasting. One thing we have to acknowledge is that all forecasts are wrong, to some degree. Only on the rarest occasions does the market act as we predicted. Nevertheless, being almost right is better than not knowing or being totally wrong. To manage human capital for tomorrow, you need HR metrics that are inherently predictive.

VALUE HIERARCHY

Each type of report has a certain value, depending on what we want to know. Yet all things being equal, there is a value hierarchy within reporting and analysis. Exhibit 11.3 is an illustration of that hierarchy.

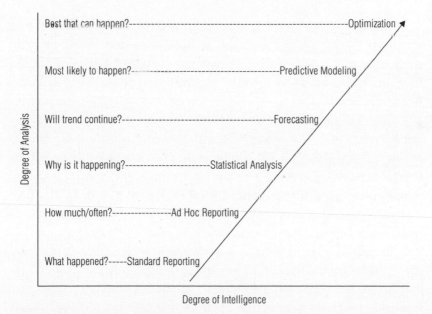

Exhibit 11.3   Report Value Hierarchy

Only since about 2010 has predictive analytics appeared on most HR agendas. Nevertheless, it is becoming more popular, even though fewer than 25% of HR departments have more than a passing experience with it. Analytics is not magic. It is applied in the same manner as other problem-solving, decision-making tasks.

A good way to start is to develop a prediction scenario. This can include projected values based on given assumptions. Depending on how complex and how important the HR issue is, you may have to make a proposal to obtain funding. In such cases, you should use leading indicators to show expected future outcomes. Common leading HR-related outcome areas include

- Leadership
- Engagement
- Readiness
- Attrition
- Learning and development
- Culture (great place to work)

Leadership improvement always attracts favorable attention. You can tie it to engagement because without respected leadership you cannot generate engagement. Then, increasing engagement should have an effect on QIPS (quality, innovation, productivity, service). Readiness ensures that there will be little or no break in performance if a mission-critical person leaves. High rates of attrition are danger signals predicting that production and customer service will suffer if attrition is not corralled. Of course, culture is the bedrock on which everything rests. Learning and development investment is a strong indicator of future performance. Culture shifts affect almost all other indicators and correlate with "great place to work" variables, such as trust, pride, respect, fairness, camaraderie, and credibility.

The question is, will your solution positively affect costs, time cycles, productivity, quality, or employee satisfaction? Quite often, the data are so clear that you can make a prediction with just four-function arithmetic: add, subtract, multiply, divide. This can yield ratios and percentages that do the job.

However, there are times when you have to apply statistical methods to predict the value of your intervention. Look for correlation and causation by applying structural equation modeling tools:

- Regression analysis
- Factor analysis
- Correlation analysis
- Multivariate analysis of variance
- Covariance analysis

This should not deter you, no matter what your level of statistical knowledge is. You can always hire a graduate student out of economics, industrial and organizational psychology, or statistics programs to run the data. Students often are very happy to work part time for the experience and a small wage.

HR REPORTING

The way you report your data is almost as important as the data itself. Remember, reporting is story telling. Make your report simple, interesting, and insightful. The essential component is that it should present actionable business-related data. Reports on HR's headcount, budget, and number hired or trained are not what management wants.

I prefer an integrated approach to reporting. By that, I mean, when appropriate, the report should include strategic, operational and predictive, or leading indicators related to one another. A C-level executive should be shown how your project is of strategic importance. That is, how it affects corporate QIPS. Then you show the operational driver that you have solved and how it positively affects internal cost, time, quantity, quality, or employee reactions. That leads to strategic level gains. Finally and hopefully, you should report how this will affect one or more of the leading indicators listed previously. At that point, you are truly presenting predictive analytics. Exhibit 11.4 is a diagram of the concept. If you want to take it to the next level of prescriptive analytics, you need to run optimization analytics to show how the many variables are connected and interdependent.

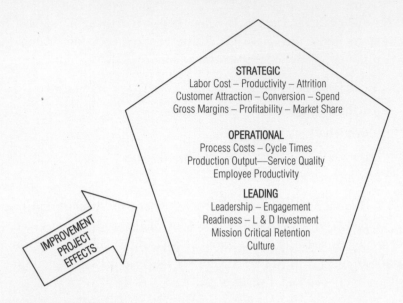

Exhibit 11.4 Integrated Reporting

In this type of format management, one can see the simple connections. That is the most essential aspect, from HR's standpoint. It solves the issue regarding how do HR programs and employee behaviors affect financials?

HR SUCCESS THROUGH ANALYTICS

In his book *The New HR Analytics*, Dr. Fitz-enz presented powerful metrics for quantifying the contributions of human capital to an organization's bottom line, as well as illustrated how to predict the continuing value of present and future human capital investments.[1] The book included chapter contributions from dozens of HR and business thinkers and executives and was fortified with cutting-edge HR tools for growth-directed organizations to focus HR on the next step in strategically aligned human resource planning. One of the coauthors, Jesse Harriott, contributed a chapter (with Jeff Quinn and Marie Artim) on how HR analytics was effectively applied to Enterprise Rent-A-Car.[2]

Enterprise approached Monster Worldwide to help in the decision-making process of where to locate a new customer contact center. The new contact center would need to handle more than 10,000 reservations and customer service calls per day. The services provided by the contact center would include reservation assistance and customer support. The company believed that through predictive analysis of Monster's real-time labor market information, it could find the city most suitable for its new center. This led ultimately to the selection of the site and the future success of Enterprise's call center.

Enterprise Holdings, ranked No. 21 on *Forbes'* Top 500 Private Companies, owns and operates more than 1 million cars and trucks, including the largest fleet of passenger vehicles in the world, under the Alamo Rent A Car, Enterprise Rent-A-Car, and National Car Rental brands. As North America's largest car rental company, Enterprise Holdings operates a network of more than 8,000 car rental locations worldwide. It leads the industry with more than a third of all airport business in the United States and Canada. *BusinessWeek* ranked Enterprise as a "Best Place to Launch a Career" for four consecutive years. Enterprise believes almost exclusively in promoting from within—another attribute that has contributed to its excellent reputation among recent college graduates.

Monster has a global footprint that reaches more than 60 countries and more than 80 million people each month. In the United States, visitors to monster.com perform more than 150 million job searches in a month and upload more than 40,000 resumes per day. Enterprise has worked with Monster for many years as a recruiting partner and as a source of human capital analytics.

To assist Enterprise with its site selection, Monster conducted a multipronged analysis to aid in decision making. To analyze potential sites efficiently, Monster first helped Enterprise identify a short list of three to six locations that were analyzed in detail to make a site recommendation. This was done with a mix of factors, including

- Unemployment rate
- Payroll change
- Rate of economic growth
- Concentration of desired occupations in each market
- Typical annual salary of desired occupation

After three to six locations had been selected for consideration, the next step was to evaluate and compare the talent pool across the locations. This was done in several ways:

- **Calculate the talent density for each key occupation.** Talent density is the total number of people working in an occupation in a location, divided by the total workforce for that location, multiplied by 100. This is used to help the company understand how difficult it would be to recruit talent in one location compared to another.

- **Compare a national job search index to a local job search index for each occupation.** The job search index is the total number of job searches by occupation and location, divided by the total for that location, multiplied by 100. It is a direct measure of job-seeking activity, an indicator of how likely a person with a particular occupation in a specific location is to apply for a job opening.

- **Prepare a talent profile for each key occupation.** In the course of evaluating a local market, it is important to understand the profile of the people the company might be recruiting. In some cases, factors to profile include mobility of talent, full-time versus part-time workers, career level, education level, and pay demands.

In the same way that it is important to evaluate the supply of talent, it is equally important to evaluation the demand for talent. The demand for talent represents the amount of competition your company will experience should it choose to enter the local market. Therefore, knowing the demand trend is crucial to understanding how successful a major recruiting initiative will be in each market. In order to evaluate the supply for Enterprise, Monster did the following:

- Evaluate posting trends over time for each key occupation.

- Calculate the talent demand index for each occupation. The talent demand index is a calculation of the number of job postings over the total number in the occupation workforce, multiplied by 100.

- Consider supply versus demand. Look at the labor conditions for each of the markets by plotting the markets in a graph showing a simple talent-market plot. This will help you identify the relative competition for talent in each market.

Monster also summarized the economic conditions for each market as an aid in understanding the economic backdrop for each proposed site. Monster included the following in each market summary:

- Unemployment and payroll trends
- Major industries and employers of the region
- Rate of economic growth or decline in the market
- Basic demographics of the workforce
- Economic incentives for companies to locate in the region
- Cost of facilities/office space in the market

Another important step was to evaluate the potential competitors for talent in each market. This was done in several ways for Enterprise:

- Use job posting trends to identify close competitors' presence and recruitment activities in each location being considered.
- Identify which industries hire the most for the occupations Enterprise needed Identify and profile top companies in each location being considered.

Monster followed the previous analytical framework to provide insights using current and historical data to support Enterprise's decision on a contact center location. As a result of the thoughtful consideration of many factors, Enterprise selected a market for its contact center for several reasons, including a strong labor supply relative to demand and its proximity to a university, which provided a consistent source of educated and skilled employees who have flexible schedules and need part-time opportunities. Employees at the new center handle more than 10,000 reservations and customer service calls a day for Enterprise, National, and Alamo. The performance of the contact center has been outstanding, with high customer-resolution rates and high employee and customer satisfaction. The care and diligence that Enterprise exercised in analyzing all of the factors in selecting a site led to a successful site implementation and resulted in a desirable business outcome.

Another example of analytics in HR from *The New HR Analytics* focused on UnitedHealth Group (UHG). Human resources challenges are complex and numerous. Health-care organizations are particularly stressed with hiring and retaining qualified medical personnel, such as nurses, lab technicians, and pharmacists. The 24/7, year-round nature of the industry makes human resource challenges even more acute. Applying predictive analytics enables HR departments to be ahead of the curve in identifying staffing and performance opportunities and to anticipate problems before they happen. In effect, by using the predictive analytics model in day-to-day HR operations, health-care companies can be more effective in running the business of talent.

UHG is one of the largest health-care operators in the United States, with access to more than 340,000 physicians and 3,200 hospitals, and whose policyholders submit tens of thousands of health claims and related documents daily. UHG uses predictive analytics to improve patient care through better human capital management in an increasingly challenging environment.

Workforce performance management can significantly enhance health-care financial and operational performance. Therefore, UHG determined that migrating to a talent management solution that leveraged predictive metrics would be the best solution for company performance. In UHG's example, the company sought to improve its internal hiring processes on a global scale. This includes increasing international focus on employee hires, especially in its India offices.

"Using a predictive analytical model, we can better analyze the employers that people came from and the sources we hired from. As a result, we can determine if there's a specific company that has a high percentage of quality of hires, and we then know that that's a company we may want to target. In terms of sourcing and recruitment, this is useful information for us, as it may lead to better hires in the future," says Michelle Fernando, the UHG manager of international recruitment operations.

By using predictive analytics and having metrics available on a global scale, UHG is better equipped to improve the quality of hires and staff retention worldwide. Predictive analytics, coupled with technology tools, has helped UHG break down silos and streamline operations and has allowed management to have centralized, real-time access for mission-critical information

Another example of using analytics in HR from *The New HR Analytics* is the Ingram Content Group. The Ingram Content Group (ICG) provides a broad range of physical and digital services and has been a partner to publishers, booksellers, and libraries for more than four decades. ICG leads the industry in physical distribution, supply chain management, and fulfillment services with access to all markets, both domestic and international. On average, ICG ships 2.4 million units each week to more than 85,000 customers from four distribution centers.

Employee turnover had been a chronic problem for Ingram's distribution and fulfillment division for years, rising steadily until it hit a rate of 81.7% enterprise-wide at the end of 2002 and 102% in the flagship distribution center in La Vergne, Tennessee. For operations/logistics leaders, the revolving door of talent was disruptive in their efforts to operate at best-of-industry standards. For the rest of the C-staff, the attitude was one of resignation; in essence, high turnover in the operations groups was viewed as a fact of life.

For operations/logistics leaders, excessive turnover disrupted their ability to effectively manage their facilities. Intuitively, they all knew that there was a significant human capital expense negatively affecting the bottom line. HR under the leadership of the chief human resources officer, Wayne Keegan, had been tracking turnover data and benchmarking against the data provided by the Department of Labor for Wholesale Trade. However, this practice alone was not capturing the financial impact of excessive turnover in terms that would prompt management to make a cost/benefit determination of focusing the attention, resources, and efforts of the organization on this matter.

Partnering with operations/logistics colleagues, Keegan analyzed the key operational and financial metrics for their divisions: cost per unit, or CPU. Production standards had been established for the majority of the positions, so HR evaluated the labor costs in relation to unit/line production standards.

From their collective experience, they knew that there was a significant gap between a tenured departing associate and a newly hired replacement, regarding production output versus production standard.

As a rule of thumb, they had accepted a 30-day ramping-up period for the average new hire to perform at standard. However, this assumption had never been validated though a scientific production analysis. An analysis of the average production rates for new hires in 2002 revealed that the ramping-up time in achieving the production standard was greater than assumed.

For every replacement of an associate with six months or more of service, who was averaging 106% of production standard, the newly hired replacement initially performed at an average of only 50% of standard, 83% at three months of service, 95% for months three to six, and finally achieved the production standard after six months of employment. Clearly, there was a dramatic drop in productivity for each separation incident, and the challenge was to craft a metric that would capture that financial impact. They came up with the following metric for their human capital value model:

$$\frac{\text{Average new hire unit}}{\text{Line labor separation}}$$

$$\text{Production} - \text{Production 0–6 mos.} \times \text{Costs}$$
$$= \text{Expense standard service}$$

Applying this formula, they found that the average cost of lost productivity was $3,652 per separation incident.

Additional work was also done to identify what factors were driving the high turnover, establish the metrics to measure the impact in order to determine which factors warranted attention, and then craft the intervention strategies and track the effectiveness of the strategies once they were implemented. All of these metrics were listed on the HR dashboard and communicated to leadership on a regular basis.

As a result of the analytics and subsequent interventions, within five years turnover for the operations/logistics groups dropped steadily from 81.7 to 25.5%, thereby achieving a cost savings tied to added productivity of $13.4 million during the five-year period. By 2006, the operations/logistics group's total turnover was less than the Department of Labor for Wholesale Trade benchmark and thus reported the first year of no expense tied to excessive turnover.

Maximizing a company's human capital is a key competitive factor for success. If human resources leaders are to be effective and to add value in support of this effort, they must operate as business leaders who happen to concentrate in the field of HR. The language of the C-staff and the boardroom is numbers. Analytics applied to human capital issues is essential in providing the predictive data that will allow leadership to manage this valuable asset more effectively.

At the end of the day, we want HR to generate business intelligence. Your HR data should show connections and indicate the most effective direction for future investments. If you want to lead your organization, you need a seat at the table. Given today's technology tools and statistical applications for collecting and manipulating human capital data, there is every opportunity to put together the information that can own the table. You can have the most valid, relevant, compelling intelligence at that table, if you want to do it.

NOTES

1. Jac Fitz-enz, *The New HR Analytics: Predicting the Economic Value of Your Company's Human Capital Investments* (New York: AMACOM, 2010).
2. Jesse Harriott, Jeffrey Quinn, and Marie Artim, "Leveraging Human Capital Analytics for Site Selection: Monster and Enterprise Rent-A-Car," in Jac Fitz-enz, *The New HR Analytics*.

CHAPTER 12

Social Media Analytics

By Judah Phillips

"Over the last few years, social media has turned marketing on its head. Everyone is rushing to 'engage' with their customers and potential customers in the social space. But social media is just like other forms of media. It can be measured. No matter what your business objective, your social media tactics can be measured, analyzed and optimized. Most importantly, you can, and MUST, measure the ROI of your social media activity."

—Author interview with Justin Cutroni, analytics evangelist, Google

Social media analytics is a type of digital analytics (see Chapter 9) and represents a shift in the way analysts, brands, agencies, and vendors think about data, analytics, and research. Social media has also facilitated a shift in the way that people interact with one another through digital technologies. Social media analytics can help you make sense of the shift in order to focus on what is most important for your organization, as well as on how to generate economic value through analysis of the meaningful and relevant signals in social media data.

Social media, in the context of this chapter, refers to the massive directional change across the globe in how people are creating, producing, editing, sharing, exchanging, conversing, collaborating, befriending, and consuming information. Social media, such as blogging, and video sharing on sites such as YouTube, Twitter, Facebook, Pinterest, and Kibits, has become pervasive across media and within social constructs (such as the family) in ways only hypothesized by futurists 15 years ago—and social media became a reality only during the last 8 years.

Early ideas on social media date back well before the dotcom implosion of 2000 to radical thinkers such as Ted Nelson, who created the term *hypertext* (as part of his Xanadu project) and coined the term *Intertwingularity* in the 1970s to mean the complexity of interrelations in human knowledge. Nelson wrote in *Computer Lib/Dream Machines*:

> Everything is deeply intertwingled. In an important sense
> there are no "subjects" at all; there is only all knowledge,
> since the cross-connections among the myriad topics of this
> world simply cannot be divided up neatly.[1]

I bring up Ted Nelson (and suggest you review his work) because social media will expose you to seemingly wild concepts and technologies that will cause you to question their business validity. I encourage you to question the business applicability and validity of social media. You can read other early thoughts about social media, such as *The Cluetrain Manifesto* or *The Tipping Point* by Malcolm Gladwell.[2] These books, concepts, and social constructs help form a basis for understanding social media, its underpinnings, and how to create economic value from it.

If Nelson's concept of Intertwingularity appears irregular, odd, or simply dumb to you, then gather up your courage. SMA is a niche field of digital analytics with many oddly named concepts (for example, velocity, centeredness, betweenness) that can (or cannot) be applicable to your business. Throughout this chapter, we will review

- **Social media concepts.** Useful business concepts and terminology are discussed in this section, with the goal of slicing some of the wheat from the large amounts of social media concept chaff.

- **Brand or direct response.** "To brand or not to brand?" is a question that may be befuddling executives in charge of social media. Learn about what's important to a manager when it comes to determining a social media analytics strategy based on brand, direct response, or both.

- **Social media analytics.** Brand and direct response analytics for social media are discussed. A high-level discussion of techniques, best practices, and examples are reviewed.

- **Social media tools.** In this section, the common features of social media analytics tools are discussed—and a framework for social media tool selection is identified.

- **Reporting**. Social media reporting has much in common—and should be considered a subset—of digital analytics reporting, which was covered in Chapter 9. This section reviews best practices, common pitfalls, and helpful communication strategies for social media reporting.

- **Social media listening and engagement**. Two concepts core to social media analytics, listening and engagement, are discussed.

- **Social media analytical techniques.** Applications of method and technique to scoring social media data are discussed. In this section, learn about more complex and advanced forms of social media analytics.

- **Social media is offline and incremental.** A primary business goal of social media and thus social media analytics is to understand the incremental impact on the business of bringing people together offline as a result of "online" social media in a positive way for enabling commerce and culture.

SOCIAL MEDIA IS MULTIDIMENSIONAL

Social media is a contemporary phenomenon based on the mainstreaming of the Internet and the pervasiveness of inexpensive Internet-enabled devices and innovative new technologies that allow for cheap communication, in real time, across distances of complex information in many different formats. Yet social media isn't new. Smoke signals, messages in bottles, carrier pigeons, wall paintings, stone sculpture, and other forms of historic communication are all, in various and different ways, social. Thus, while it may be easy to think of social media as *only* something that occurs online, it is important to understand that while enormous value is and can be created socially online, we must realize that social media also drives offline behavior. As a result, the analytical goals for many social media measurement strategies should likely include the measurement of offline behavior. As an example, consider that social media analytics must take into account the following scenario:

- A consumer is exposed to a social media advertisement across multiple social media channels.

- The consumer is identified to be a customer of the advertiser, who is considered desirable to be reached and possibly open to being reactivated into a consideration and purchasing cycle.

- The potential customer reads but does not click on the ad and begins to explore blogs, consumer reviews, product reviews, and the advertiser's Twitter feed and finally decides to "like" the advertiser's Facebook page.

- The potential customer is retargeted on Facebook by the same advertiser—several weeks later—and the customer clicks on the Facebook ad to land on a Facebook page where some part of the page is controlled by the advertiser (and thus the brand being advertised).

- The potential customer clicks through the Facebook page on a specific link that leads to the advertiser's site, where the overall brand messaging and promotional offer are enforced.

- The potential customer makes an appointment or a reservation online to visit the advertiser offline in its physical retail store and subsequently makes a purchase in the retail store.

In this example, an existing "cold" customer is reawakening by a social media advertising campaign but does not respond to that campaign.

Instead, the customer begins to consider the brand and the purchase. Several weeks later, through retargeting in a different social media channel, the person is taken through a series of digital experiences that go from one site to another—and eventually to an offline experience.

What may be surprising is that every step in the social media sequence described previously is not only possible, it is happening right now across many different industries—from automobile dealers to retail stores. What may be even more surprising and shocking is that it is possible to track every single step described here from the ad being served, then being seen, the time between exposure and retargeting, and all the way through the funnel on the social media platform and across domains to the final conversion event. What may be the most shocking is that given the social graph being developed by companies such as Facebook and Google, it is not only possible to collect, track, measure, and analyze almost every single behavior in the sequence, but it is also possible to join that advertising data (and the related behavior) back to the social graph that contains every bit of information ever collected and made available (by you and opt-in/opt-out) on any social media site. Consider also that the social graph can be joined to other third-party repositories, such as consumer credit data, financial data, and other personal data, and the implications for analytics are enormous.

UNDERSTANDING SOCIAL MEDIA ANALYTICS: USEFUL CONCEPTS

Just as Facebook redefined existing vocabulary, such as *friends* and *like* and Twitter with the words *tweet* and *twitter*, social media analytics requires learning a new vocabulary. Social media vocabulary terms run the gamut from academic (betweenness) to slightly absurd (*conversions*). Thus, I think it is helpful to identify some, but not all, of the vocabulary to understand social media and social media analytics. It is likely you may have heard, used, defined, or criticized the usage of some of the buzzwords. That said, social media is like the Internet in the mid-1990s: people are making up new words to explain new concepts.

While new ideation can be met with criticism, it is important to keep an open (but critical) mind in social media and toward the vocabulary, concepts, and constructs. Social media is only beginning to go mainstream—and the jargon will filter out (brick and click, anyone), but for now, it is helpful to speak the same language to drive the shared economies and markets. The following social media vocabulary will be helpful for social media analytics:

- **Listening**. Refers to the process by which consumer, brand, or business actively monitors social media data using a social media tool or technology. Listening may be as simple as reviewing a Twitter feed or more complex, such as automatically categorizing massive volumes of incoming text-based social media data from multiple social media sites into logical categories.

- **Engagement**. Refers to the ongoing and continuous process of actively participating and communicating across one or more social media channels, either in private (Facebook, outside of Timeline, MySpace) or in public (Twitter, outside of private accounts, YouTube). Engagement for businesses could take the form of offering promotions on social media, responding to criticisms, actively messaging about new products, or casually participating in the dialogue on sites that are popular for customers of the brand.

- **Participating**. When your business starts and stops intermittently, keeps shifting social media strategies, channel switches, and generally is not consistent across social media, then you and your business are not *engaging* but are simply *participating*.

- **Lurking**. Brands (and consumers) that spend resources (and thus time) passively observing what's going on in relation to their brand, products, or PR across one of more social media channels without *participating* or *engaging* are said to be *lurking*.

- **Social media platform**. The digital experiences that enable socialization on the Internet. The primary examples of the social media platform are Facebook or Twitter.

- **Social media tool**. Any tool, free or paid, that performs some useful social media analytics function.

- **Word of mouth (WOM).** WOM marketing is a concept known to global marketers and refers to people spreading the word to people they know regarding your product or service. WOM is enabled by social media; thus, WOM measurement models have usefulness for social media analytics.

- **Virality**. The idea that concepts can be rapidly communicated quickly across great distances (and cultures) illustrates what is meant by "virality" and "viral marketing."

- **Social bookmarking and linking.** From del.ico.us to bit.ly to tinyurl.com to e-mailing to SMS to applications and widgets that send content (via links or text) to people we know (our "friends!"), these reference tools are commonly known as social bookmarking and linking.

- **Social sharing.** In countries with high-speed Internet access, wireless, and mobile technologies and governments that allow it, people are sharing whatever they can think of—from pictures of their vacation on Photobucket to news articles from the *New York Times* to videos of a conference on YouTube to random images found on Pinterest.

- **Privacy**. Scott Mcnealy from Sun Microsystems once said, "You have no privacy, get over it."[3] Was he right, wrong, both right and wrong? Learn why privacy and the answers to these questions are important for social media analytics.

- **Copyright laws.** Huh? What are those? Ask Kim Dotcom from MegaUpload.

- **Influencers**. A term referring to the people who have the power to affect your business (both positively and negatively), along with their social media handles/accounts, blogs, and other digital experiences.

- **Social networking.** A macro term for the sum collection of interpersonal connection activities across social media, including social sharing, bookmarking, and linking that are done across social media platforms and measured across social media tools.

- **Twitter, Facebook, and Google+.** These big three global social platforms are very important sites for social media and necessary to measure.

- **Social applications.** A new term, as of 2012, that refers to mobile applications that are primarily based on social and online collaboration over mobile devices, which are also GPS location–aware, regardless of physical location.

- **The incrementality of social media.** When tracking and measuring the impact and outcomes of social media using analytics, it is absolutely essential to consider not only brand and direct response but also the impact of *incrementality* of the social channel on the business. The concept of incrementality means that for certain brands (large brands, mainly), social media does not help them sell more product (think beverage companies or banks); thus, understanding how social media adds incremental value is important. Do not attribute all social media direct response or revenue to social media; measure the *incrementality* of social media—of incremental signups, registrations, downloads, white papers, members, and orders and tie the impact directly back to profitable revenue or cost reduction. Note that the concept of incrementality and first-product learning from social media for smaller, local, and regional brands can be quite high, regardless of incrementality.

IS SOCIAL MEDIA ABOUT BRAND OR DIRECT RESPONSE?

Business activities that require expense and overhead need business justification. Social media, which is often tied to marketing or PR, must answer this question to qualify the type of analytics that is necessary to measure the social media campaign/product/experience and measure the business outcome. I had a chance to speak with Jascha Kayakas-Wolff, the chief marketing officer of MindJet, and he had this to say about social media analytics: "The promise of social data is to connect the anonymous with the known. As a marketer, there is very little that is more important to me and my organization's success."

Whether a business should be listening and engaging in social media is an "it depends" answer. While the author of this chapter strongly believes that all businesses should judiciously be using and measuring social media, it is obvious that every business has a level of social media listening and engagement that is right for it. Such decision making and the impetus behind it are beyond the scope of this book, but in order to frame social media analytics, a business must define which of the following (or some other reason) social media is to be used for:

- **Brand.** Social media channels (and their data) can be used to attract, message, encourage favorability, promote satisfaction, and act as variables for media mix and other marketing models that help identify brand equity, impact, and other higher-order consumer and shopping concepts.

- **Direct response.** Social media channels (and their data) can be used to engage directly and convert new and existing customers via promotions, offers, games, advertising, and other ways to directly interact and engage over the social channel. It is even possible to target types of customers from which you want a response and track them from social media to your website or another digital experience (such as a mobile application).

When determining a measurement strategy for social media, the strategy must be tightly aligned with the overall business goal of the social media campaign. Tying direct response to profitability is less challenging than is tying the impact of digital advertising campaign on Facebook to a change in favorability or satisfaction.

SOCIAL MEDIA "BRAND" AND "DIRECT RESPONSE" ANALYTICS

Social media is certainly about "brand" and is in fact essential to brand identification, awareness, and equity in the twenty-first century. If you or your brands aren't on social media, do you really exist?

As someone who measures social media—or those who aspire to manage and/or understand social media analytics—it is important to agree on definitions. A definition, and certainly not the only and an arguable definition, of "brand" is the following:

> The sum culmination of all the inputs, thoughts, feelings, and experiences whether real, virtual, or imagined perceived by an entity about another entity.

I think it is important to emphasize the words *entity* and *sum culmination* in the previous brand definition because when measuring the notion of "brand" in social media, we need to consider that brands are not only corporate but are personal and associated with real people.

Consider the impact of social media reviews for hotels on TripAdvisor or Expedia. How do you read them? Do you believe them? How have such reviews affected your decisions about commerce or influenced your conclusions about the brand?

The guidelines for social media analytics begin with understanding that with brand measurement, one is attempting to quantify the qualitative, which is often, at best, an educated estimate and at worst, value destroying.

Many advocates of social media also believe it is the channel responsible for a significant part of direct and indirect revenue for new and existing brands. While this may be true for the cornucopia of new and interesting social media companies that hope to attract members, qualify their audience, sell to advertisers, and thus create value, it is less so for more traditional companies.

Although, undoubtedly, some legacy companies have success driving new and incremental revenue from social media advertising and other activities in the social channel, only 7 million of the total dollars generated on cyber Monday in 2011 (the Monday after Thanksgiving in the United States) came from social media.[4] That said, revenue is being and can be generated on social media, especially from social advertising campaign integrated with offline components.

However, social media is an excellent channel through which to drive "direct response" action that expresses an intention of interest, such as reading an article, watching a video, rating a product, or learning about a service. "Direct response" is any social media activity that activates a target entity and compels that entity to perform a desired action. Again, the vocabulary I use in this definition is precise, with several key words: *target entity, compels,* and *desired action.* It is crucial to understand that social media direct response analytics involves:

- **Targeting entities,** such as customers, segments, cohorts—and even slicing and dicing these entities into their constituent attributes, such as demographics, psychographics, firma-graphics, or financial-graphics.

- **Compelling entities** via social media into listening, partici-pating, and engaging. The social media team must aspire to influence positively the business by creating compelling con-versations, content, and social experiences (both online and offline) that help generate economic value via by increasing brand equity or revenue (or reducing cost).

- **Desired actions** are the goals, steps in the funnel, and con-versions in the social media experience that create the economic value. Desired actions for direct response must tie to financial metrics, such as revenue and profit.

Social media analytics should be articulated by a series of steps that are necessary for measuring the impact of brand and direct response from social media within digital experiences. Thus, consider the following instruction set for building out the effective social media analytics:

1. Answering the following questions:
   - Do I want to affect the brand awareness, favorability, satis-faction, and equity?
   - Do I want to measure the behavior and outcomes of behavior across time?
   - Do I want to measure new or existing customers?
   - What financial metric (such as profit) do I hope to move through the actions that come from my brand analysis?
   - What direct response activities is social media meant to drive?
   - What are the goals, funnels, and conversions within the social media channel itself (that is, in the advertising or on Facebook directly) and within the digital experience that is controlled by your business (such as your mobile application or website)?

2. **Identify and document a full set of social media activities for the brand.** A simple task, you think? It may be when you are not accountable for doing so across multiple lines of business and in less complex and "interwingled" corporations.

3. **Identify and document the social media event and actions within the digital experience that you want to measure.** See Chapter 9 for more details.

4. **Identify the financial model and relevant business justification for the social media campaigns.** The analytics team must put the data and its analysis in appropriate and relevant business context. Analysts must interact with stakeholders in other departments, such as finance and senior management, to understand the financial underpinnings, and thus the business justification, for the social media campaign. The financial data and business justification will provide helpful context and data input for your analysis.

5. **Assign values by tying the social media campaigns and each action to an estimated *revenue* value in the context of your "brand."** Several methods exist for associating a monetary value with an event—from using a spreadsheet and manual data entry to more elegant approaches, where behavioral data and events, transactional events, and financial value are integrated and reportable in a unified way.

6. **Analyze the impact of the "sum culmination" of total social media activities, each campaign, and each action.** It is important to start with large, simple key performance indicators. Then break the totals into segments that make sense, both to your business and within the context of your industry. For example, if the goal is "profit" or "revenue," then an analyst can deconstruct the drivers in social media. It is possible to attribute site or mobile traffic to social media and corresponding purchases or downloads. Thus, one might look at the number of orders, the order conversion rate, and the profitability of each social media campaign in which social media–referred traffic went to the site; then segment the social media audience by attributes by which you already segment your audience, via new segmentation specific to social media, and even segment by newly collected behavioral data from the campaign.

7. **Estimate the incremental financial benefit (such as revenue, cost reductions in customer service, cost of sale,**

marketing, and so on) for each social media brand activity. A simple activity for financial analysts, but when digital behavioral data (and associated events and conversions) are brought into the equation, this comparison becomes harder to execute but remains entirely possible.

8. **Communicate the results to stakeholders in the context of the initial financial model and business justification of the social media strategy.** Again, the importance of having a socially intelligent analytics team is paramount. Your team members will have to leave their offices and cubes and communicate analytical results, outcomes, and recommendations to stakeholders and clients. As we have discussed throughout this book, the ability for an analyst to tell data stories in a way that makes sense (politically, emotionally, organizationally) in a business relevant way is an essential skill.

9. **Use the data collected for social media to affect other marketing models, such as brand trackers, media mix, attribution, and propensity models, using a statistically rigorous method.** Successful execution of effective social media analytics is entirely possible in a highly customized, value-generating way for your global, national, and local business—by yourself, with your team, or with external help. A successful outcome using the previous framework rests entirely in the execution and capabilities of the analytics leadership and team.

SOCIAL MEDIA TOOLS

Social media tools refer to the ever-growing and vast collection of technologies that exist as stand-alone software or software-as-a-service that collects, stores, measures, reports, or analyzes data from social media, whether in real time or latently. Social media tools are also sometimes provided by social media platforms (e.g., Facebook Insights, Twitter Analytics). Social media tools are numerous, and as such your business may benefit from an independent social media consultant that will be familiar with the most efficient and effective tools.

Guidelines for digital analytics tool selection can be reviewed in Chapter 9, and many of those steps apply to social media analytics tools as well. However, the guidelines for social media analytics tool selection that are reviewed in this chapter are a more customized instance for identifying and understanding the feature set of a social media analytics tool and its applicability for helping you create value from social media. When evaluating a social media analytics tool, you should consider the following factors:

- **Users**. Determining how the analytics team will use the social media analytics tool is common sense—or is it? Does the tool need a dedicated admin? Are the user roles customizable? How many users will you have and in what roles? How is user security handled?

- **Listening and engagement features**. Discover the way social media analytics listening and engaging can be measured. Are conversations threaded? Are data captured in real time? Can you respond to social media channels within the tool itself? What type of metadata or other data from different social sources is available to use?

- **Search.** The heavy textual nature of social media communications (and even the transcripts of videos and the tagging of objects, such as pictures and Web pages) require excellent search capabilities. Make sure to learn about the nuances of social media search analytic features in each tool. What technology is being used for search? What languages? Automatic categorization, clustering, text analysis? What about strange words with multiple meanings in different languages or geographies? Query language? Cost per search? Use lists of key words? Filter results? Drill-down? Save? Rerun? E-mail results? Natural language? Boolean?

- **Sentiment and text analysis and categorization**. Identify the features for text mining and analysis—and determine how customizable it is. Discuss with customer references if the tools for text mining are helpful or lacking in some way. How does the tool handle linguistic nuance and cultural differences? Text mining is an area that can easily "wow" people because it so easy to understand—and the potential to help business so powerful—yet the best text analysis does not come out of the box (yet)—so dig deep on text analysis and how it is handled when words have multiple meanings, in different cultures (with different semiotics), and across different languages (in one, multiple, or within one country).

■ **Data access and integration.** Social media data alone has value, but the value can be truly unlocked only by integrating it with other data. Integration with CRM systems, third-party data vendors (comScore, Rapleaf), data enhancers (Experian), data from large platforms (Google and Facebook), and customer data (in CRM systems) is possible, but social media tools are nascent in support as of 2012. Determine how the data, once collected, is stored and summarized. For how long? At what cost? Who owns it? Can data be accessed without leaving the tool and by the tool itself? What partners exist, and what proven-use cases can be demonstrated where data were accessed, extracted, transferred, and loaded to and/or from the social media analytics tool?

■ **Systems integration.** At a more macro level than data integration, entire systems can be linked together and their operations orchestrated to generate business value. Adobe Genesis, Webtrends Connect, comScore Social Analytix, and Salesforce .com's integration of the social media monitoring provider Radian6 are all examples of systems integration that are possible at the vendor or customer level.

■ **Customization and growth**. Social media is dynamic and evolving organically; thus, social media analytics tools must provide features that allow for extensibility and scalability of data collection, processing, reporting, and analyzing data. In addition, the features for listening, participating, engaging, and managing social media analytics must continue to evolve. How is the tool supporting the inevitable fast pace of change in twenty-first-century social media?

■ **Tracking, reporting, and analysis.** Can the social media team's time and activities be tracked in the tool? Message archiving? Scheduled engagement? Dashboarding? Scheduled reporting? Usage of other data from third parties?

Beyond the previous social media analytics tool selection framework, I have found it helpful to ask questions in the following focus areas when selecting social media analytics tools:

- **Partner information,** such as: What vendors complement your product that you have worked with before?

- **Product road map,** such as: What are the five primary focus areas for product development within the next 12 to 18 months—and what features are being released during the next two fiscal quarters across how many releases?

- **Competitive information,** such as: Who are your main competitors, and why do they win deals over you?

- **Organizational support,** such as: Do you provide free training and support when deploying your tool?

- **Financial information,** such as: Is your company profitable, and does it have positive cash flow?

- **Pricing data,** such as: Can we do a free proof-of-concept? How much does it cost to listen back as far as one year ago? Does it cost to perform features on a "cost per X" basis?

- **Customer references,** such as: Can we speak with the customer who has been using the tool the longest?

By framing your selection criteria along the dimensions discussed in this section, you will best position your company for understanding the pros and cons of whatever set of social media tools you select.

SOCIAL MEDIA ANALYTICAL TECHNIQUES

The flow of data is endless and, as a result, can be overwhelming, especially in the field of social media. In this section, we outline some basic techniques for the analysis of social media data that we have found to result in the greatest business impact. Certainly, this section is not exhaustive but should give you an idea of where to start.

Social Media Listening

Listening on social media can be defined as the process by which a social media team monitors one or more social media channels in a timely way, using technology in order to understand how to generate revenues or reduce cost for the organization from social media analysis.

One of the main activities for a social media team will be listening to what is being said (and why, how, where, and so on) across social media channels. As a result, analysis must be done where social media data collected through listening can be parsed to help you understand what people are saying about your brand, your products, your people, and your competitors. Analysis of listening data is also necessary to stay current in the ongoing conversations, which can change rapidly and in which you may want to participate and even engage. The goal, of course, is to understand past and present action in way that you can use it as input for detecting, interacting with, and predicting the future business outcomes (possibly in an automated way).

When you begin to measure listening, make sure to tie past and current social media activities to the analytics, as well as back to the expenses incurred and the revenue generated from the social media activities.

Social Media Scoring

Advanced analytical and statistical technique can be performed on social media data; however, the data most often must be prepared in some way before it is useful for statistical processing. The data can often be dirty and noisy—and must be processed to ensure conformity and integrity over time (social media data definitions change, even those from vendors). Oftentimes, some level of data verification, integrity checking, and data smoothing or pre-processing before statistical analysis is necessary. Thus, extra time must be budgeted in any project plan when the goal is to data mine social media data for any statistical or machine learning application.

Social media scoring is the process whereby one or more proxy values are assigned to events and actions within the social media—on the social media platform, within the campaign, and on the site/digital experience. Actions such as those that a known customer performs within a portion of Facebook to the specific behaviors on your site can be allocated a score. For example, a click may be worth a score of "1," a completed form may be worth a score of "2," while an order may worth a score of "3."

A simple scoring model may assign a score to each action, track the actions by a known customer segment or a specific known customer (via CRM), and sum them up across all segments or customers. In addition, it is possible to score specific social media channels against one another, based on customer behavior and revenue/profit generated from them (in ways somewhat similar to offline catalog or retail category management). In this way, it is entirely possible to incorporate social media scoring of not only social media exposed and referred customers but also the impact of the social channels used by customers. In addition, integrating this data, research, and analytics into and unifying it with traditional offline data is what the world's most innovative companies and consultants are doing right now.

Social Media Modeling

Social media modeling can involve social media scoring but, of course, does not require scoring as a necessary component. Social media modeling refers to the process of creating models by using applied statistical methods to measure and/or predict the impact of investment in social media listening, participating, engagement, promotional and pricing activities; tactics and strategies on sales (revenue), profit, and expenses; and high-order concepts such as awareness, favorability, and satisfaction.

Social media modeling and the variables used in the models are helpful for improving the efficiency of your social media buy and for understanding and determining the best social channel for marketing your products (e.g., does Facebook create more value and better return than YouTube?). Thus, social media modeling is helpful when creating, implementing, executing, maintaining, and closing business activities. Techniques for social media modeling can range from simple correlation analysis to more complex types of regression models (with their inherently risky assumptions) and decision tree techniques.

Social Media Text Mining

Text mining helps social media analytics because the technology can help sift social media–generating text into logical categories or clusters that can be evaluated qualitatively against quantitative business metrics. Social media analytics can involve the application of social media tools to understand the patterns and trends in the text data. Text-mining features in social media tools are often met with skepticism from practitioners, but because the technology is so complex, it is not surprising that the future of text mining and text analytics is bright.

Future social media analytics will benefit from improvements in text mining's many complex and interesting features and techniques, such as sentiment analysis and pattern extraction categorization. Digital and social media analysts worldwide are looking for improvements in social media analytical tool features, such as automated extraction of keywords and their synonyms; merging similar social media conversations, based on clustering, evaluating, and analyzing relationships between concepts and ideas extracted from structured and unstructured text; and the automated recognition of relationships in the text created across social media channels based on parsing, analyzing, and reporting the meaning of social media conversations.

SOCIAL MEDIA ANALYTICS AND PRIVACY

The implications of social media on the evolution of human society are enormous. Facebook has nearly one billion members—and is larger than many countries. That is why, when doing social media analytics, business leaders and data analysts must remember that it is not only their goal but their responsibility to be mindful of data privacy. Social media analysts are largely left to self-regulate their analytical activities—in much the same way the social media analytics tool vendors are left to self-regulate their innovations. That is why it is important to also apply ethical principles to social media analytics, to ensure privacy and the application of social media tools and analytics in a way that positively promotes not only global commerce but also human society.

I suggest several rules when dealing with social media data, whether behavioral, transactional, qualitative, quantitative, first or third party, and private or anonymous:

- **Be *absolutely* transparent about what data you collect and how you collect it by creating and frequently updating a privacy and data usage policy and prominently displaying it on your site.** Write it in English, not legalese, and keep it simple, comprehensible, and summarized. If needed, link to a more formal legal document.

- **Understand and be able to provide, on request, a list of the tracking and measurement technologies currently deployed on your site.** Such a simple idea is hard to execute and deliver—especially at globally distributed enterprises—but smart companies should create and maintain a list of all social media (and digital) tracking and measurement technologies deployed on the site and have that list ready for review when requested.

- **Publish a simple metadata document that people, both externally and internally, can review that describes the social media data being collected and how the data will be used.** For every technology deployed, the vendor should be providing a document answering the following questions: (1) What is this technology? (2) What data are being collected? (3) How are the data being used? And (4) How do I view, modify, and prevent my data from being collected? These answers can be used to craft your policy and privacy statements relevant to social media and the analytics that support it.

- **Create formalized governance around measurement, tracking, and advertising technologies and involve cross-functional representatives from teams across your company.** It was discussed in detail in Chapter 4 that companies using any analytical technology should have a data governance council. Teams from research, analytics, legal, marketing, sales, and technology should participate to ensure that best practices are adhered to.

- **Enable easy and logical "opt-out"** and, in the best case, only allow tracking and targeting to be "opt-in" for social media—and all digital tracking in general.

- **Eliminate all unnecessary data collection while regularly reviewing the data you have collected and delete unneeded data.** So much data can be collected, but very little is actually useful, insightful, and actionable (UIA). Figure out what is UIA, generating profitable revenue, then delete the rest.

- **Don't exploit new technologies in tricky ways that attempt to circumvent a user's choice or perception of privacy.** For example, do not use Flash to reset cookies after the user deletes them and do not use hacks to store cookies forever.

- **Represent yourself and your companies in industry organizations** such as the Analytics Research Organization (ARO, www.thearo.org) and Interactive Advertising Bureau (IAB).

- **Make your voice heard by writing to your senator or congressperson.** The heart of a democracy is the citizen's voice. Imagine the potential for understanding and alignment that could be achieved if the thousands of readers of this article wrote an e-mail, made a phone call, or advocated in the public domain positively for our industry. If you do not speak up to protect your livelihood and business, no one is going to do it for you.

KEY TAKEAWAYS

- Social media analytics is part of digital analytics but has its own vocabulary and nuance that must be learned. All brands should experiment judiciously with social media in a nonrisky, honest way. Some marketers have postulated that if your brand is not on social media, then "does it exist?" Thus, social media should be considered a channel for maximizing the reach of your brand to new and incremental audiences—as well as attempting to compel new and existing customers to respond directly to your campaigns. Social media measurement is not only about simple metrics and basic counts of social behaviors and activities. Social media requires an understanding of virility and viral marketing, word of mouth marketing, and a comprehension of the differences between using social media for branding or for direct response. Social media analytics can be used to track social media-referred prospects and thereby enhance media mix modeling. Social media tools often exist separately from other digital analytics tools; however, some tools have the ability to integrate with digital analytics tools by sharing data.

■ Social media measurement teams use social media platforms for "listening" to the stream of conversation across one or more social media channels. Some tools allow for the social media team to "engage" directly with the social media audience.

■ More advanced and powerful tools have functionality for searching social media streams (both live, as they occur, called "filtering," and post data collection), features for sentiment analysis, methods for gaining access to and integrating data across systems, and functions for team collaboration, scheduling, and workflows. Social media teams often use these tools to identify and communicate with "Influencers."

■ Choose your partners for social media analytics with heightened care and diligence, because a lack of standards and consistency exists in the industry.

■ The best social media measurement and analysis focuses on the profitability of social media activities. Profitability analysis requires knowledge of the cost of social media campaigns and the associated revenue. Make sure to look at the cost, revenue, and profitability of social media campaigns in aggregate total and segmented by campaign.

■ Social media scoring is a technique that can help a brand understand the value of social media behavior by assigning proxy values to events and behaviors in the social stream.

■ Socially enabled, location-aware mobile applications are common. As a result, companies have access to more data today than in the past about people preferences, thoughts, activities, locations, and emotions. As a result, all companies and people who do social media analytics must consider the impact of privacy in data collection and analysis.

NOTES

1. Ted Nelson, "Intertwingularity," "Ted Nelson," http://en.wikipedia.org/wiki/Intertwingularity.
2. F. Levine, C. Locke, D. Searls, and D. Weinberger, *The Cluetrain Manifesto: The End of Business as Usual* (New York: Cluetrain, 2000); Malcom Gladwell,

The Tipping Point: How Little Things Can Make a Big Difference (New York: Little Brown, 2000).

3. Scott McNealy, quoted in Polly Sprenger, "Sun on Privacy: 'Get Over It,'" *Wired*, January 26, 1999, http://www.wired.com/politics/law/news/1999/01/17538.

4. IBM press release, "Record Online Thanksgiving Day Shopping Paves Way for Strong Black Friday Retail Sales, Reports IBM," November 26, 2011, http://www-03.ibm.com/press/us/en/pressrelease/36100.wss.

CHAPTER 13

The Competitive Intelligence Mandate

"What enables the wise sovereign and the good general to strike and conquer, and achieve things beyond the reach of ordinary men, is foreknowledge."

—Sun Tzu, on *The Art of War* (500 BC)

As discussed throughout this book, effective business analytics is about integrating different types of information across your organization in order to address critical questions and help your company achieve its key business objectives. Gaining insight about your competitors through intelligence gathering may seem like common sense to you; however, it is amazing how many companies do not formalize this process or make it part of their strategic business analytics initiatives. What is more common in organizations is that with everyone moving so rapidly, keenly trying to satisfying customers and running the organization, people tend to concentrate more on the analysis of internally focused business problems than on an outward scan.

For example, one of the coauthors, Jesse Harriott, recalls a time in the late 1990s when he was working with a well-established background verification company as a consultant, helping it use fact-based strategies to increase its new customer acquisition rates and decrease its existing customer attrition. The company provided pre-employment background investigation services to different types of organizations, mostly to its HR departments. It provided services such as drug testing, criminal background checking, and employment verification services. At that time, the company had noticed a gradual declining trend in its ability to retain customers, as well as in its ability to acquire new customers. To the company, it made no sense because the economy was strong, and the rate of hiring was increasing. The company asked Jesse to use an analytics- and research-based approach to help it figure out the explanation and recommend strategies for how to reverse this trend.

During the discovery phase of the engagement, Jesse met with several people across the organization, including the CEO, to gather information, as well as to understand what tactics had been tried. There was a great deal of detailed customer data and sales data available, and that had been used to try to understand the decline. The company had also experimented with a number of tactics to retain customers, such as price discounting and offering additional services, but had not seen any of these approaches stem the tide of declining customer acquisition and retention in a meaningful way. The company had been in business for more than 20 years and seemed to feel secure in its belief that it offered a strong service at a fair price to its customers. After several meetings, Jesse went away amazed at one thing—no one had raised a discussion about the competitive situation, other than to say that their competitive position was strong. There was no ongoing competitive intelligence or focus on thinking strategically about how competitors may be affecting the business trends. Jesse wasn't sure at the time, but he thought the area of competitive intelligence might just be the blind spot that was contributing to the company's decrease in customer retention and acquisition.

Jesse and his team started by doing some in-depth customer interviews, as well as researching the competitive landscape. What he quickly discovered is that this company was being affected by its failure to monitor and integrate competitive intelligence into its analytics process. Specifically, customers indicated that new competitors were offering the same services at similar pricing but were able to offer a much faster turnaround time, because they were using digital sources for much of their background verification services. Furthermore, reports were being delivered to customers electronically via the Web and through e-mail. Customers liked the speed and convenience of gaining access to the reports this way, and it allowed them to reduce their time to hire, because background checks were returned more quickly, compared to waiting for a report via fax or traditional mail. Jesse and his team summarized these issues for the client and provided specific recommendations for how to consider adjusting service delivery in order to exceed the turnaround time of new competitors. He also recommended that they design and package background services for key company types and occupational roles in order to differentiate even further from the new competitors in the market. Finally, Jesse and the team recommended that their client set up an ongoing formal competitive intelligence function to ensure it stayed ahead of the competition and avoid future similar circumstances. As a result of implementing these recommendations, the company was able to reverse the declining customer trend and actually surpassed previous company customer growth records.

The previous example is just one illustration of why it's important for your business analytics function to integrate competitive intelligence as part of the information to help address your critical business questions. For some of you, it may mean establishing a formal competitive intelligence (CI) function in your department; for others, it may mean leveraging an existing CI function somewhere else in your organization. Either way, during the remainder of this chapter, we outline some competitive intelligence best practices, as well as principles to help guide the structure of the CI function in your own organization.

COMPETITIVE INTELLIGENCE DEFINED

When some people think of competitive intelligence, they form an image of a somewhat shady practice where people lie, cheat, and steal and use every means of dishonest corporate espionage to learn what the competition is doing. Nothing could be further from the truth.

Competitive intelligence gathering is neither dishonest nor something for which your company should be ashamed of engaging in. Competitive intelligence is really just the analytical process by which publicly available information is collected and transformed in an ethical manner through analysis into valuable insight regarding competitors' market position, performance, capabilities, and intentions for use in tactical and strategic business decisions. The quality of your firm's competitive intelligence will be a function of several factors, the most important of which is the effectiveness of the CI processes you put in place across your organization.

The key objectives of your competitive intelligence organization should be the following:

■ Anticipate and provide an early warning for trends that could negatively affect the business.

■ Identify trends early on that represent an opportunity for company growth or improvement.

■ Stay current on competitor activities to enable your company to effectively differentiate itself in the minds of customers.

■ Build a collective and actionable corporate knowledge base to enable fast decision making.

■ Inform and stimulate strategic planning through the dissemination of intelligence across the enterprise.

■ Create a collective knowledge system whereby intelligence across the company can be easily obtained and used by your company.

These may sound like intimidating goals, but they are all attainable with thoughtful planning and execution. In terms of what type of competitive intelligence you may gather, it will depend heavily on your industry, but at a minimum you should consider capturing the following:

■ Competitor press releases

■ Social media and Web channels

■ Investor relations activities/earnings

■ Competitor customer perceptions

- Industry articles and news
- Competitor product performance
- Changes in bids, proposals, and sales tactics
- Key executive activities
- Patent/intellectual property activities
- Joint ventures/strategic alliances, mergers, and acquisitions
- New product developments

We hope you now understand what competitive intelligence is and why it is crucial to incorporate into your business analytics discipline. Now, let us turn our attention to the best ways to implement competitive intelligence in a manner that enables insight and action against your key business objectives and achieves the goals outlined previously.

PRINCIPLES FOR CI SUCCESS

Successful competitive intelligence hinges on many factors and can be a complex undertaking, depending on your organizational structure, the number of markets you compete in, and the maturity of your organization. Shortly after coauthor Jesse Harriott joined Monster Worldwide in 2002, he formed Monster's first competitive intelligence initiative. He was the executive sponsor for that initiative for almost 10 years; following are his five key principles for CI success, some of which were learned the hard way. We will explain each one in detail.

1. Executive sponsorship
2. Alignment with business objectives
3. Strong communication systems
4. Relationships matter
5. Bias to action

The first key to an effective CI program is executive sponsorship. You must have at least one senior leader who believes in the importance of competitive intelligence and understands that CI is a must, not a luxury. This support must be ongoing and revisited on a regular basis in order to maintain it. To identify the leaders most likely to support your efforts, think about the people in your company who would benefit the most from CI. For example, if you have a direct sales force, its leadership frequently will be big supporters of CI because the sales reps come in direct contact with the competition on a regular basis as they try to win and retain business. If you don't have a direct sales model, then marketing can often be the next place to look. Because the marketing organization is responsible for differentiating your products or services effectively, marketing leadership will have a keen interest in staying current on competitive developments, how customers think about competitors, and marketing messages from competitors in the marketplace. Another leadership area in which to look for support can be product. An effective product organization will want to understand competitors in great detail, because product leadership is responsible for bringing products to market that meet the needs of your customers. There are certainly others in the organization who will benefit from competitive intelligence as well, such as public relations, customer service, strategy, business development, and technology.

The second key to competitive intelligence success is alignment with key business objectives. We covered this topic in detail in Chapter 3, yet it is especially important in the collection of competitive intelligence. Most of competitive intelligence will come from people in or closely connected to your organization. You will require their cooperation as the "feet on the street" to understand the nuances of competitive developments. This will require ongoing communication and relationships with multiple departments. Therefore, your CI initiatives must be very closely aligned to the objectives of the departments you will rely on, to make their cooperation more likely. For example, if your sales organization is focused on a new push into the Phoenix market, and you can use CI to help the sales organization understand the local competitive environment in Phoenix, you are more likely to gain the ongoing support and cooperation of sales leadership.

The third key to successful competitive intelligence practice is to have strong communication systems funneling information into and out of your CI function. Although you can leverage plenty of non-human information, such as reports, online data streams, social media chatter, third-party reports, and industry data, there is no substitute for the direct human feedback of your employees, customers, partners, and suppliers. Therefore, having communication strategies that make it easy to systematically capture information from these groups is crucial.

For communication within your company, each organization is different, but sometimes something as simple as one e-mail address where anyone inside your company can send competitive information or his or her perspective on competitor activities can be very effective. It is essential to promote and reward people for providing information, so consider calling out leading CI information providers within your company on a periodic basis, letting their peers inside the company know what a good job they have done. If you have a more open organization, consider a private Web-based community stream, where anyone inside the company can review, post, and respond to competitive information he or she has seen or heard. This can be very effective for leveraging the collective intelligence of groups, rather than your CI team piecing information together, one by one. However, you must be sensitive and monitor regularly to ensure that people inside the company are aware of what competitive intelligence is ethical to possess and what is inappropriate to possess. The Society for Competitive Intelligence Professionals (www.scip.org) has a great deal of helpful information regarding what is considered ethical and what is consider unethical.

In terms of communicating CI back to those inside your company, consider a monthly CI update where key developments and information are synthesized for prominent leaders across the organization. Also, consider "learning lunches" on important competitive intelligence topics, where people can come to learn and provide feedback on strategic topics, such as a new competitor products or marketing initiatives. Finally, maintain a regular self-service repository where vital competitive intelligence can be consumed and used across the company. However, keep in mind, some competitive intelligence may not be appropriate for some audiences, so permission controls are crucial.

To establish channels of communication for gathering competitive intelligence from people close to, but outside, your company, consider periodic one-to-one customer feedback sessions, customer focus groups, customer events, industry trade shows, and industry groups as ways to keep the information flowing regarding the competition. If you establish a reputation among your customers and partners that you are genuinely interested in how your company is doing vis-à-vis the competition and how you can improve, you will be surprised at how much insight they are willing to provide. Just remember, it is never okay to misrepresent your identity, your company's identity, or the purpose for gathering feedback.

The fourth key to competitive intelligence success is that your relationships matter. If you are going to drive competitive intelligence collection and usage, you must form strong relationships with both the people who provide you with the critical information and the people whom you serve within your organization. Those strong relationships are what will enable you to react quickly to industry developments, mobilize your network to gain context regarding what you have learned, and get the organization to listen to what you have learned. Relationships are cultivated over a period of time; they do not happen instantly. Therefore, you must first build a track record of your competitive intelligence activities that are affecting the departments and the people with whom you want a strong relationship. For example, have you been able to help your sales organization win business? Has your information enabled product to develop a leapfrog technology product? Has your work uncovered a lesser-known industry player for your business development team that led to a winning partnership? It's these types of consistent wins that will help ensure that your competitive intelligence gathering works at full steam and continues to affect your organization. I had a chance to sit down with Ellen Julian, the former global director of competitive intelligence for Monster Worldwide. She emphasized repeatedly that "having strong relationships inside the organization is the unspoken key to CI success." Ellen asserts, "The information gathering and synthesis must be cutting edge and business relevant, but failure to have the right relationships across the organization will mean a slow and ineffective CI response to threats in the marketplace."

CASE STUDY

COMPETITIVE INTELLIGENCE IN THE PHARMACEUTICAL INDUSTRY

A pharmaceutical company was hearing complaints from physicians about the time it took payers (insurance companies and government programs such as Medicare) to reimburse them for one of the company's drugs. As a consequence of this slow payment, there was a danger that physicians would switch to competitive therapies for which they could get paid more quickly. However, the company faced two serious obstacles when trying to address this problem:

1. The company had no idea what the source of the slow payments was. (Was it one specific payer? Was it one specific clinic? Was it because the company's drug was unfamiliar to the payer and the hospital billing staff as a whole?)

2. The company did not have any data on physician-payer billing cycles, because it was not a party to those transactions.

To help overcome these roadblocks, the company turned to a pair of outside vendors (Market Strategy Group and Medical Present Value) that could bring the relevant data and analytical skills to bear. Together with these vendors, the company then set about defining what it needed to know.

- How long do payers take to reimburse clinics for our drug and for competitive drugs?

- Are payers more likely to reject claims for payment of our drug vs. competitive drugs?

- Are there specific payers that are particularly slow pays and/or who are highly likely to reject?

- Are there specific clinics that are particularly likely to be paid slowly and/or that are highly likely to have their claims rejected?

- Who *and where* are these payers or clinics?

This last question was important because the company would ultimately end up working to correct any problems through its sales force, which was organized regionally. By thinking through not only what the company wanted to know but also how it was likely to act on any findings, the company was able to identify early on a key aspect of the analysis—that it would have to be done regionally.

(continued)

As a practical matter, this meant that a lot of the value in the analysis actually came from a combination of the company's own internal data (in this case, on sales regions) with third-party data on billing and payment dates. The melding process was simple—a single translation table placed clinics from the third-party data in the company's sales regions. This one linkage allowed all of the other third-party data to then be placed in the company's sales regions. Although this translation table was created manually, it was created early in the analytical process and thus allowed the entire data set to produce integrated results for all manner of queries.

When the analysis was complete, the company discovered that its drug was in fact reimbursed only a day or so more slowly than competitors' drugs, and that it was no more likely to be rejected. Even though the average reimbursement cycle was about the same as competitors', there were some outliers—one payer and one clinic took more than 60 days to resolve several of their claims. These findings meant that the company had a perception problem with regard to its drug's reimbursement cycles (a difference of 1 day in a cycle that is typically 20 to 25 days is not generally viewed as important by most clinics and physicians). As a consequence, the company took two sets of actions:

1. To deal with the physicians who were concerned about long reimbursements, the company incorporated a few simple bullet points about payment cycles into its sales collateral (here, it helped to mention that the underlying data was from a third party, because that increased its credibility) and wrote a few similar talking points for the sales force. Although a significant amount of analysis really boiled down to only a few sentences, that, more than some complex graphs and displays, was what was appropriate to neutralize physicians' objections.

2. For the few outliers that did take a long time to pay, the company was able to identify the payer and the clinics and work specifically with each to ensure that future reimbursements would be handled smoothly.

In addition to answering the core question about reimbursement cycles, the company found that doing the reimbursement data analysis actually created a new data set for it that it could use to answer other questions. Using the data set to answer questions about the frequency of the dosage, the relative reimbursement amounts, and so on, only further increased the ROI on the effort to solve the original problem.

Source: Sims Hulings, partner, Market Strategy Group, LLC, www.mkt-strat.com.

The fifth key to competitive intelligence success is about your insights having a bias to action. In other words, information you collect, analyze, and distribute should clearly lead to or imply action. If your information is merely "interesting" or "wow, I didn't know that," you aren't doing your job. Your information must spur the business to be inclined to react and take a new action. The information you provide should create a decision point, whereby business leaders now must decide, "Okay, where do we go from here?" For example, if you provide analysis of a press release that a competitor just issued regarding a new product or service via e-mail, your internal customers may find it compelling and interesting, yet may take little action. However, if you provide an analysis of the press release, plus outline how the new service compares to your organization's existing services, and you quantify the market size for those types of services and then you also schedule a learning lunch for your key sales managers to provide their reactions directly to your company's product managers, then you are much more likely to lead the organization to a decision point. Any time CI can be used to create a bit of angst inside the organization, you are more likely to get the organization to consider its options and take appropriate actions.

Now let us consider a hypothetical illustration of how a formal CI process should work.

Let us imagine that Wizbang Company makes tablet computers and sells them online. It enjoys a majority market share percentage for online sales of tablet computers. The company has a few competitors, but none, it believes, offer the price and service it offers. The company is happy with its market position and has no formal competitive intelligence function. Now imagine that UpandComing Technology, Inc., has a small but profitable online tablet computer business; it runs its own website and doesn't enjoy the sales that Wizbang enjoys. UpandComing Technology is perceived as a minor threat to Wizbang.

Inside the Wizbang organization (without a formal and coordinated CI function), the following is observed across different departments regarding UpandComing Technology:

- The CMO reads a press release that UpandComing signs an agreement to sell its products at a large retail chain.

- The investor relations manager reads in the latest 10-Q that UpandComing has acquired XYZ Tech, a tiny technology company that makes computer hardware.

- At a technology trade show, a Wizbang sales rep hears that UpandComing's newest computer will have a lower price point than Wizbang's.

- A Wizbang customer service representative hears from a customer that UpandComing will be giving away its newest monitor as soon as it comes out, with the purchase of a new computer.

Separately, these facts range from "who cares" to "interesting," but none sets off significant alarm bells. Now what if Wizbang had a formalized CI function that took this information and added to it the following:

- A search of the *patent database* reveals that UpandComing has several patents on high-resolution retina display monitor technology for tablets.

- Found at the same trade show mentioned previously, UpandComing's newest tablet computer is being released in six months and a promotion for free 3G access will run at the launch.

- A search of the UpandComing job openings reveals that it is hiring technology support managers to work in satellite offices located inside a large retail chain partner.

- Calls to UpandComing's talent recruiting partners reveal that the retail chain is the very well-known Target corporation.

In the previous case, the CI professional is able to take seemingly unrelated pieces of information and piece them together to create deeper and more relevant insights with a bias to action. With all of this information, the CI professional prepares a report for the Wizbang CEO with the following information:

UpandComing is launching a new tablet PC in 6 months that has a lower price point than Wizbang's. It will be giving away

3G access with every purchase. It will sell this tablet at Target stores and most likely on the Target website, increasing its online visibility by 500%. Service for UpandComing will be enhanced by new in-store tech support reps in Target stores.

We think it's obvious that the Wizbang leadership would much rather learn this information months in advance, as opposed to the day the UpandComing press release comes out. Even if the CI interpretation isn't completely accurate, the information has exposed a potentially huge threat to Wizbang's market share and a possible opportunity to beat UpandComing to the punch. This hypothetical example is a simple illustration of the effect of a high-impact formalized CI function. In reality, things can be more complex, but the biggest point in this example is that information starts to have context when all of the pieces of data are grouped together. The corporate environment is multilayered and includes, but certainly isn't limited to, competitors, customers, suppliers, social and economic trends, technology, and the possibility of mergers and acquisitions. The level of success you achieve in business analytics will be directly related to how intimately you know your competitors and what's going on around them.

We hope this chapter has convinced you of the importance of CI and the need to integrate it into your business analytics strategies and activities. Whether you currently have a CI function or do not, we encourage you to discuss CI with your leadership team in an effort to make sure you get the most impact for all information available to you in your business analytics efforts. We know that the integration of competitive intelligence will make your business analytics efforts stronger and more effective than ever before.

KEY TAKEAWAYS

- Competitive intelligence is an integral part of an effective business analytics practice.
- Failure to integrate CI can result in wasted time and resources against company initiatives that will produce no results.

- There are five principles of CI success:
  1. Executive sponsorship
  2. Alignment with business objectives
  3. Strong communication systems
  4. Relationships matter
  5. Bias to action
- Strong relationships within your company are an often-overlooked component of CI success.
- Integrating CI effectively into your business analytics requires a strategic approach to information gathering and analysis.
- Effective CI requires the integration and synthesis of seemingly unrelated pieces of information that lead to a call for action.

CHAPTER 14

Mobile Analytics

By Judah Phillips

"Mobile is the next frontier of businesses, and 'there's an app for that' has gone from an advertising catch phrase to an expectation. The Internet boom of the 1990s and early 2000s caught a lot of businesses by surprise. While the quickest profited, there was enough lag in the industry for people to play catch-up. Nobody is going to be surprised by the mobile boom. Make sure you're not playing catch-up."

—Author interview with Raj Aggarwal, CEO, Localytics

Mobile analytics, like social analytics, is another form of digital analytics (see Chapter 9). Mobile analytics has much in common with Web analytics, yet it also has a certain uniqueness, peculiarity, nuance, and technology that is specific to "mobile." Even more confusing is that mobile analytics may also include social analytics. Any portion of the marketing "funnel" can be touched by a mobile device, and any mobile application can touch another digitally enabled application. Thus, while mobile analytics is similar to site (Web) analytics, in terms of data collection, basic concepts, measurement, reporting, and analytical approach, it has complexity, in that mobile analytics must take into account two different constructs of mobile behavior:

1. **Mobile sites.** These are slimmed HTML (5), WAP, WML, or other Internet-enabled user experiences that can be rendered on any mobile device that does not require a special installation of a "mobile application" for engaging a visitor. For example, visiting the Google website using your iPhone.

2. **Mobile applications.** This is a stand-alone user experience delivered across one or more closed or open proprietary systems, such as iOS, Android, and RIM, on which a digital experience is presented for engagement by a visitor. Mobile applications are software programs downloaded to a mobile device. The game Angry Birds is an example of a mobile application.

Measuring mobile applications requires following a similar decision-making methodology, as has been discussed throughout this book, of aligning your analyses against your organization's critical business questions and objectives such that your analytics will lead to action. Analysis of mobile begins by asking the following questions:

- **Are we measuring a mobile site and/or a mobile application?** Mobile sites tend to be slimmed-down websites with a user experience that fits the mobile screen. Functionality on mobile sites may be reduced when compared to the website. As a result, applied analytics on mobile sites can be similar to websites—and should take metrics, reports, and analytical approaches from site analysis. Mobile applications can mimic and replicate site functionality but are often stand-alone in terms of features, flows, and content from counterpart websites or mobile sites. Mobile applications may also be stand-alone with no site counterpart. Some applications can spawn a browser when being used, which represents another type of mobile analysis—one where the crossover from application to site must be measured.

- **Why does the mobile site and/or application exist?** Crucial to any measurement and analysis effort is understanding the critical business objectives. Mobile is no exception.

- **Should we be measuring the same metrics across mobile experiences that we do for other digital experiences?** Mobile analytics does contain some different vocabulary, but not much is different from the concepts discussed in Chapter 9.

- **Do existing data definitions, data, reports, and analytical approaches already exist in my company (or elsewhere) that can be reused?** Relevant tacit and explicit knowledge from experience in other projects should be applied to any mobile project.

- **Does the team have sufficient resources to engage in a mobile data collection, reporting, and analysis effort?** Mobile analytics does require some new and different analytical technologies and processes.

- **Has the analytics team set expectation and gained approval from the other teams as necessary for analytical success when executing a mobile analytics project (such as IT, engineering, and QA)?** Mobile analysis, as with any digital analysis, will require data collection, which will need definition/specification from the analytics team and sufficient technology team resourcing. Senior management buy-in, and support for mobile analytics may be necessary, given the resourcing required.

- **What are the key business questions that need to be answered by the analytics team for stakeholders who can actually make or influence changes to the mobile site and/or application?** Like other analytical efforts, the capability of the analytics team to get the data, reporting, and analysis in the hands of the people who can take action on it in a timely manner is important; thus, it is an essential step to consult those stakeholders and determine their business questions and goals for mobile analysis.

- **What are the best possible ways for communicating answers to business questions about mobile?** Communication strategies for mobile analysis should use existing processes, as discussed in Chapter 15; however, your team may need to create additional "mobile-only" reports, self-service environments for querying mobile data, and custom analyses for "what if" and "what else" mobile business questions.

CASE STUDY

VOXY AND LOCALYTICS

Voxy, an innovative language-learning company that uses mobile technology and gaming mechanics to turn media and real-life content into language lessons, employs a push notification strategy to encourage users to interact with its app. The notifications foster repeat usage and remind users that new articles are available to help push people along their path to learning English. Pushes are sent on a regular basis, and Voxy uses app analytics provider Localytics to optimize notifications for maximum user engagement and retention.

App Analytics: Daypart and Location Analysis

Taking advantage of insights into user patterns provided by Localytics' daypart and location analyses, Voxy optimized its push notification strategy to coincide with its Brazilian users' most active times of day. The changes immediately delivered dramatic improvements. Peak user numbers exploded, with users being reminded that they want to use the app at just the right moment. In addition to the initial spike, Voxy's long-term retention rose as well. Second-week user retention improved by 120%, growing from 23% to 51%.

Optimizing In-App User Flow

In addition to getting the most out of its regular push notifications, Voxy must continually analyze, optimize, and adapt to improve in-app user flow. Voxy's desired action from users who launch its app for the first time is for users to complete registration and reach Voxy's personalized dashboard.

App Analytics: Screen Flows and Conversion Funnels

Voxy uses the Localytics screen flow functionality, breaking out visual representations of how its users interact with its app. With screen flows, Voxy can look at a particular screen in its app and see both what users do on the screen and where they go afterward.

Voxy's registration process was originally multistep, a process that asked users to self-identify their level of English comprehension in order to customize their Voxy experience. However, users appeared to be confused by the process. Screen flow analysis showed that many users were confused, cycling back and forth through some of the signup pages. Only 20 to 30% got to the primary dashboard.

In response, Voxy redesigned its registration process to make it more streamlined and easier to understand. After launching the redesign, the percentage of users reaching the registration dashboard rose from 10 to 20% to 80 to 90%.

Voxy is an example of a data-driven company dedicated to using app analytics tools to optimize both its users' experience and the success of its apps.

Source: Raj Aggarwal, CEO Localytics.

In these questions are much of the crucial foundational knowledge you will need to know as soon as possible to begin successfully executing a mobile analytics project. In some cases, obtaining all of the answers will be hard, if not impossible; however, that is no excuse for not trying to answer them.

The mobile experience, of course, shares many of the elements of user experience and applied theoretical frameworks, such as the Eisenberg Brother's Persuasion Architecture or Gary Angel's excellent work on Semphonic's Functionalism.[1] People, however, do behave on mobile devices differently than on websites because of the screen size and the way users interact with mobile devices (via keys or by touching the screen). Thus, the analysis of the mobile experience must accommodate for new modalities of user input, types of funnels and flows that lead to conversion of desired actions (e.g., opening an account, making a purchase).

As with all analytical pursuits, Matt Cutler, the CEO of Kibits (www.kibits.com) recommends business leaders not overestimate the importance of mobile in the long run. Matt quotes Paul Saffo, of the Institute for the Future, about "macromyopia" or the "general human tendency to overestimate the short-term consequences of a profound new technology and underestimate them in the long term."[2] Business leaders should note the concept of macromyopia when thinking about mobile strategy, in the same way mobile analytics needs to be considering as only one channel—albeit a very important channel—across the digital analytics ecosystem.

In the future, it is entirely possible and quite likely that all devices will be wirelessly connected to the Internet (and thus also Internet-enabled) in large mesh networks across almost all human landscapes and living spaces. Televisions, refrigerators, dishwashers, home alarm systems—all Internet aware, all devices on which human behavior will occur. It is entirely possible that mobile analytics may become digital analytics or at least, in the future, will no longer be a differentiation between doing mobile analytics and digital analytics. For the benefit of clarity, I seek to explain in this chapter how mobile analytics, at the time of this writing, stands alone but is still a part of site and social analytics in the larger frame of digital analytics.

UNDERSTANDING MOBILE ANALYTICS CONCEPTS

Mobile analytics has concepts that should be defined and standardized, based on industry agreement across vendors, consultants, practitioners, and global industry associations. Until then, here is a helpful list of mobile concepts and their definitions:

- **Screen view (or page view).** A more contemporary and modern term for the viewing of content on the screen of a mobile device that may or may not be connected to the Internet at the time of viewing. Most businesses are still reconciling and struggling with Web analytics. Many businesses are stuck in the technical quagmire of tagging—and are still learning how to understand the difference between visitors and visits and what page views are in the world or RIA, AJAX, HTML5, and other rich, dynamic client-side experiences. Thus, the analytics industry is ready, but the general stakeholder who consumes analysis may not be ready.

- **Scan-through.** The transition from QR code embedded either online or offline, in digital or traditional media. QR code, once scanned by a mobile device, can render a user experience. When you scan a QR code with your mobile phone, the browser opens up with the site. A QR code is just like a "click through" only the user has to scan the code. Hence, it's called a "scan-through." In Asia, QR codes are well understood and are used ubiquitously but are much less frequently used in the United States.

- **API.** Application programming interface. Mobile data collection often requires the use of customer APIs specific to the vendor technology implemented directly into site code. APIs are used to collect data in mobile applications and mobile-specific website experiences when JavaScript is not possible for data collection. Mobile APIs are only restricted to a technology choice by the vendor. Software development kits (SDKs) are provided by mobile analytics vendors for data collection in languages such as Objective C, JSON, REST, and so on.

- **Site crossover.** When a mobile site or an application links back to a nonmobile site, such that the mobile experience crosses over to the website and renders a similar but different experience in a browser. For example, some mobile applications may require registration on the website in order to use the mobile application. In this case, user registration and signup may occur after clicking on a link in the mobile application and opening Safari or Chrome. This crossover from mobile to browser is necessary to measure.

- **Stitching.** Linking together what people do on mobile devices as those devices travel across distances. As one travels, a mobile device hops across the different towers, which can sometimes cause data anomalies. For example, cookies may get deleted or the IP address changes. Most mobile analytics software has functionality to help "stitch" together these breaks/disjointed streams.

Other digital analytics and social analytics concepts defined in Chapters 9 and 12 are relevant to mobile analytics and should be reviewed. Think how to apply the concepts outside of this chapter to mobile analytics. For example, mobile sites and applications also have visits, visitors, events, and conversions.

HOW IS MOBILE ANALYTICS DIFFERENT FROM SITE ANALYTICS?

Mobile analytics shares concepts both technically and analytically with digital analytics and can have similar analytical approaches, as well as frameworks applied to it, as to other digital experiences. Given this, why is it important to differentiate "mobile analytics" and call it out as a separate channel in digital analytics that, like social analytics, requires specialized knowledge and skills? Mobile analytics is different from other channels for digital analytics, such as social, interactive TV, gaming, and sites for the following reasons:

- **Mobile analysis often involves location-based segmentation.** The ability to segment your mobile analytics data by country, region/province, city, state, zip code, DMA, MSA, and other geographic constructs is necessary—and will likely be asked for.

- **The data collection on mobile platforms and in mobile experiences tends to use more complex programming languages and methods for collecting data.** In most cases, mobile data collection will involve using a software development toolkit (SDK) with an API. It may even be necessary to add libraries or other code to your mobile application to cache data when the application is offline.

- **Mobile data collection integrity must be ensured.** The accuracy of mobile data (and thus the veracity and relevancy of any analysis) can be easily affected by externalities related to carriers and wireless providers.

- **Mobile applications and other rich experiences may have features and capabilities that you can gain access to offline.** Mobile applications enable richer and different functionality than is available on live mobile websites, thus making them more challenging to measure.

- **Mobile analytics data may be incomplete.** Be careful setting expectations on mobile analytics because stakeholders may want identical rigor and depth of analysis on the mobile experience as on the main site experience. In these cases, allocate resources where revenue is at risk and to the digital channel with the most profitability.

- **Mobile analytics requires additional tools.** Mobile analytics is measured by internal tools deployed and operated by analytics or technical resources in brands, but also by audience measurement firms and third-party data vendors with a full complement of professional services. Although vendors of digital analytics platforms, such as IBM, WebTrends, and Omniture, have features and capabilities for mobile analytics, a class of software exists, named mobile analytics software, that was developed specifically for the mobile channel. Explore stand-alone software or SaaS mobile analytics vendors, as well as the larger analytics vendors who offer mobile analytics as a complement to their large digital analytics offerings.

■ **Mobile applications are not searchable.** For example, you can't search Google.com for the text and content in iPhone mobile applications in the same way you can for websites. As a result, sentiment analysis and text mining may not be possible. Android and iOS have different levels of openness on their platforms, which affects the way mobile analytical data have to be collected.

■ **Mobile applications may have restrictions on the type of data collection.** iOS has more stringent terms for mobile data collection than other platforms do. Collecting mobile data for aggregating the data and reselling it (audience measurement) can have obstacles on certain mobile platforms. Instrumenting mobile applications to collect data that helps the company improve a product or sell advertising is generally always allowed.

■ **Mobile experiences may incorporate other digital analytics channels.** The mobile experience may transition between the mobile application and the traditional website. It is not uncommon for a mobile application to spawn a browser for enabling some functionality, which, for one reason or another, requires a browser and a website.

■ **Mobile experience advertising requires specialized measurement.** Just as mobile analytics is a subset of digital analytics, mobile advertising has its own theory and nuance when compared to online display advertising. It is important to incorporate data about mobile advertising into media mix models.

A PERSPECTIVE ON MOBILE MARKETING

It has become something of a punch line to declare this "the year of mobile," because that's something that marketers and pundits have been saying for about five years running now. To me, though, there is a simmering revolution in mobile marketing. It ties into the thread of "mobile/social/local," and it is a true marketing evolution.

It is axiomatic that, like politics, all marketing is local. Yet what does local really mean? Historically, what it has meant is, there is some line drawn around a geographic area, and everything inside that line is a local area— whether it's a DMA, a store trading area, a radio metro, or an MSA. Local means all of the people and marketing variables inside that line. It's a sort of metaphorical lasso tossed around the waists of consumers bound together by the happenstance of proximity.

Traditional media such as TV, radio, print, and even direct mail and couponing have all developed around this model of localism; indeed, the DMA is actually a marketing geography specifically defined by how TV broadcast signals are distributed. Newspapers, billboards, TV stations, radio stations, and, to some extent, magazines are all dependent on distribution within a predefined "local" area. Advertising messages are pushed through these forms of media to people inside the local geography.

Yet mobile is wholly redefining "local." Instead of the concept of localism being the people inside a circle, mobile is turning local into a small circle drawn around the individual consumer. Each of us takes our own personal trading area with us wherever we go. Mobile is the key to delivering messages into that "trading area of one." That's why mobile is a game changer.

The consumer worth the most to a restaurant is the consumer who is five minutes away from that restaurant. Because of geo-location and micro-targetability (think Foursquare), mobile allows advertisers of any size to target the specific consumers who are, by current proximity, in their immediate target audience right this minute.

So far, much of mobile advertising has looked like traditional media advertising, writ small for the screens of mobile devices. Once all of the tools and the marketing infrastructures are in place to fully support messaging to the trading area of one, we'll suddenly find ourselves smack dab in the middle of the decade of mobile.

Source: Josh Chasin, chief research officer, comScore, Inc.

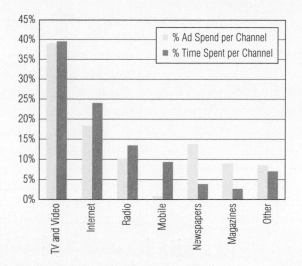

Exhibit 14.1 Time and Ad Spend for Various Media
Sources: www.emarketer.com/blog/index.php./numbers-major-media-ad-spending/;
www.emarketer.com/PressRelease.aspx?R=1008732.

IMPORTANCE OF MEASURING MOBILE ANALYTICS

Mobile is part of digital analytics. It is simply another channel to consider in the media mix, similar to television or radio. The importance of mobile is often completely underestimated, especially in the area of brand or advertising impact. The data in Exhibit 14.1 show the time spent on mobile compared to the time spent on other channels in the context of advertising spend in those channels.

Notice the large gaps in the bars of the histogram between print-related media and mobile in Exhibit 14.1. One could hypothesize from this data that advertising spend on the mobile channel will increase to close the gap between time spent on the mobile channel. The ubiquity of mobile devices, the affordability of wireless technology, the emerging VOIP (voice over IP) and advanced satellite technologies that are enabling mobile coverage across all countries on Earth indicate that more capital will flow into the mobile channel—and especially into advertising. The gap between ad money spent on mobile and time spent on mobile will narrow to look like that of television or radio.

In that gap and the closing of it lay possible huge revenue opportunities for companies innovating with big data science and statistical and machine learning and data mining the mobile channel. It's a gap, a revenue opportunity, and a new market that simply can't be ignored. This market is worldwide and growing—and the analysis of the mobile channel, when tied back to revenue, profit, and/or reduced expense, is absolutely required to compete in the mobile space. Those companies that understand why mobile analytics is important will be at an advantage against competitors as they innovate the future mobile business, advertising, and digital experiences that will create our shared mobile future.

MOBILE ANALYTICS TOOLS

Mobile analytics tools are similar to digital analytics tools. These tools allow for data collection, processing, reporting, visualization, and possibly even analysis. The best tools allow for the mobile data to be extracted from the tool and even integrated with other digital or traditional data.

Tools for mobile analytics are divided into the following categories:

- **Internal mobile measurement tools** are deployed either via software installed and maintained by IT in a data center or provided by a vendor as software as a service (SaaS). For example, WebTrends and Localytics.

- **External mobile measurement tools** are third-party data vendors who collect, aggregate, report, and offer analysis to customers from proprietary systems. For example, Groundtruth and comScore.

Because mobile is another digital channel, many of the same principles apply for determining how to select a mobile analytics tool as apply for selecting a digital analytics tool (see Chapter 9). Nuances on the mobile channel make it worth identifying the following challenges to collecting, reporting, and analyzing mobile data:

- **Data collection.** Not all mobile browsers execute JavaScript, so the most common method for collecting analytics data doesn't work across all devices. Thus, vendors offer us choices for data collection. Current mobile analytics offerings include image-based data collection methods, packet sniffers, server-side "no tag" implementations, and log files.

- **Unique visitor identification** is an issue, due to lack of cookie support and the changing of IP addresses. IP addresses on mobile browsers can change as they switch from tower to tower. In addition, many mobile devices will take the IP address of the gateway, making all of the devices look the same "person." Compounding the difficulty in assessing "uniqueness" is that not all mobile devices support cookies. As many of you know, in Web analytics, cookies are helpful in defining uniqueness and in mobile analytics are helpful in weaving together sessions when the IP address changes mid-session. The fallback method in analytics, when you can't use a cookie, is IP address/user agent. Thus, if you can't set cookies and the IP address and user agents are identical, then how do you identify uniqueness? That's the challenge. Interestingly, packet sniffing as a data collection method has an advantage here because some devices pass unique IDs (such as the phone number) in the HTTP header. When you can detect a unique value in the header, you can easily detect uniqueness.

- **Handset capability detection.** Companies that want to identify whether the device supports WAP pushing, streaming video, ringtones, downloading video clips, and so on, need to carefully select a measurement tool in order to ensure that these attributes are available.

- **Phone and manufacturer identification.** Databases from WURFL and DeviceAtlas can be used to identify phone and manufacturer device attributes. Larger vendors are further behind on integrating these data into their current offerings, whereas the smaller niche players are making use of it.

- **Screen resolution detection.** Mobile Marketing Association's guidelines for the four "standard" screen sizes may carry enough weight to push an often neglected or misunderstood site analytics concept, screen size, into part of the conversation for guiding user experience and interface design for mobile applications.[3] Screen size has been reported by site analytics tools for many years, and given the importance of creating compelling and persuasive experiences on mobile devices, it can be helpful to look at your audience's mobile device screen size.

- **Traffic source detection.** Determining the source of traffic, such as search, e-mail, direct entry, RSS feeds, and marketing campaigns, can be challenging in the mobile space.

- **Geographic identification.** Where are the visitors viewing your site coming from? And what does the mobile audience environment "look like" in each country? From this information, you can extrapolate country specifics for mobile site and application optimization and localization. Yet not all devices enable geographic detection because the gateway's IP address is used, rather than a GPS signal. If geo data are important to you, make sure you ask vendors that you are researching how they collect the data and what are the limitations.

Although many challenges still exist in collecting and reporting mobile analytics data, the industry is much further along than we were last year in delivering solutions in this space, and it's evolving rapidly. Still, vendors need to do a lot more work to improve the precision of the data they are collecting and the overall data about the mobile experience that they are reporting.

As you look toward purchasing the best solution for your company's needs, carefully consider the data you need to collect and report for analysis and judiciously choose the vendor that provides the most appropriate and extensible data collection and reporting capabilities that fit your business goals.

BUSINESS OPTIMIZATION WITH MOBILE ANALYTICS

You can create economic value in your business through applying mobile analytics in the following ways:

- **Determine the size of your mobile audience**, their unique demographic and psychographic characteristics, and their preferences for your products or services. Take it to the next level and identify your deduplicated audience across site and mobile—or all digital channels.

- **Use data to identify what types of content, experience, programs, and products to offer on your site.** Similar to the analytical product optimization with site analytics, use mobile analytics to enhance and improve your mobile products.

- **Use mobile analytics and behavioral data to feed other systems.** Digital analytics requires data integration across multiple channels, such as mobile.

- **Combine mobile analytical data with other market research or analytics.**

- **Incorporate mobile analytics data into your media mix model and attribution models.** This work requires data integration between your mobile channel data and other channels.

- **Determine the potential lifetime value of a new mobile customer**—or the incremental impact of the mobile channel on existing customer lifetime value. Apply traditional analytical methods, models, and techniques to the mobile customer, such as lifetime value (LTV)—as part of and segmented out from overall customer LTV.

- Although the mobile channel will only grow in prominence and importance over time, it's important to remember that as you do mobile analytics, it is only one channel of digital interaction with your brand. It is a unique channel with complexity across open and closed platforms, yet it is measurable and, if aligned to your business objectives, can provide valuable insight regarding your customers' digital experience.

KEY TAKEAWAYS

- Mobile analytics is a subset of digital analytics with unique concepts, which requires investment resources (people, training) and new or additional technology for capturing, reporting, and analyzing mobile data.

- Mobile analytics includes the measurement and analysis of both mobile sites and mobile applications. The analytics approach you take when measuring a mobile site or application is different than when measuring a site; however, best practices from site analytics should be reused whenever relevant and possible.

- Mobile analytics has new vocabulary that includes screen views, scan-throughs, and crossovers and will require using software development kits (SDKs) and application programming interfaces (APIs).

- Mobile analytics includes tools that can be run internally by a company or externally by a vendor. These tools have differentiated features for competitive analysis but may report conflicting and overlapping data, such as visitors.

- Mobile analytics has challenges and nuance, due to the proprietary open or closed nature of mobile platforms (such as iOS and Android), which brings additional complexity to the accurate collection of mobile data when compared to other digital channels.

- Mobile analytics can be used to optimize business. The data can be combined with site and social data or data from traditional analytics. Mobile data can be used for targeting and as input to larger marketing automation systems that use location for detecting, interacting, messaging, and (re)targeting people or customers.

- Mobile analytics may no longer need to be called out in the future as a subset of digital analytics because all Internet-enabled devices will be in an "always on" state, constantly connected to a wireless cloud or personalized mesh network, which moves with them wherever they go—allowing for highly personalized human experiences on a technology backbone. Thus, mobile analytics will likely be subsumed by digital analytics. Make sure to read about Saffo's concept of macromyopia.

NOTES

1. Bryan Eisenberg et al., "Persuasive Architecture: How to Get You Visitors to Take Action," grokdotcom.com, www.grokdotcom.com/persuasive-architecture.htm; Gary Angel, "Functionalism: A New Approach to Web Analytics" White paper, Semphonic, July 2006, www.semphonic.com/resources/wpaper_005.pdf.

2. David S. Isenberg et al., "SMART Letter #63," November 26, 2001, http://isen.com/archives/011126.html.

3. "Mobile Marketing Best Practice," Mobile Marketing Association, http://www.mmaglobal.com/bestpractice.

CHAPTER **15**

Effective Analytics Communication Strategies

"The single biggest problem in communication is the illusion that it has taken place."

—George Bernard Shaw

The success of any business or organization depends largely on how effectively its employees or members communicate. Whether it is at home, at work, in private, or in public, communication is the centerpiece in human relations. It enables and drives the quality of the relationship between people. Politicians, for instance, at any level of government—local, state, or federal—understand the power of effective communication and always focus in this area to ensure they have the right message delivered to the right audience. Why? Well, the content of the message and the ability to deliver it will influence perceptions, attitudes, and opinions and eventually shape the context in which actions can take place. Thus, failing to effectively deliver the message could undermine one's capacity to lead and get things done.

We have all heard at some point comments about companies eager to improve the communication skills of their C-level executives. Most of those companies understand the need to connect with their audience, the need to bond with their staff to get their message across the entire organization. Failing to get out the message that resonates with the audience (communicate effectively) can have a huge impact on the company brand, on employees' morale, and on the overall productivity of the organization.

The majority of large corporations are equipped with corporate communications teams. The key mandate of the communication team is to design effective messages and help the company connect with its employees, with its customers, or with the general public. Although politicians and organizations are all staffed with communication teams to disseminate information to their audiences, interestingly, analysts usually do not have any communication strategists; however, the most important area of their role includes effectively communicating with others, communicating their findings to a variety of audiences at different levels of the organization—more important, communicating analytics to executives. Similar to how it affects politicians, the quality of the analytics communication can have an impact on a career in analytics; it can make or break the execution of the findings and ultimately affect the company. If the message does not get to the right audience in the right way, the company will not be able to drive the change that reinforces analytics culture across the company.

In fact, most analysts are not traditionally known to be "good" and "effective" communicators. It is only recently that effective communication has become part of the curriculum, training, and education in analytics. Communication is an inherent part of the job. The ability to communicate clearly with peers, as well as with internal and external customers, is crucial to analytical success. End users need to understand the messages from the analytics team in order to take action, often changing their business processes. Therefore, the level and quality of the communication from analytics can have tremendous influence to drive the adoption and execution of the findings. From our experience in working for a variety of industries, we notice that there is often a communication gap between analysts and executives: analysts frequently complain about their findings not being used or not having any impact on the decision-making process, while executives claim that they have no clue about what the analytics team produces or simply say they can't use any analytics. Communication is probably one of the most undervalued analytics tool. It is a challenge some people in the analytics community are facing, and it can draw the line between an effective analyst and a typical analyst.

Your typical analysts focus mostly on doing their job, which could be anything from report creation to dashboard development to building predictive models. Most of them believe that their job ends once they send the results to their internal clients. In effect, they forget to effectively communicate their findings with their end users and do not realize that after sending the results, one portion of their job is finished, while the next portion of their job has just begun.

An effective analytics professional is one who will be able to bring the job to the next level by putting together communication material in order to convey the findings to end users, empowering them to act on the findings on all levels of the organization. For instance, if the analytical objective was to predict customer attrition, an effective analyst will not simply send to marketing a list of customers with the likelihood to churn. He or she will also summarize the reasons why customers are leaving the company in a way that people can read and understand, including what actions are needed. He or she will also present, explain, and answer questions about the findings to target groups to ensure that the key messages come across and that action will be taken based on the findings. An effective analyst will also illustrate the dollar value of taking the analytical recommendations.

COMMUNICATION: THE GAP BETWEEN ANALYSTS AND EXECUTIVES

We have seen examples of gaps in communication effectiveness between executives and analysts in multiple countries across the globe. Following are five typical quotes that exemplify the most common forms of analytical miscommunication:

1. "Oh, I didn't know we have that!" said a C-level sales executive, talking to the analyst about a report he'd received from the marketing manager on Fortune 1000 leads ranked by employee size. Yet in reality, this report was sent to him every quarter, but he never looked into it.

2. "I don't even know if they are using the list I have been sending every month!" said an analyst complaining to her manager that her job has no impact on the decision-making process.

3. "I didn't know you were also working on that list!" Communications between two analysts in different groups within the same company. The two analysts were working on producing the number of customers to call for a renewal campaign, one sitting in sales operation and another sitting in marketing analytics teams.

4. "I produce this every month, and I sent you the list last month!" said an analyst talking to a marketing manager who was asking for an insight that had been repeatedly sent to him for months.

5. "We receive this report every Monday from the analytics team. I don't even know what it's about and what to do with it. I simply archive it," said a sales manager.

All of the aforementioned examples have a common denominator: a communication gap between groups and within groups. That communication gap consists of the lack of effective communication that creates a duplication of efforts and a lack of actions taken from the analytics that is provided. In the previous examples, we clearly see some internal communication issues, where analysts in same group are not talking to one another or have duplicated their efforts and are working on the same requests in parallel. Also seen was a communication issue where a lot of data had been sent to different levels of the organization but was not being used.

Therefore, building an effective analytics solutions is not sufficient. We need to have people leveraging the analytics that is produced to make smarter decisions, address business challenges, and solve business problems. This will only happen if, once the analytics are completed, the findings and recommendations are clearly communicated to people who will take business action. Only communications can drive the intelligence obtained from analytics and empower the people within your organization. Empowering people means talking to them effectively in their language and sharing with them how the solutions could help them address the core business challenge. Empowering people is about having a clear strategy to communicate with them to close the analytics loop by effectively communicating findings with end users that can put analytics to work. Empowering people is about bridging that communication gap between analysts and informed decision makers. In this chapter, we will review what goes into an effective analytics communication strategy.

In the next sections, we will define effective analytics communication strategies by introducing the SELLING concept because effective analytics communication strategy is really about SELLING analytics findings to others. We will also provide some best practices on how to communicate analytics to executives.

AN EFFECTIVE ANALYTICS COMMUNICATION STRATEGY

From the analytics perspective, effective communication refers to the ability to convey information to the target audience. It is the activity of sharing analysis findings. It is about telling others what happened. What is happening? What will happen? And how does one's finding help the stakeholders address their business challenges? In effect, it is the ability to disseminate information effectively to others in a way that makes sense to your audience. Effective analytics communication strategy is about using simple words, sentences, tables, graphs, and other visual cues to represent the knowledge imparted from the data. Communicating findings from analytics involves "connecting the dots" between the overall business challenge down to what we observe and create from the data into insights that are relevant to the different stakeholders.

Effective communication also entails packaging a core message that reflects analytics' overall objective strategy, findings, purpose, and mission to convince key stakeholders and prepare them to embrace analytics and execute on the findings. It helps to frame the scope of analytics and set expectations for each stakeholder. To this end, one important tool to develop is an analytics communication plan that can synchronize organizational units and align resources to deliver a common core message from analytics. To be effective, an analytics communication plan is based on the SELLING concept as defined by the following:

Set clear goals for the analytics solutions.

Evaluate the target audiences to whom you have to convey the findings.

Lay out key findings and messages you would share with the audience.

Localize channels and tools you would use to deliver the solutions/findings.

Identify resources that you need to involve and to target, in order to implement analytics.

Normalize the time frame to deliver an update of the solutions.

Get feedback on, and the performance results of, analytics.

Set Clear Goals for Analytics Solutions

No matter what the deliverable (for example, whether you are providing a simple list of customers, a dashboard, a segmentation analysis, or a list of scored customers), you should begin by asking yourself, What is the "true" end goal? All effective analytics communication tries to influence other people to make them think differently, act differently, and interact differently with customers. Always take a second look at the deliverable, and ask yourself whether it meets this intent.

Make sure to have a clear sense of your communication purpose before communicating:

- What do you want your findings to do?
- What do you want from people you are addressing?

Nothing is more important to the success of any analytics solution than linking its findings to the business objectives that it seeks to address. As we discussed in previous chapters, analytics should always be tied to concrete business challenges, such as to

- Increase customer acquisition.
- Reduce customer attrition.

- Increase average spend per customer.
- Increase sales productivity.

Ask yourself what you can do to help your organization achieve its core objectives. For example, in churn reduction, the objective of the analytics solution is to provide the business with recommendations from your findings to address customer attrition. The goal of the analytics, in this case, is to help the company achieve its retention objectives. Analytics will achieve that goal by communicating clear answers to the following questions:

- Why will customers attrite?
- When will they attrite?
- Who are the customers who will attrite?
- What actions need to be taken with analytics?

Evaluate the Target Audience

In today's era of digital information, the explosion of data has created the need to leverage the knowledge that can be obtained from data. With almost every company and at all levels of the organization, people are looking for analytics to support their decision-making process. Therefore, the communication strategy needs to reinforce the focus on speaking the language of each audience and, more important, focus on what each level needs or wants to know, receives, and acts on. How will people leverage the solution to perform their daily activities? You should know your audience and identify their needs to ensure that you tailor the key messages when talking to them. We encourage using a "top down" approach because executives will provide the necessary support and sponsorship to drive the change that analytics solutions require, in order to put analytical intelligence in action.

From our experience in delivering analytics for companies operating in more than 55 countries around the globe, we noticed that analytics requirements and usability vary across all levels of the organization. Usage, we have found, is not only localized but is often based on roles and responsibilities. Therefore, the communication strategy should take these factors into account and adjust the message for each of the following roles and functions within your organization:

Roles
- C-level executive
- Vice president
- Director
- Manager
- Customer service representative (CSR)
- Sales service representative (SSR)

Functions
- Sales
- Marketing
- Services
- Management
- Product
- Finance
- Operations

Once you identify your target audience to whom you plan to communicate your findings, you should start building your talking points and crafting your key messages for each target group.

Lay Out Key Findings and Messages

It is important to lay out the main findings and messages that you want to share with the audience. The primary message should really be a story that you will create to share the findings. Think of it this way: if your stakeholders need to remember a few essential things from your analytics communication, what would they be? This is one of the most crucial steps in the analytics communication process, and it is not always managed effectively. Crafting the message from the deliverable means articulating the findings in a simple and actionable way to make sure stakeholders will understand the findings and act on them. As a reminder, the message should always be tied to the organizational business challenge and has to be simple and actionable for your stakeholder. From our expertise in delivering analytics to a variety of executives, we have noticed several major themes. Specifically, to get your message across with the most important group (executives), we recommend the following:

- Avoid using technical language.
- Don't try to teach them analytics; the business trusts you and expects you to master this area for them.
- Hone your elevator speech: be simple and deep; executives are looking for simple, actionable findings.
- Money talks. Always bring analytics to the bottom line:
  - Increase in revenue.
  - Reduction of cost increase.
  - Increases in the average spend per customer.
- Leverage clear visualization. Once again, a picture worth thousand words. The use of visualization can also help convey the message.
- We recommend using as few bullets as possible to summarize key findings.

For instance, in telecommunications, it is always better to explain why a customer will attrite, instead of talking about R square or any goodness of fit statistics of the regression model. Rather, say in four bullet points why this is happening. For example, maybe your findings indicate that customers attrite because

- The number of dropped calls has increased.
- The handset is pretty old.
- Billing errors are on the rise.
- They have reached out to the service team for help an average of seven times without the problem being resolved.

The second step is to provide actionable information to marketing and services so that they can work to intervene and prevent customer attrition. You need to convince them to use your findings by

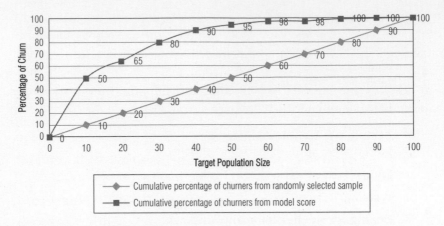

Exhibit 15.1 Cumulative Gain Chart: Model Score vs. Random Selection

communicating the value of using analytics (such as the predictive model). For example, the gain chart (Exhibit 15.1) will help convey the power of the predictive model. It would explain how the proactive intervention of marketing or sales could increase the return on investment (ROI). Exhibit 15.1 illustrates that by targeting only 10% of the universe of companies, leveraging the predictive model would help capture 50% of the churners.

Locate the Delivery Channels, Tools, and Activities

Like any product that is sold, successful analytics solutions are those that are being used by stakeholders at all levels of the organization helping the company solve its business problems. Therefore, it is imperative to ensure that analytics solutions are delivered to the most appropriate audience via the right channels using the right tools and activities. End users of the analytics should be categorized in groups according to what actions they will be taking with the analytics. This will help determine the best medium to communicate analytics to them.

In terms of activities, we recommend setting up some regular communications and updates with each of the target audiences, as well as tailoring tools and activities to each level of the audience that is targeted.

Delivery channels and tools could include:

- Navigators (a go-to person in analytics in charge of gathering analytics requests from business partners and communicate findings)
- Executive update through PowerPoint presentation
- Visual (graph, map, picture)
- Presentation to managers and end-users
- Lunch and learns
- Web applications tools
- Internal newsletter, monthly or quarterly
- Analytical brief
- Central repository
- Project plan summary (resources roles and responsibilities)

As an example, Exhibit 15.2 illustrates the communication channel delivery tools and activities across three levels in the organization for customer scoring (that helps to identify what companies are more likely to attrite).

Identify Resources that You Need to Involve and to Target

After securing what channel you should use to deliver analytics effectively, it is important to identify what resources are involved. This is crucial because it will ensure that all communications channels are leveraged and that the message is consistent across every level of the organization. It will also help set legitimate levels of expectations while communication is taking place with the right audience.

One of the authors, Jesse Harriott, who leads the Global Insights team at Monster, introduced the concept of navigators to make sure that communication between the Global Insights team and the Monster business partners in more than 55 countries was effective in all regions where the company operates leveraging analytics. What is a navigator? The navigator is a dedicated resource in the analytics team, generally a good communicator who serves as the bridge between

Solutions	Audiences	Channel	Tools	Activities
Scoring	C-Level Executive	Navigator	■ Executive PowerPoint Presentation ■ Executive Tools ■ Executive Dashboard or Web Application	■ Meetings ■ Executive One-Pager ■ Newsletter
	Manager	Navigator	■ Manager PowerPoint Presentation ■ CRM System, Where the Info Is Available ■ Sales Manager Dashboard	■ Regular Meetings ■ Project Plan
	Sales and Service Representatives	Navigator	■ PowerPoint Presentation ■ CRM System, Where the Info Is Available ■ Sales Dashboard	■ Regular Meetings ■ Project Plan

Exhibit 15.2 Delivery Tools and Activities for Customer Scoring

business partners and the analytics team. His or her role helps both the analytics team and the business. Whenever a business partner from marketing, finance, product, sales, or services has a request, this individual channels it through the navigator who will work with the target analytics resources to make sure the request is satisfied. For the analytics team, the dedicated navigator communicates analytics findings and messages to the business partners. For the business partners, the navigator gathers their requests and assigns them to the appropriate groups in the analytics team that will take care of the actual analytical work. Once the analysis is completed, the groups discuss the findings with the dedicated navigator and potentially with other analysts as well. A navigator, as described in Exhibit 15.3, is a facilitator between groups. Using a navigator to identify resources and communicate with the business partners should prevent any derailing from the business focus and ensure that the message is being delivered on time and, more important, that the solution is actionable and is put into execution by the stakeholder.

Normalize the Time Frame

Once resources are identified, we recommend that you document an analytics project plan jointly with other functional teams. This should be in place as the reference guide to manage the project from start to finish. Involving cross-functional groups early will secure their commitment and streamline the adoption and usage of the solution

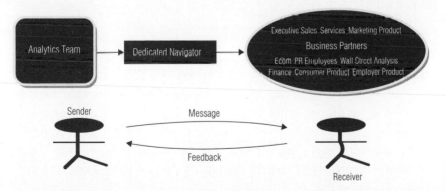

Exhibit 15.3 Analytics Team Engagement Model: Communication via the Navigator

produced. It will also set and manage expectations about the details of the solutions and timeline for delivery. More important, the project plan helps ensure that analytics delivers what it promised.

Get Feedback and Track Results

As part of the two-way communication process, we have found it very useful to get direct and honest feedback from end users of the analytics solutions. Therefore, we recommend that you formally and informally survey your customers, clients, and other partners about analytics you have delivered. Ask about their perceptions of what you do well. What is working? Identify obstacles that exist in adopting the analytics solution, which will also help optimize your communication plans.

Also, tracking the results is a key component of any analytics solution because it leads to the ability to communicate the value of analytics to the organization. For example, when predicting customers' attrition rate using analytics from our model and explaining how to prevent this attrition, we can show that by increasing the retention rate by 3%, it results in an additional $4 million of revenue. Results tracking can also help evangelize other groups in the organization that are not using analytics and can convince them to adopt the analytics plan.

Exhibit 15.4 summarizes the SELLING concept framework that we covered in an earlier section. It is useful guidance for an effective analytics communication strategy.

ANALYTICS COMMUNICATION TIPS

Although business analytics is about creating value, we have seen throughout this book that putting analytics to work requires a need for change. In turn, change management requires sponsorship from the executive team, and, as we all know, the execution of the intervention prescribed by the analytics team is not always owned by that team. Hence, in order to work with and through other teams, effective communication is the essential tool. Therefore, within the framework of communication and change management, you should consider the following items:

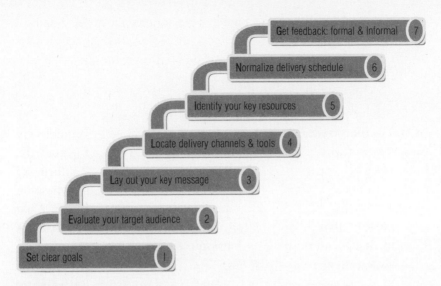

Exhibit 15.4 The SELLING Strategy for Effective Analytics Communication

- Get commitment and the buy-in from target audiences to adopt the solutions.
- Achieve consensus on how to put analytics to work in the organization.
- Achieve consensus on how to deliver the solutions.
- Review and prioritize the business challenge.
- Prepare the audience for the change.
- Plan the timeline accordingly.
- Set the right expectations.
- Manage changes.

Communication is the biggest challenge some analysts face. It is sometimes their pitfall, simply because analysts primarily care about doing analytics, and it is sometimes difficult for them to get out of their analytics comfort zone. To communicate analytics effectively, analysts need to really spark their audience's interest and attention, by focusing on what is important to them. Following are some tips on how to communicate analytics:

- Have a communication plan.

- Include an agenda.

- Know your audience.

- Put the findings in context.

- Use examples that everyone can relate to.

- Have key talking points or key messages.

- Use simple and clear tables, graphs, charts, and other visual cues.

- Formalize recommendations, takeaways, and next steps.

- Allow time for questions from stakeholders, to obtain feedback.

- Realize that the audience members' level of understanding varies, based on their background.

- Present the information differently to different people.

- Communicate well to promote the benefits of analytics.

Communication is a crucial step in analytics implementation and analytics delivery. Successful implementation is always supported by an effective communications plan and strategy.

COMMUNICATING THROUGH MOBILE BUSINESS INTELLIGENCE

The use of mobile devices has exploded during the last 10 years. With larger screen sizes, faster download speeds, and application development, the mobile device as a business tool has become a reality. Business decisions and sales are now frequently made outside of the office—at the airport, in a hotel lobby, or at an industry conference. This change in business behavior presents another communication channel in which to deliver your team's analytic tools and insights. Analytics can no longer rely on being able to simply send insights via a PowerPoint deck or Excel files. Mobile communication channels are becoming increasing important, as business users desire timely and effective analytics that is available on the go.

Howard Dresdner (a former Gartner research fellow) is bullish on mobile as a communication channel for business analytics, saying, "In the future mobile BI will not only be a growing fact but will become the main form of delivering for business analytics and the focal point of the entire industry." He believes that mobile BI (business intelligence) will fundamentally become the new platform for business intelligence.[1] Aberdeen outlined the drivers underpinning the adoption and implementation of mobile BI:

- Ability to achieve a competitive advantage.
- Can increase the productivity of mobile workers.
- Ability to eliminate delays in alerting key decision makers to critical information.[2]

What is mobile BI? Mobile BI is the process of providing actionable and interactive business intelligence solutions via a mobile phone or device such as smartphone, a tablet, or a portable computer. Being able to gain access to, read, write, and visualize KPI dashboards, analytically driven alerts, predictive analytics model results, segmentation, customer data, and other analytics via a mobile phone is the promise of mobile BI. Mobile BI offers people the flexibility to efficiently gain access to BI insights to drive the business. Mobile BI is typically achieved via software that extends a desktop BI application so that it can be used on a mobile device. However, sometimes mobile BI is delivered through customized mobile interfaces developed internally.

Mobile BI provides ready-to-use information wherever your end users happen to be located. Effective mobile BI must optimize a traditional BI report so that it can be accessible and viewed easily on a small screen. For example, critical KPI alerts with spark line trend graphs are an ideal application of mobile BI. We believe there are several benefits companies can achieve by embracing mobile BI as a communications channel:

- Helps increase the efficiency and productivity of mobile workers.
- Helps enable faster business decisions through people having access to critical information.
- Reduces the time to inform decision makers.
- Is usually a competitive advantage (for the time being).

■ Can help sales reps in the field strengthen customer relationships.

■ Helps save time because field workers do not need to power up a different device to gain access to important information.

Gartner predicts that 33% of BI functionality will be consumed via mobile devices by 2013.[3] Therefore, we recommend that your organization embraces mobile BI as another communications channel that can help demonstrate the value of analytics to your business.

 KEY TAKEAWAYS

■ Effective analytics communication strategy is the ability to convey findings to stakeholders, making sure that the message is tailored to the audience's role and responsibility.

■ In this new era of big data, the key to assessing, managing, and harnessing that data intelligence lies in the ability to effectively communicate analytics to decision makers. Winning with analytics requires effective analytics communication at all levels of the organization.

■ Intelligence that is not shared (or is shared with only a few people) is not valuable. A broad communications strategy will enhance the business impact of your analytics considerably.

■ Effective communications is an undervalued analytics tool, and sometimes analysts may not be great communicators. They believe that providing a list or a PowerPoint presentation is getting the job done. We argue that it is just the beginning.

■ Effective communication entails packaging a core message that reflects analytics' overall objective strategy, findings, purpose, and mission to convince key stakeholders and prepare them to embrace analytics and execute on the findings. It helps frame the scope of analytics and set expectations for each stakeholder. To this end, an analytics communications plan should synchronize organizational units and align resources to deliver a common core message from analytics.

■ Analytics is effectively communicated when it leverages a communication plan based on the SELLING concept:

■ Set clear goals for the analytics solutions.

■ Evaluate the target audiences to whom you have to convey the findings.

■ Lay out key findings and messages you would share with the audience.

■ Localize channels and tools you would use to deliver the solutions/findings.

- Identify resources that you need to involve and to target.
- Normalize the time frame to deliver an update of the solutions.
- Get feedback on, and the performance results of, analytics.
- To be effective, analytics should have a navigator who helps ensure smooth communication between stakeholders and the analytics group.
- Effective analytics communication always provides a clear answer to a business question, not merely another piece of data.
- The analytics communication should focus on the business impact of the findings. If the information doesn't help lead to an action, don't provide it.
- We also provided some best practices when communicating analytics to executives: speak their language, always bring it back to dollars, use your best elevator speech, avoid technical details, and use clear analytics visualization.

NOTES

1. Lachlan James, Dresner: Mobile Business Intelligence to Transform BI Industry," *Dashboard Insight*, April 6, 2011, http://www.dashboardinsight .com/articles/business-verticals/dresner-mobile-business-intelligence-to-transform-bi-industry.aspx.

2. Andrew Borg and David White, "Mobile BI: Actionable Intelligence for the Agile Enterprise," Aberdeen Group, December 2010, http://www.dataskill .com/pdf/Aberdeen%20-%20BI-Mobile.pdf.

3. "Gartner Says New Relationships Will Change Business Intelligence and Analytics," Press release, Gartner, January 6, 2011, http://www.gartner .com/it/page.jsp?id=1513714.

CHAPTER **16**

Business Performance Tracking

Execution and Measurement

"A little knowledge that acts is worth infinitoly more than much knowledge that is idle."

—Khalil Gibran

Business performance tracking is part of the Business Analytics Success Pillars (BASP) framework we introduced in detail in the second chapter of this book. The BASP framework is made up of the following pillars:

- **Business challenge pillar.** The most pressing business problems that you seek to address using analytics.

- **Data foundation pillar.** The data that will support the analytics process.

- **Analytics implementation pillar.** The logistics of how to execute analytics systems and processes in a way that addresses your business challenges.

- **Insights pillar.** The key to business impact, and often the most difficult step, lies in the ability to take raw data and turn it into a compelling narrative that addresses specific business challenges and results in business actions.

- **Execution and measurement pillar.** Analytical intelligence must be put to work to provide tools and guidance that lead to business actions and must have the ability to track the impact of those actions.

- **Distributed knowledge.** There must be a conscious and concerted effort to communicate, disseminate, and make analytics available broadly across the organization.

- **Innovation pillar.** Analytic teams must be aggressive in the use of new ideas or methods to address business challenges and go beyond customer expectations.

In this chapter we will focus on the execution and measurement pillar. Our goal is to elevate the discussion on how to monitor, measure, and analyze the business performance of actions taken by the organization. Every business decision or action has implied questions for the future, in order for the company to understand whether there was a successful business outcome. The execution and measurement pillar is also about effectively following up on the results of actions based on decisions across the entire organization. Business performance tracking and measurement should be an integrated process that assesses the performance of analytics-driven changes.

In the previous chapters, we discussed the predominance of big data in today's business environment, and we underscored that big data offers opportunities to do things that could not be done before. We outlined that big data has also added another layer of information that's available, to capture new metrics and to deepen a company's understanding of customers' feedback reactions, needs, and preferences.

Media fragmentation and the pervasiveness of social media have increased customers' demands and expectations, creating unprecedented competitive pressures on companies. This phenomenon has resulted in an accelerated rate in which data creation, transfer, analysis, and response are processed. In addition, the more transparent business environment enables data to affect corporate accountability and often leads to higher customer expectations, because companies are now competing for the same customers. Needless to say, these conditions do not offer most companies a second chance to get it "right," because everyone is monitoring those interactions. To maintain their competitive advantage, forward-looking companies are leveraging analytics to realize their core strategies and business objectives.

As noted in Chapter 15 on effective analytics communication, analytics should be action oriented. We also underscored that effective analytics communication is about getting feedback and tracking the results. Then, within the analytics implementation pillar, we highlighted two key elements that really drive analytics implementation: (1) the transformation of data into intelligence, and, (2) more important, the staff's response on the intelligence produced. Both production and execution of the intelligence are needed to make up business performance. However, this is not enough; we also need to measure, monitor, test, and tweak the results of the solutions to justify the return on investment (ROI) in the short and long term.

From our experience implementing analytics in more than 55 countries and working with a broad spectrum of executives, we noticed that the most important step in the process of production and execution of intelligence is the measurement of the results. Why? Well, as Peter Drucker says, "If you can't measure you can't manage."[1] Building an analytics solution without implementing a measurement process to track the results is a recipe for failure. And because the insights of analytics should lead to actions from the organization, measurement is key in order to monitor the success or lack of success. Our experiences, coupled with interviews we recently conducted to enrich this book, pointed us to the conclusion that a company's response to its analytics is the foundation of the business performance. Our approach covering business performance execution and tracking is five-fold, as outlined in the process seen in Exhibit 16.1.

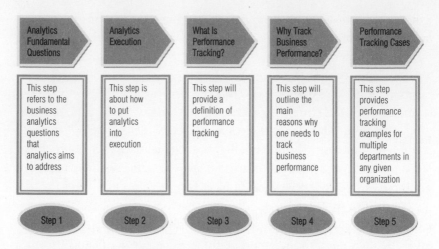

Exhibit 16.1 Business Performance Five-Step Process

ANALYTICS' FUNDAMENTAL QUESTIONS

Before addressing performance execution and tracking, we believe it is important to go back to the basics and review the fundamental business questions that analytics aims to address. We will then evaluate how those questions resonate into business actions. Regardless of the organization, business challenges that analytics must address often fall into one of the following categories:

- Reduce cost
- Increase market share
- Increase customer retention
- Increase customer acquisition
- Increase profitability

The fundamental questions remain the same and are about analyzing, understand, monitoring, measuring, and planning:

- What has happened?
- What is happening now, and why is this happening?
- What will happen?

Once completed, analytics findings can then be shared with the rest of the business. Those findings provide answers to the

Functions	Past	Present	Future
Analytics Team	What happened?	What is happening, and why is this happening?	What will happen?
Executive Team	How did we do?	How are we doing?	What should we do?

Exhibit 16.2 Advanced Business Analytics Questions

aforementioned questions and are directed toward a clear business outcome. Exhibit 16.2 illustrates how analytics questions are translated into fundamental business questions that will drive the execution of the company's strategy and address its business challenges.

The future side of Exhibit 16.2 (What will happen? What should we do?) is the main focus of this chapter; it is the key aspect of performance tracking and execution. This is because the goal of business analytics is to predict or anticipate the future of a business action or circumstance. In turn, that prediction will inform the execution of the business response from each department to create a positive and profitable customer experience.

ANALYTICS EXECUTION

Once analytics solutions are delivered by the analytics team to address core business challenges, the execution of the analytics is the next step. The decision makers and stakeholders who have championed the cause should ensure that any follow-up business actions are taken. Execution makes or breaks the company's benefit from analytics. If you don't execute and take action, you will not see the full benefit of analytics and will also be at a competitive disadvantage from other companies that are acting on analytical insights. This is one of the reasons that analytics execution shouldn't be relegated to a single department; it should include all sections of the business that affect the customer experience.

As an illustration, let us consider an analytics project where the business goal is to increase customer coverage through new customers, as well as increased retention of existing customers. The analytics execution for that project should be based on a strategy that includes two principal tools:

1. The executive customer experience one-pager, and
2. The segmentation grid/matrix.

The customer experience one-pager in Exhibit 16.3 provides information that gives a 30,000-foot view of the suggested solution and measurement of analytics execution. It is made up of two major components. The first component is an outline of the customer relationship management (CRM) stages: it lays out customer life cycles from prospect to churn. The second component is the core of analytics execution and tracking, which includes

- Business goals
- Analytics solutions
- Actions/execution
- Metrics /data elements
- Benchmark and measurement
- Time frame

With the customer experience one-pager, every department involved in the ultimate customer experience will begin to see how it can leverage analytics for each customer's stage and with each customer segment. In turn, new analytics findings should drive subsequent response, enabling the organization to be flexible and use coordinated efforts across departments. This one-pager, properly shared across the organization, will enable synchronization of customer relationship management analytics action and, more important, coordination and effective execution and tracking of the performance. This plan will help outline what each team should be doing and what other teams are doing with the customer. Executives can also get a blueprint of CRM analytics activities from every department of the organization.

The second component of great analytics execution, in our example customer coverage project, is the segmentation grid. Major customer touch points, such as sales, marketing, and customer services, must have coordinated actions on the insights provided by the

CRM/LCM	CRM Status	Prospect	Candidate	Customer		Inactive/Churn
	CLC Stage	Reach	Acquisition	Conversion	Retention	
	CLC Objective	React	Acquire	Convert	Retain	Win Back
Analytics Team	Goal					
	Solutions					
	Action/Execution					
	Metrics/Data Elements					
	Benchmark/Measurement					
	Time Frame					
Functional Team(*)	Goal					
	Solutions					
	Action/Execution					
	Metrics/Data Elements					
	Benchmark/Measurement					
	Time Frame					

(*)Functional Team includes: Marketing, Sales, Customer Service, IT, Finance, HR, Product, Operations

Exhibit 16.3 Customer Experience One-Pager

analytics team. Many forward-looking companies have embraced analytics to compete, and one of the cornerstones of their strategy is segmentation. Why? For companies to become responsive to different types of customers, the needs of those customers must be defined and contrasted. Based on our experiences with a broad spectrum of organizations in multiple industries, we have found that scoring and segmentation of customers and prospects is not only very effective, it should be considered a best practice. Time and time again, it has been found that the segmentation approach leads to the better customer execution, because it "models" customer behavior and sets expectations for better servicing, prioritization, and, ultimately, customer experience.

The segmentation grid is a tool to illustrate the insights from customer scoring on two axes. It looks at the propensity to convert (Exhibit 16.4) or churn (Exhibit 16.5) as a function of customer lifetime value (CLTV). By mapping the percentage of your customers who

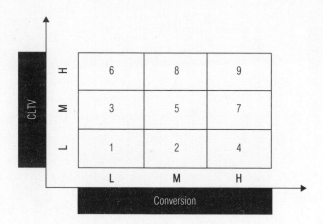

The Y-axis is the CLTV: Customer Lifetime Value

The X-axis is the Conversion: Propensity to Convert

The letters H M L stand for

H: High   Segment 9: High Conversion and High CLTV

M: Medium   Segment 8: Medium Conversion and High CLTV

L: Low   Segment 7: High Conversion and Medium CLTV

Exhibit 16.4 Customer Prospects Segmentation Grid

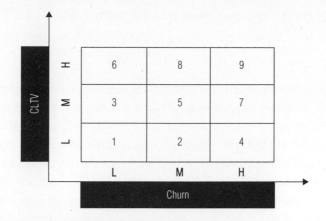

The Y-axis is the CLTV: Customer Lifetime Value
The X-axis is the Churn: Propensity to Churn
The letters H M L stand for

H: High   Segment 9: High Churn and High CLTV
M: Medium   Segment 8: Medium Churn and High CLTV
L: Low   Segment 7: High Churn and Medium CLTV

Exhibit 16.5   Customer Churn Segmentation Grid

fall into each of the different groups, it gives you a perspective on which prospects are most likely to turn into customers, as well as which customers are most likely to stay with your company long term. The focus of the grids in these two areas is to ensure that the organization treats each customer in a strategic manner by rewarding certain behavior, while having a basic service level to ensure a positive customer experience.

In Exhibit 16.4, the segmentation grid for prospects, it highlights the likelihood of converting a potential customer to an actual customer, plotting this against CLTV. When you look at your customers in aggregate in this manner, it will help your organization prioritize acquisition strategies to drive CLTV and increase conversion. It helps focus the organization on the most-likely-to-convert prospects. It helps lead to future actions by stimulating the questions. What will happen, and what should we do? Propensity to convert and CLTV for the three segment groups can be described as

- High likelihood to convert includes micro segments 7, 8, and 9.

- Medium likelihood to convert includes micro segments 4, 5, and 6.

- Low likelihood to convert includes micro segments 1, 2, and 3.

The segmentation grid in Exhibit 16.5 is focused on existing customers, rather than on customer prospects. It shows the likelihood for an existing customer to stop being a customer. This type of scoring and analysis enables the prioritization of targeted retention strategies toward your existing customers. It helps focus the organization on the most likely to churn customers. By looking at the percentage of your customers in each group, you can gain perspective regarding the stability of your customers to continue doing business with your organization. By taking action on the insights in this type of grid, hopefully you will reduce your customer churn rate. The grid can be thought of in three segment groups, described as the following:

- High likelihood to churn includes micro segments 7, 8, and 9.

- Medium likelihood to churn includes micro segments 4, 5, and 6.

- Low likelihood to churn includes micro segments 1, 2, and 3.

Using these two grids, your business analytics team can provide multiple insights to help identify at-risk customers, as well as the most attractive prospects. Providing actionable intelligence that the company can put into effect is key. That actionable intelligence in our hypothetical example of increasing customer coverage may include:

- For customer retention: a stack-ranked list of all customers with their likelihood to churn, including possible explanations or theories for the reason.

- For prospects: a stack-ranked list of prospects who will convert to being customers, including the reasons.

Marketing, sales, and customer service can leverage those findings to prioritize their acquisition and retention activities.

After getting customers and prospects scored and segmented, as described, we can now introduce the execution process. For each functional group or department, execution is about building up analytically based activities and "treatments" to serve these segments, based on the scoring prioritization. In the following, brief examples of

Department	Business Challenge	Analytics Solutions	Execution/ Actions	Measurements
Advanced Analytics	Reduce Customer Churn	Build churn predictive models to identify who are customers who will churn. Why and when?	Provide the target list of most likely to churn customers prioritized by other variables.	-Model performance -Increase customer retention.
Marketing	Reduce Customer Churn	Leverage churn predictive model's findings to develop some proactive retention offering and messaging for every segment.	Send target marketing CRM campaigns to every customer's segment (at-risk to churn).	Track: -Response rate -Renewal rate -Increase in customer retention and loyalty
Sales	Reduce Customer Churn	Leverage churn predictive model to prioritize activities on high CLTV and high likelihood to churn customers in high segment.	Prioritize daily activities to reach out to at-risk customers based on scoring and segmentation. Optimize the coverage model.	-Intensifying touches on highly scored account. -Renewal customer -Renewal amounts -Renewal rate and loyalty
Customer Services	Reduce Customer Churn	Leverage at-risk customer scoring as described on table to prioritize proactive retention activities.	Prioritize daily activities to proactively reach out to those customers based on the scoring and segmentation; leveraging predefined offering and messaging for inbound calls.	-Number of outreaches to at-risk customers -Number of at-risk satisfied customers -Overall customer satisfaction

Exhibit 16.6 Outreach Execution Table: Customer Churn

analytics execution in marketing, sales, and customer service teams are provided.

- **Analytics execution in marketing.** Marketing execution means that marketing, for instance, will send its campaigns based on the segment score of the existing customers who are more likely to attrite, starting with the high group (9, 8, 7) and then the medium group (4, 5, and 6).

- **Analytics execution in sales.** From the sales team's perspective, execution is about prioritizing its customers' touch points to maximize revenue in high-value segments. The sales team could also optimize sales headcount planning and its account coverage models.

- **Analytics execution in customer service.** Customer service should have a special outreach program to target those considered at risk but who are valuable customers.

Actions across all of these departments should be integrated, as described in the "Outreach Execution Table" in Exhibit 16.6, where we have used churn reduction as an example. For example, a contact strategy using a given set of business rules ensures the coordination of efforts across all relevant departments of the organization and helps ensure that the customer is not bombarded with contacts from multiples channels. This approach is one that is customer-centric, not product-centric, and necessitates a certain process and incentive structure.

BUSINESS PERFORMANCE TRACKING

Performance tracking analyzes the success of a company's initiatives or activities by comparing what actually happened to what was planned or predicted. We outlined that analytics implementation requires changes in the way people do things. We started the book with the analytics challenge, and, more important, we underscored that the ultimate goal of any analytics project is to address critical business challenges. Yet a key question remains: after implementing analytics, have we seen any business changes? To answer that question, we have to measure the results of analytics-based actions. Therefore, business performance tracking asks questions such as

- Have we seen any changes in the way that sales representatives cover their territories?
- Have we seen any increase in customer retention?
- Have we seen any increase in customer acquisition?
- Have we seen any increase in the average spend per customer?
- Have we seen any increase in customer up-sell?

Performance tracking is not only the measurement of analytics solutions at work. It is also about managing the evaluation of the impact of the analytics business solutions and is a closed feedback cycle. It is an ongoing quality improvement process, where the tracking of the solutions delivered versus the results achieved, based on a specific set of key metrics or indicators, is constantly evaluated.

For instance, if the business goal is to reduce churn, we need to evaluate whether the churn has actually decreased after the implementation of the proactive program. Likewise, if the business goal is about increasing the market share, the measurement of number of new customers or the amount of new revenue needs to be captured. This can also be applied to other areas of the organization—for instance, recommending that sales reps engage in certain kinds of activities to optimize revenue. Tracking these activities through key performance indicators, such as the number of phone calls on a daily basis, can guide performance measurement and be related to revenue. Although we know that nothing in life is perfectly linear, we are trying to convey that certain analytics-based actions can affect the bottom line, while others might not.

Why have business performance tracking in analytics? Because we know that analytics execution requires a change of business processes, and in order to understand the impact of the change, you have to be able to implement and measure it. As Gary Cokins recalled in his book *Performance Management*, balanced scorecards developed by Robert Kaplan and David Norton recognize the shortcomings of executive management's excessive emphasis on short-term financial results.[2] He also added, "Performance measures motivate people and focuses them on what matters the most." Bruno Aziza and Joey Fitts have also noted that business performance is the key enabler of intelligent business execution. They summarized that intelligent execution falls under three core capabilities: monitor, analyze, and plan.[3] From our experience, the benefits of performance tracking include but are not limited to the following:

Benefit 1: Return on investment (ROI) tool. Performance reporting is a tool and a manner by which one can justify investments and provide relevant meaningful answers to the following cost-benefit business questions:

- Was it worth investing in business intelligence resource tool solutions?
- Was it worth spending money in marketing for traffic?
- Was it worth it to pay for a TV ad?
- Was it worth it to run a marketing CRM campaign?

Measurement of the ROI is key to help us understand the success of an initiative. It also helps in building a business case for a request for additional funds and resources. Tracking the results helps stakeholders evaluate their efforts and tactics and adjust them when necessary. With performance tracking, a company can forecast and monitor productivity and profitability and become an innovator.

Benefit 2: Organizational goal settings and reinforcement. Because performance managements start with a company's goals and objectives or a business challenge, measurement is crucial across the entire organization. It helps set up some goals of the business intelligence solutions and generates people's interest and belief across the entire organization.

Benefit 3: Change management engine. Performance management offers the ability to properly implement analytics and leverage it. It provides an opportunity to assess your company's capacity to undertake analytics implementation. What are the strengths and weaknesses? Because performance execution and measurement are an integrated process involving multiple departments, performance management helps identify the different types of risk, in terms of resources, to achieve the target goals.

Benefit 4: Adoption, incentives, and rewards. The process of adoption is important, because it measures how the organization manages change as a whole and embraces new processes. As a result, it is essential that this process is managed and rewarded accordingly. Incentive for change must not only be promoted but must also be rewarded internally. This should help to

■ Increase the adoption of analytics.

■ Help sell analytics to other groups by sharing what is working and other best practices.

Benefit 5: Enhanced accountability. Setting up clear goals to be achieved and measuring the results will definitely reinforce accountability at every level of the organization that is involved. Accountability drives a change in behavior and usually helps get things done. It could also help redefine roles and responsibilities, based on business expectations on achieving the business's core objectives. Reinforce accountability, productivity, and efficiency by improving ownership and appraisal.

Benefit 6: Value of leading with analytics. It also helps demonstrate the following attributes of advanced analytics: validity, reliability, credibility, and functionality. It helps reinforce credibility and visibility with its underlying results. It helps you ensure that the entire organization sees the added value of analytics. And reinforcing accountability shows the contribution of everyone in the organization toward the end goal.

Benefit 7: Progress tracking and updates for stakeholders on the value of analytics. Measuring the progress and results over time gives a company the opportunity to assess and improve analytics quality, as well as people's underlying actions and activities. It helps a company evaluate whether the changes dictated by the analytics solutions are working. It also helps a company track progress and improve the quality of the service delivered to internal and external customers.

In the following sections, we outline some performance tracking cases and how they work across sales, marketing, customer services, and other departments in the organization. Depending on the business goal you seek to address, there are countless data elements, metrics, and measurements that could be monitored, measured, and analyzed, and you can find several books that fully cover business performance. Our objective is just to share some simple examples of performance execution and measurement best practices, based on specific business goals and using a defined set of metrics. For each of the departments, the following approach will be used to discuss performance execution and tracking:

- Overview of the department and key responsibilities
- Analytics-based actions to address goals and objectives
- Executing and tracking the performance using a target goal as an example
- Performance tracking and execution table summary

ANALYTICS AND MARKETING

Most companies spend a significant portion of their overall corporate budget on marketing. Responsibilities of the marketing department vary, depending on the industry, the size, and the corporate structure. For some, marketing is the big spender "cost center," while for others, it is a strong "revenue generator." In today's fast-evolving competitive marketplace, the predominance of business analytics, in tandem with the proliferation of data availability and technology, challenge the old notion of "spray and pray" marketing. Marketing is no longer expected to be only a creative center, but is also expected to be a strategic partner that is driven by analytics to support the overall customer acquisition and management process. The recent global recession has increased marketing accountability, while at the same time, companies reduced their marketing budgets. As a consequence, greater results are expected with fewer resources, and the need for transparency and accountability rules. Today, marketing departments have to track the return on every major investment they engage in. Whether it is branding, advertising, or driving the overall strategy by stimulating growth and rewarding customers, forward-looking marketing departments must leverage analytics to achieve their key objectives. Depending on the corporate structure, key responsibilities of the marketing department may include

- Owning the brand
- Managing customer relationships
- Focusing on customers' experience
- Planning the overall company business strategy
- Managing the company's market mix: product, promotion, placement, and price
- Supporting sales, service, and distribution partners
- Managing the competitive strategy
- Managing external company communications

MACYS.COM SEES WHAT'S IN STORE FOR CUSTOMERS

CASE STUDY

After more than 80 years in business, Macy's Inc. is one of America's most iconic retailers. With annual revenues exceeding $20 billion, Macy's enjoys a loyal base of customers who come to its stores and shop online each day. To continue its legacy of providing stellar customer service and the right selection of products, the retailer's e-commerce division—Macys.com—is using analytical software from SAS to better understand and enhance its customers' online shopping experience, while helping to increase the retailer's overall profitability.

To more effectively measure and understand the impact of its online marketing initiatives on Macy's store sales, Macys.com increased its analytical capabilities with SAS Enterprise Miner, resulting in an e-mail subscription churn reduction of 20 percent. It also uses SAS to automate report generation, saving more than $500,000 a year in comp analyst time.

Ending "One Size Fits All" E-Mail Marketing

"We want to understand customer lifetime value," explains Kerem Tomak, the vice president of analytics for Macys.com. "We want to understand how long our customers have been with us, how often an e-mail from us triggers a visit to our site. This helps us better understand who our best customers are and how engaged they are with us. With that knowledge we can give our valuable customers the right promotions in order to serve them the best way possible.

"Customers share a lot of information with us—their likes and dislikes—and our task is to support them in return for their loyalty by providing them with what they want, instantly," adds Tomak. Macys.com uses Hadoop as a data platform for SAS Enterprise Miner.

Initially, Tomak was worried that segmenting customers and sending fewer, but more specific, e-mails would reduce traffic to the website. "The general belief was that we had to blast everyone," Tomak says. Today, e-mails are sent less frequently but with more thought, and the retailer has reduced subscription churn rate by approximately 20%.

As competition increases in the online retailing world, Tomak says there is a push toward generating more accurate, real-time decisions about customer preferences.

Targeted Analytics-Based Actions to Address Marketing Business Goals

From the customer-centric perspective, marketing activities and business goals are tailored to the customer's stage in the life cycle. For the purpose of this discussion, let us consider the following analytics-based marketing objectives:

- **For prospects.** Increase customer touches using the stack-ranked list of prospects to contact, based on predictive analytics models.

- **For candidates.** Increase conversion by leveraging predictive analytics to target the most likely to convert prospects.

- **For customers.** Increase customer retention using predictive analytics to identify which customers are most likely to leave and proactively use retention campaigns to keep and protect those customers. Also, increase existing customer spend. Because not all customers are equal, predictive analytics will provide a list of the best customers to target for up-sell and cross-sell opportunities. It is important to note that the role of predictive analytics will really help identify the who, when, and why to enable prioritization of marketing activities.

Execute and Track Performance Using a Marketing Goal as an Example

Let us assume that the target goal is to increase new business by 10%. To execute CRM activities to achieve the target goal, the marketing team may leverage prospect scoring, as described on Exhibit 16.4. The segmentation will help prioritize and tailor marketing's acquisition campaigns. Once the execution of the campaigns begins, we need to track and evaluate. How did we do? What should we do to improve? In this case, the marketing goal was to increase new business by 10%. The tracking should following the execution path and assess how we did with the customer segments—for example, comparing the new business three months before and three months after the segmented campaigns. The performance tracking will simply assess whether this goal was achieved by looking into conversion three months before and three months after.

Many data elements are important to track from a marketing perspective, but the following are additional metrics based on our selected business challenge of assessing customers at different lifecycle stages:

- Percentage of increase in new customers
- Number of marketing campaigns
- Marketing spend
- Marketing spend per lead
- Number of qualified leads
- Number of converted leads
- Percentage of increase in customer retention
- Percentage of increase in conversion
- Percentage of increase in average spend per customer
- Percentage of increase in up-sell

Those metrics could be tracked on a weekly, monthly, quarterly, and yearly basis. The important trends to monitor and analyze are

- Week over week change, coupled with analytics, to understand where and why
- Month over month change, coupled with analytics, to understand where and why
- Quarter over quarter change, coupled with analytics, to understand where and why
- Year over year change, coupled with analytics, to understand where and why

The focus should be on comparing and benchmarking those metrics against the targets that the marketing department has set. After following the analytics recommendations, marketing managers will have the strategic intelligence they need to follow the steps to measure the impact of their actions.

KEY TAKEAWAYS

- To be effective, business performance tracking should be an enterprise-wide initiative culture that enables intelligent execution across all departments of the organization. Therefore, performance tracking and execution should enable

  - Customer service to optimize call center and staffing levels, identify problem areas that need attention, and respond more effectively to customer service calls.

  - Sales to better manage the pipeline and track key opportunities, plus effectively forecast revenues and transactions.

  - Marketing to monitor and measure the efficacy of CRM campaigns and make some adjustments to maximize the response rate.

- We outlined that forward-looking companies have embraced analytics to compete, and one of the cornerstones of their successful execution strategy is the segmentation approach that regroups their customers into meaningful segments. Why? Well, today, this trend is becoming the norm, because customer requirements and characteristics are divided into smaller and smaller micro segments that require organizations to become responsive to the needs of more and more customer categories.

- Effective successful business performance execution shouldn't be relegated to a single department; it should include all sections of the business that affect a customer's experience. More important, an analytic execution should also be based on a strategy that includes two principal components:

  - The customer experience one-pager and

  - The segmentation grid/matrix.

- In this chapter, we outlined that business performance tracking is an integrated process that includes analytics and people's actions, and it is about measuring the outcome of what we predicted would happen.

- The main objective of analytics is to address key business challenges, and business performance analytics is about benchmarking how you performed against your goals. After anticipating the future with analytics, performance tracking will provide a state of

  - How did you do?

  - How are you doing, and why?

  - What should you do?

- We also discussed that performance tracking should be linked to business objectives to ensure that results, when measured, could help improve the target goal.

- For marketing, business performance tracking requires going through micro segments and assessing how the company performed in every specific segment.
- We provided a performance life-cycle matrix that helps businesses synchronize performance execution and measurement across all functional groups in the organization.

NOTES

1. Robert D. Behn, "On the Philosophical and Practical: Resistance to Measurement," *Bob Behn's Public Management Report*, vol. 3, no. 3, November 2005, http://www.hks.harvard.edu/thebehnreport/November2005.pdf.
2. Gary Cokins, *Performance Management: Integrating Strategy Execution, Methodologies, Risk and Analytics* (Hoboken, NJ: John Wiley & Sons, 2009).
3. Bruno Aziza and Joey Fitts, *Drive Business Performance: Enabling a Culture of Intelligent Execution* (Hoboken, NJ: John Wiley & Sons, 2008).
4. Christine Moorman, blog post, "How Much Firms Spend on Marketing," *The CMO Survey.org*, November 2011, http://www.cmosurvey.org/blog/how-much-firms-spend-on-marketing.

parts that make up the Business Analytics Suite

CHAPTER 17

Analytics and Innovation

"Innovation distinguishes between a leader and a follower."

—Steve Jobs

I n this chapter, we cover analytics and innovation, one of the seven pillars that make up the Business Analytics Success Pillars introduced in Chapter 2. To succeed in today's fast-evolving competitive marketplace with consumers who are more informed and increasingly demanding, we have underscored that successful companies must harness advanced business analytics to meet their business challenges. To maintain their competitive edge, those companies need to analyze their data (big and small) coming from multiple sources and transform it into actionable intelligence. This intelligence not only provides a competitive edge but also makes critical issues visible to decision makers, enabling them to detect problems, better plan for the future, and identify opportunities to develop and improve products and services. Effective business analytics provides companies with the information necessary to differentiate their products and services from the competition. In other words, it enables them to innovate.

Companies must constantly improve their customers' experience and their products and services through innovation. Analytics can help facilitate this innovation in countless ways, including helping the organization understand the dynamics of the market, determining what other companies are doing in the way of innovation, figuring out what customers want, and helping the organization think about issues in different ways. In order for analytics to affect innovation in the organization, it must be innovative in its approach, tools, and delivery of analytical insight. This also necessitates that analytics integrate disparate data sources for the organization, in order to provide a complete and insightful perspective.

Bruno Aziza pointed out in Microsoft's blog that analytics and innovation are sometimes perceived as opposing concepts.[1] "Many argue that innovation cannot be reduced to a set of processes or, even worse, a set of metrics." There are countless books covering innovation, and very few of them mention analytics or the pivotal role that analytics can play in the innovation process.

Our goal in this chapter is to address the intersection between analytics and innovation and illustrate how forward-looking companies have been leveraging advanced business analytics to stoke innovation. We will also attempt to outline the importance of innovation within analytics itself and identify the common traits of innovative companies. Therefore, in the next sections we will discuss

- What is innovation?
- What is the promise of analytics and its impact on innovation?
- What makes up innovation in analytics?
- What is the intersection between analytics and innovation?
- Why are analytics and innovation crucial for success?
- What are the common characteristics of innovative companies?

WHAT IS INNOVATION?

After the financial crisis in 2008, the majority of companies were seeking new ways to get back to profitability. Innovation was seen as a key way to make this happen. Innovation is the creation of better or more effective services, technologies, products, processes, or ideas that are accepted by markets, governments, and society at large. Roy

Luebke's article titled "Peter Drucker on Innovation," from the blog *Innovation Excellence*, underscored that Drucker identified seven sources of opportunity that will ultimately drive innovation:

1. The organization's own unexpected successes and failures, and also those of the competition.

2. Incongruities, especially those in a process, such as production, distribution, or incongruities in customer behavior.

3. Process needs.

4. Changes in industry and market structures.

5. Changes in demographics.

6. Changes in meaning and perception.

7. New knowledge.[2]

Oftentimes, there is confusion about the difference between innovation and creativity. To be clear, creativity is about coming up with great ideas, whereas innovation is about bringing those creative ideas to life through execution and converting the ideas into a successful business. In the book *The Other Side of Innovation*, Dartmouth professor Vijay Govindarajan outlines very convincingly that an organization's capacity for innovation is its creativity multiplied by its execution. Research on Fortune 500 companies found that organizations believe their companies are better at generating ideas than they are at commercializing them.[3]

It is important to underscore the process of innovation: how companies innovate and what really drives them to do it. There are several definitions about how companies innovate, but the definition that we found very practical, simple, and straightforward is the one from TED (technology, entertainment, design) conference founder Richard Saul Wurman. TED is an invitation only event where the world's leading thinkers and doers gather to find inspiration. When Wurman was asked to define innovation, he referred to the first TED conference he organized: "In order to innovate one needs to add or subtract."[4] When he organized the first TED conference, he said, "Everything I did was subtraction." He took away panels, dress codes, politicians and CEOs, long speeches, silos, and the podium.

It would be a disservice to discuss innovation without looking at Apple. In 2003, when Apple introduced the iPod with the iTunes store, the company revolutionized portable entertainment, creating a new market and completely transforming the Apple business model. According to an article published in the *Harvard Business Review*, "Reinventing Your Business Model," in just three years, the iPhone/iTunes combination became a nearly $10 billion product, accounting for almost 50% of Apple's revenue.[5] Apple's market capitalization catapulted from $1 billion in early 2003 to more than $150 billion by late 2007. The success story of Apple is well known, but what's less known is that Apple was not the first to bring a digital music player to the market. A company called Diamond Multimedia introduced Rio in 1998. Another firm, Best Data, introduced the Cabo 64 in 2000. Both products worked well and were portable and stylish. So why did the iPod, rather than Rio or Cabo, succeed? Apple took a good technology and wrapped it up in a great business model. Apple's true innovation was to make downloading digital music easy and convenient—the iTunes store. What Apple did was to draw a line directly between the recording artist and the consumer through a commerce platform and a recommendation engine. More than a manufacturer of a good device, Apple became a gateway for the distribution of content through podcasts, iTunes, audiobooks, and the like.

In order to achieve this objective, the company built a groundbreaking business model that combined hardware, software, and service via the iTunes platform. This set Apple ahead of the curve in the consumer market. The idea was a game changer for the company and for consumers. As Steve Jobs said when introducing the iPod, "You are able to carry your entire music library in a little box." Similar changes took the industry by storm when Apple introduced its first smartphone, the iPhone. In just a couple of years, Apple's share of the smartphone segment outpaced competitor RIM's Blackberry figures. RIM pioneered the smartphone industry, and the main iPhone features that really appealed to consumers were the touch-screen feature, along with the intuitive and user-friendly high-resolution screen. Those key innovations brought Apple to where it is today.

WHAT IS THE PROMISE OF ADVANCED ANALYTICS?

In the previous chapters, we outlined that advanced analytics includes three major steps:

1. Unlocking
2. Prediction
3. Optimization

In today's business environment, companies are inundated with data from multiple sources, including market data, chat and e-mail data, sensor data, Web data, servicing data (warranty claims), social media data, mobile data, and call center data, just to name a few. Here, the unlocking step is to convert, integrate, and streamline these data in order to detect problems/opportunities, analyze strengths/weaknesses, measure performance, and track success. Advanced analytics aims to provide a complete knowledge of the market, the product, the services, the technology, and, more important, the overall performance level of the company versus its competitors and the market as a whole. However, in the process, advanced analytics can also help businesses understand, identify, and test seeds of innovation.

To be able to innovate, companies need to analyze their performance in the recent past and the present and then also be able to anticipate the future. Basically, the company needs to understand where it came from, how it is performing today, and how it plans to perform in the future. Not only is it crucial for companies to understand their markets, products, customer service, and technological capabilities, companies must also understand the competition.

It is imperative when thinking of innovation to understand what your competition is offering. Competitive knowledge can be provided by the competitive intelligence team within your organization, a topic that was covered in detail in Chapter 13. Using analytics, the competitive intelligence team helps companies find out about their strengths and weaknesses. That team is also instrumental in better identifying areas of innovative products and services. Because the team has an ear to the ground, team members know what customers want and also know what the competition offers.

Properly leveraged, the proliferation of data coming from multiple sources should provide insights that should enable companies to listen to the voices of their customers and understand their needs and wants, but, more important, to spot areas of opportunities that can improve the current business model, to enable them to compete and win against the competition by offering or creating new products or services.

WHAT MAKES UP INNOVATION IN ANALYTICS?

The explosion of Internet, social media, mobile, and other digital information, as well as technologies to capture, process, and analyze data, provides a broad spectrum of opportunities for companies to innovate in analytics. Our experiences in working with innovative companies, enriched by interviews recently conducted with industry leaders, enabled us to see five frontiers in analytics that companies can take advantage of, in order to help them innovate:

1. Innovation from the analytics team resources
2. Innovation from combining data
3. Innovation from predictive analytics
4. Innovation from unstructured data analytics
5. Innovation from the integration of intelligence

Innovation from the Analytics Team

Innovation from the analytics team can come from three core factors:

1. Team member empowerment
2. Analytics business planning
3. Regular off-site meetings

Empowering analytical employees to question the status quo and to change existing processes is an important driver for analytical innovation. For example, one of the authors, JP Isson, usually grants 15% of the time to all team members to think about new analytics solutions or ideas to better support the business. As a result, some great innovative ideas have been shared and discussed with the team. One of those creative ideas was an innovative solution from a team member who leveraged data from people searching for jobs on Monster's site and provided tools to the sales force and the customers who helped them inform recruitment advertising strategies.

The second activity from the analytics team that can stimulate innovation is putting together a biannual business plan. The team members must be encouraged to take their planning the extra mile toward being proactive in building new solutions to help the company that are based on internal and external customer input. By talking to customers, they will understand what their most important business problems are and therefore be able to build solutions that address those challenges and provide business value to the company in the process.

For instance, at Monster, we have customers who post a job, looking to hire a talented candidate. Often, they do this with limited understanding of the most effective strategies for posting that job. The analytics team helped Monster innovate by creating a Web interface that informed customers of the most effective ways to post specific types of jobs that would lead to the greatest response. This was unlike anything that competitors in the industry were doing and led to Monster seeing a shorter sales cycle and increased retention rates. This also helped create increased customer intimacy and customer satisfaction.

Off-site meetings are also part of the activities from the analytics team that can spur innovation. Taking time away from the daily pressures of work and encouraging your team to think creatively about new analytical solutions they can put into action can yield great ideas. However, in order to have a productive off-site meeting, it's important to have some structure and focus the team on the key business challenges that require their analytics innovation. For example, during an off-site meeting, the Monster Insights team came up the creative idea of a Global Customer Knowledge tool. Because Monster serves multinational companies in more than 55 countries, it was sometimes a challenge to get a unified view of the customer. We designed and created a Global Customer Knowledge tool during one of our off-site meetings that would enable users to see key customer data all in one place, providing a 360-degree view of customers from top to bottom. This helped increase the sales, productivity, and effectiveness of our international sales organization.

Innovation from Combining Data

Innovation from data is about the way we approach data and the way we use it. Operating in the big data environment, top-performing companies are using new approaches to integrate data from multiple sources in innovative ways. This provides a full view of the customers to enrich existing key performance indicators (KPIs) and helps to better monitor, measure, analyze, and plan customer behavior. This includes voice of customer, customer site experience, customer tracking, customer usage, and buying behavior. Traditional KPIs on a traffic increase could be enriched by positive comments from blogs or opinion sites regarding a company's campaign or new product. Innovative data gathering could also stoke innovative predictive analytics.

Innovation from Predictive Analytics

There is a lot of innovation stemming from predictive analytics in today's new business environment. Innovation in predictive analytics is about how it's built and how it is used. For example, to predict customer attrition, traditionally analysts built predictive models based on customer spend history, customer usage, and customers' demographics. Yet new data sources available today provide additional power to include new information, such as customers' social media activity, Web behavior activity, customers' comments, feedback, e-mails, blogs, review sites, and opinion sites to enrich the existing models but also to create new models based on this new type of data. One of the authors, JP Isson, conceived and implemented the Global Business Intelligence Scoring Model at Monster that includes a variety of customer data, market data, Web activity behavior data, macro-economic data, customer buying history, customer online behavior, Internet penetration, and seeker activity data to predict company attractiveness and company potential. Predictive models that leverage additional data can be used in innovative ways by targeting customers at the right time, at the right location, and through the right channel. In the case of Monster, the innovative implementation of predictive analytics led to

- Increases in customer retention
- Increases in marketing/CRM productivity
- Increases in sales productivity (sales was able to prioritize retention and acquisition activities based on the scoring)

Innovation from Unstructured Data Analytics

Unstructured data analytics that includes document analysis, e-mails, blogs, and voice of customer analytics offers a wide range of ways to innovate in analytics: first, by providing some additional insights to traditional analytics, but, more important, by providing data to enrich existing predictive models and create new models for acquisition and retention. The centerpiece of innovation from the unstructured data analytics is its predictive component. Leveraging unstructured data analytics at Monster, we created a keyword search tool by building a predictive model to match seekers' search activity to employers' behavior. We provided the business with a seeker/employer predictive tool that offers keywords used by seekers to employers, enabling them to adjust their jobs' posting descriptions to facilitate the largest responses from seekers.

Innovation through the Integration of Intelligence

In today's business environment, with data intelligence from multiple sources, intelligence integration or data convergence is the lifeblood of innovation in analytics. Cutting-edge companies are leveraging ways to understand, explain, and predict customer behavior by combining site analytics with social media analytics, with mobile analytics, with predictive models powered by text analytics, with customer buying behavior, with information captured via CRM systems, with information gathered via conversations with the service team, with e-mail exchanges, with customers' site reviews, with site behavior, and with social media behavior, among other sources. This is offering a much more comprehensive view of customer intelligence that enables fast and innovative customer-centric activity. Much of the critical information can also be delivered via mobile devices to make sure decision makers can quickly leverage the findings and address any potential issues.

INTERSECTION BETWEEN ANALYTICS AND INNOVATION

We outlined in the previous sections that to innovate, companies need to understand what to subtract or what to add to the existing product, services, and customer channel strategies. We also recalled the promise of analytics and the fundamental business questions it seeks to address. In Exhibit 17.1, we illustrate factors that make up the intersection between analytics and innovation.

Analytics' main objectives typically revolve around addressing the key questions of what happened, what is happening, and what will happen. Once you apply these questions to your product, service, or channel strategy and compare yourself to the competition, innovative ideas are likely to result, as you spot what to "add" or "subtract" in order to differentiate your company from the competition.

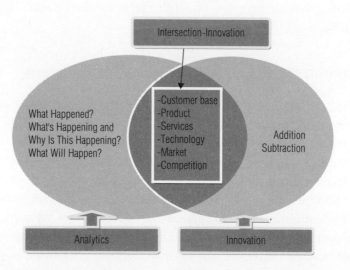

Exhibit 17.1 Analytics and Innovation Intersection

We believe the most important areas where analytics can intersect with innovation is in understanding

- The customer base
- The product
- The service
- The technology
- The market
- The competition

Getting a deep understanding of the aforementioned topics can be achieved only via the use of advanced analytics.

The execution of creative ideas can take place only if we understand what is happening in the market, what is missing, and what would appeal to customers. Analytics creates a blueprint to innovation by providing the intelligence of what to do, while operations executes the recommended actions. Only by combining these two forces are organizations able to innovate.

Great ideas are not enough; execution is the key to success. From the interviews we conducted and our experience in working with innovative organizations, the process of innovation that is based on execution can properly take place only if preliminary analytics and business operations are working in tandem. Innovation requires these two key processes to occur in concert.

Common Denominators of Innovative Companies

In sports, we know that most professional athletes share common characteristics: they are extremely focused on achieving their goals, they have strong discipline, and they work hard, practicing regularly. The same can be said for successful innovative companies. In many cases, these characteristics are what sets them apart and draws the line between those who have creative ideas and those who bring those creative ideas promptly to execution. Most innovative companies are also known to be analytical, which means that they have a data-driven decision-making process. These organizations have common denominators that drive their success. The denominators include

- Empowering their strongest asset, their workforce, by enabling a culture of innovation. Google, for instance, encourages engineers to spend 20% of their work time on projects that interest them. Some of Google's newer services, such as Gmail, Google News, Orkut, and AdSense, originated from these independent endeavors.

- Strong customer focus (they master customer satisfaction, needs, wants, preferences, and services).

- Strong product diversity (they are eager to try to expand the product lines and engage in new markets). Although every product may not be a success, innovative companies try to get ahead of the marketplace through the addition or subtraction of service delivery models.

- Strong competitive intelligence (they are aware of what the competition is doing, its strengths and weaknesses, and know how to outpace competitors).

- Strong update on trends (they understand business trends and often lead the trends).

Successful and innovative companies understand that above everything else that they do, focusing on the customer is the core of the innovative process. Listening to the voices of their customers to understand their needs and wants and leveraging analytics and operations to develop innovative products and services for their customers are the keys to their success. That ability to leverage the voice of the customer and the voice of the market and then improve or develop products and services will set them ahead of the competition. The customer is the main focus for successful and innovative companies. Here are two companies that we consider to be strong innovators.

Amazon.com

Amazon is the largest online retailer in the world and is really focused on customer satisfaction. This even starts with its logo, which is an arrow leading from A to Z, representing customer satisfaction as a smile. The company innovated by quickly focusing on a diversification of products and services to seize great areas of opportunities, to sustain growth, and increase its value. It started as a bookstore but soon diversified, selling a variety of products, including DVDs, CDs, MP3 downloading, software, video games, electronic devices, apparel, toys, and jewelry, among others. Amazon leveraged the fact that it was the most visited website by using commerce as a way to drive revenue.

In September 2011, with the explosion of the tablet market, Amazon entered this market and launched Kindle Fire, which runs a customized version of the operating system Android. The aggressively low pricing of the Kindle Fire ($199) was largely perceived as a strategy that was supported by Amazon's anticipated revenue from its content sales, which would be driven though adoption of the device. The Kindle Fire has been a successful product and is positioned well in the current tablet war. Amazon's American Customer Satisfaction Score Index was 86 in 2011. Amazon is among the top performers in customer satisfaction, just 1 point below Apple. Amazon is one of the best examples of a company that leverages analytics and operations together to lead in innovation.

Google

The leader in search engine technology and market share defines itself as a customer-centric company. "Serving our end users is at the heart of what we do and remains our number one priority," says Page.[6] Despite being perhaps the only media company in the world whose stated goal is to have its customers leave its website as quickly as possible, Google is no doubt committed to making those customers satisfied. From its inception, Google has focused on providing the best user experience possible. While many companies claim to put their customers first, few are able to resist the temptation to make small sacrifices to increase shareholder value. Google has steadfastly refused to make any change that does not offer a benefit to the users who come to the site.

Google's experience is a great example of a company committed to wowing its customers with consistent quality and innovation. Google is also a great example of a company that is leading with analytics; it quickly understands market trends and the crucial need to diversify its products and services. Google's rapid growth has triggered a chain of new products, acquisitions, and partnerships beyond the company's core search engine. Today Google offers online solutions, such as an office suite and the Android mobile platform.

With today's customer expectations, innovation has become a must—companies have to constantly put themselves into customers' minds and evolve their products and service offerings to meet those expectations. In the end, advanced analytics can pave the way for innovation and is a requirement for companies that seek to grow and sustain their competitive edge.

KEY TAKEAWAYS

- In this highly competitive new business environment, with the proliferation of digital information, analytics and innovation are the lifeblood for success.
- To innovate, as Richard Saul Wurman mentioned, one needs to "subtract" or "add." Advanced analytics is key to this process, from the macroeconomic trend to the customer's needs.
- We also underscored that the best-valued companies in the world leverage a combination of analytics and operations to become innovators. These companies share common denominators:
  - Focus on the customer.
  - Have product diversification.
  - Understand and anticipate the market and trends.
  - Have fast execution.
  - Champion a culture of analytics and innovation by empowering their best assets, their employees.
- New data offer a broad spectrum of innovation in analytics, starting with innovation from the analytics team through off-site innovation meetings; feedback from customers; innovation from the data, the way we approach the data, and the way we use data; innovations in predictive analytics that are now powered by new data; and unstructured data analytics.
- We outlined the intersection between analytics and operations; this is where we believe innovative companies simultaneously leverage both and focus on ensuring that the fundamental questions that analytics addresses (What happened? What is happening? And what will happen?) support and stoke the execution of that very innovation.
- Analytics provides key insights to the two primary steps of the innovation process:

- **AS IS analysis**. This is an overview that is covered through three major questions analytics seeks to address: What happened? What is happening? Why is it happening? At this stage, analytics helps detect problems and uncover strengths and weakness of the product, the market, the product, the service, the price, and the competition, to better plan for the future offering.

- **TO BE analysis**. This is an overview that is covered via analytics' fundamental question: What should we do, knowing what will happen? Here, analytics paves the way to innovation by focusing on what needs to be done and anticipating the future to ensure that the company's new products, services, and technology will stay ahead of the competition and provide a groundbreaking competitive edge.

- Category-leading companies such as Apple, Google, and Amazon lead with analytics and, more important, leverage analytics and operations to maximize innovation, while they outpace their competition by focusing on customer experience and on developing diversified products and services to meet customers' and market expectations.

- We finally underscore that there should be innovation with analytics itself; one should anticipate future trends and be up-to-date on new technological capacities; this includes a full integration of mobile, text analytics, cloud analytics, visualization, and high-speed computing analytics.

NOTES

1. Bruno Aziza, "Innovation and Analytics," blog post, *Microsoft Official Blog*, May 11, 2010, http://blogs.technet.com/b/microsoft_blog/archive/2010/05/11/innovation-and-analytics.aspx.

2. Roy Luebke, "Peter Drucker on Innovation," *Innovation Excellence*, July 30 2010, http://www.innovationexcellence.com/blog/2010/07/30/peter-drucker-on-innovation/.

3. Vijay Govindarajan, *The Other Side of Innovation: Solving the Execution Challenge* (Cambridge, MA: Harvard Business Review Press, 2010).

4. Richard Saul Wurman, Transcript of interview, *Infrascape Design*, January 11, 2012, http://infrascapedesign.wordpress.com/2012/01/11/richard-saul-wurman/.

5. Mark W. Johnson, Clayton, M. Christensen, and Henning Kagermann, "Reinventing Your Business Model," *Harvard Business Review*, December 2008, http://hbr.org/2008/12/reinventing-your-business-model/ar/1.

6. "Larry Page Quotes," *Inluminent*, January 7, 2009, http://www.inluminent.com/2009/01/07/larry-page-quotes/.

CHAPTER 18

Unstructured Data Analytics

*The Next Frontier**

"There is no way I'm going to let these simian creatures defeat me. While they're sleeping, I'm processing countless terabytes of useless information."

—IBM's Watson supercomputer (*Jeopardy* champion)

I n today's globally connected arena, with the explosion of the Internet and social media, unstructured data analytics is no longer a choice for any forward-looking company; it is a must. To stay current and continue to successfully operate in this highly competitive marketplace, high-performing companies are turning to unstructured data analytics, because it provides path-breaking insights on customers and market knowledge building. As we have discussed throughout this book, companies need to leverage intelligence from multiple data sources and multiple data types, both structured data and unstructured

---

*We would like to thank C. Jonathan Lehto, an expert in text analytics with more than 25 years of experience, for his contribution, assistance, and guidance in writing this chapter.

data. Gartner Research predicts that data will grow 800% during the next five years, and 80% of that data will be unstructured.[1] The overwhelming unstructured data is made up from sources such as social media data, chat and e-mail data, Web log data, location stream data, and voice of customer and voice of the market data. To maintain a competitive edge, forward-looking companies have to derive reliable and relevant insights from the ever-increasing stream of data. In order to succeed, companies need to uncover complex patterns, trends, and sentiments that will lead to strategic business actions. As part of this, companies will also need to maximize the business value that is buried in the unstructured data. Right now, companies that do this have a competitive advantage. However, in the future, it will not merely be an advantage but a requirement for doing business.

This chapter explores the evolving analytics discipline, examining the goals of business analytics in the current environment, as well as the strategies and techniques being deployed to extract, transform, load, and analyze unstructured data. Success in getting business value from unstructured data analytics is being driven by a race of businesses to survive. Within the sections of this chapter, we will address the following:

- What is unstructured data analytics?
- Why use unstructured data analytics?
- How does unstructured data analytics work?
- Why is it the next business frontier?
- Success stories of valuable companies.

WHAT IS UNSTRUCTURED DATA ANALYTICS?

Before we discuss unstructured data analytics in more detail, let's first define what is meant by "unstructured data." Unstructured data or unstructured information refers to information that does not have a predefined data model and/or does not fit well into relational database tables. Unstructured data typically have no identifiable structure and may include bitmap images/objects, text, and other data types that are not part of a typical database. Unstructured information is frequently text-heavy but may contain data such as dates, numbers, and facts as well. This results in irregularities and ambiguities, making it difficult to understand through the use of traditional computer programs, as compared to data stored in fielded forms in traditional relational databases or annotated (semantically tagged) in documents. Unstructured data cannot easily be analyzed with traditional analytics techniques.[2]

Unstructured data analytics first emerged in the late 1990s as "text mining." Early approaches treated and analyzed text as a bag of words. Text mining evolved early to use basic shallow linguistics to handle variant word forms, such as abbreviations, plurals, and conjugations, as well as multiword terms known as n-grams. N-grams are a contiguous sequence of items from a sequence of text or speech. The items in question can be phonemes, syllables, letters, or words, depending on the application. An n-gram text analytics model is a type of probabilistic language model for predicting the next item in such a sequence. Basic text analysis might also count frequencies of words and terms in order to carry out elementary functions, such as attempting to classify a document by topic. Yet at that time, there was little ability to understand the semantics or meanings of the words in context contained within a given document, as we will discuss in the next sections.

Contemporary unstructured data analytics helps address unstructured data issues that arise from unstructured content by applying statistical methods and linguistic rules to automatically assess, analyze, and act on the insights buried in unstructured text—such as e-mail and social media content, Web and call center logs, survey data, insurance or warranty claims, and loan applications.

As recalled in the previous section the variety, the volume and the velocity of big data are growing at a rapid pace. Data volumes are exploding. Globally, more people in more languages are on the Internet. Many are using smaller, voice-enabled mobile devices and, as a result, are communicating more frequently in a larger, richer data environment than ever before. However, the questions for business remain the same as they have for many years: Who are my customers? How do they make their purchase decisions? What do they want? How are we doing? What should we do in the future to remain competitive?

Organizations are using modern predictive analytics to address, in real time, the evolving needs and trends of their customers. Although *big data* is an overused buzzword, it is today's business reality and offers opportunities to do a lot more things that couldn't be done before. However, in the *2010 IBM Global CEO Study*, a survey of more than 1,500 business leaders in 60 countries, CEOs described their companies as "data rich but insight poor."[3] At the same time, the number of worldwide e-mail accounts is projected to increase from more than 2.9 billion in 2010 to more than 3.8 billion by 2014.[4]

Most of the data contained in e-mail and on the Web are unstructured data and represent a significant opportunity for companies to uncover insights regarding customer attitudes, behavior, and preferences.

Premier websites—Amazon, Facebook, Google—are constantly improving their offerings by anticipating their customers' needs. These changes are the result of advanced business analytics and turning data into actionable information through predictive models. New approaches in parallel processing are enabling novel solutions, many of which could not be done even a few years ago. Smaller mobile devices are also increasingly being driven by voice interaction. As mobile devices shrink and becomes more highly featured, voice command/control with audible response becomes a requirement. With it comes the challenge of not only doing what was asked, but also tracking the interaction for billing, reporting, quality control, and potential buying behavior. Also, increasingly, the application fulfillment is in the "cloud," complicating the unification of analytics data for analysis. For example, a typical cell phone user may consult his or her mobile device's search engine for a service nearby, such as a restaurant. Then, the individual might follow GPS directions to it, Tweet for preferred menu items, Tweet comments, and pay—all using a mobile device. Each of the Internet services is interested in the complete details of its part of the interaction. In this example, most of the "work" is performed by software that is resident on the Internet and not on the person's low-powered device. Also, much of this transaction's data is unstructured.

In addition, legal requirements (HIPAA, Sarbanes-Oxley) vary across borders for and against data capture and data retention, presenting additional challenges to unstructured data management, as the law continues to evolve to protect the right to privacy. As a result, it is necessary to determine what the data are and whether they can be used for analysis.

Structured and unstructured data commingle and complement each other. For example, information about data, or metadata, tends to be structured. Examples of structured data might be a part number or a customer ID. Unstructured data might be the voice records of a customer's interaction with a support center, survey verbatim, or search query text. Modern analytic methods work strategically with both types of data.

Today's businesses also need to develop and maintain demographic and behavioral customer profiles in order to personalize the customers' experience and anticipate their interests, wants, needs, and opportunities in real time, while the customer is engaged. Businesses need to provide personalized information, actionable immediately, while at the same time not seeming "creepy" to customers. For example, in a couple of well-known incidents, a popular vendor anticipated customers' product needs correctly by providing online recommendations, while inadvertently missing the sensitivity of the personal nature of the information, causing a consumer backlash.

THE UNSTRUCTURED DATA ANALYTICS INDUSTRY

Industry consolidation of unstructured data analytics providers is ongoing, as key technologies and even more precious patents and skilled engineers are acquired by companies with an interest in unstructured data technologies. In the search engine arena, numerous well-known vendors have been assimilated—AltaVista, Autonomy, Endeca, and FAST. Record-linking technology companies (technology to deduplicate different forms of people and place names, such as IBM, Intl. Business Machine) have also been absorbed by larger vendors. Taxonomy and information retrieval companies (for example, InXight, Teragram) have similarly been snapped up. Statistical software vendors with text analytics solutions have also been acquired.

IBM's Watson debuted as a fine example of the promise of question-answering technology. Attivio, a premier independent vendor of hybrid structured and unstructured data management, offers a solution that seamlessly integrates traditional relational database technology with the capabilities of a full-text search engine.

At the consumer level, it is possible with a small and talented staff to conduct hybrid structured and unstructured analytics, using a blend of open source and commercial software. Open source solutions include R, a statistics package, and Apache Lucene/Solr, a full-text search engine. However, the choice of implementation technology and the degree of sophistication are driven by budget, staffing, and opportunity. The solution spectrum includes custom, highly configured, distributed collection and automated analysis and reporting solutions to a modest, limited processing for key metrics on the low end. Open source technology can also be a viable option at all scales.

Against this competitive backdrop, the traditional business intelligence technologies of database and statistical analysis are converging and merging with the younger analytical technologies, such as text analytics, computational linguistics, natural language processing, and machine learning. As these solutions mature and are proven out, often by small start-ups, established companies are expected to develop or continue to acquire them.

USES OF UNSTRUCTURED DATA ANALYTICS

Whether it is for companies, research groups, public service, or government organizations, unstructured data analytics provides tangible benefits through an infinite variety of uses. Examples of the uses of unstructured data analytics include

- Increased competitive intelligence from analyzing documents, blogs, and reports from the competition.
- Voice of customer analysis from open-ended survey questions, call center logs, e-mails, blogs, or opinion sites. This can also be used to increase customer satisfaction, customer retention, and customer loyalty by reaching out to customers proactively.
- Help in maximizing a company's CRM (customer relationship management) efforts by leveraging customers' feedback analysis and taking into account customer needs and preferences.

- Increased effectiveness of customer retention efforts by providing enhanced insights from unstructured data to enrich traditional predictive retention models.

- Driving product development and adoption by analyzing early customer feedback on a product and/or analyzing warranty claims.

- Enhancing government investigation procedures, uncovering security threats and criminal actions, and detecting terrorist activities.

- Detecting patterns of fraudulent behavior. For example, Monster Worldwide uses unstructured data analysis to detect fraudulent actions and activities on its sites.

- Informing financial investment strategies.

- Enhanced drug discovery processes for pharmaceutical research companies that can explore articles, journals, patents, and other research material related to existing drugs.

HOW UNSTRUCTURED DATA ANALYTICS WORKS

As seen in Exhibit 18.1, unstructured data analytics is a five-step process:

1. Prepare unstructured data for analysis.
2. Apply linguistic statistics and machine learning techniques to the unstructured document before the extraction and the modeling.

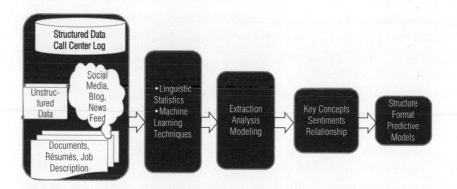

Exhibit 18.1 Unstructured Data Analytics Process

3. Extract and model the information from textual unstructured data sources.

4. Convert unstructured text into categories and structure the format for advanced analytics.

5. Transform the data into actionable intelligence to address business challenges, such as fraud detection, financial investment strategies, or consumer sentiment.

WHY UNSTRUCTURED DATA IS THE NEXT ANALYTICAL FRONTIER

The evolution of modern unstructured data analytics has been 54 years in the making. In 1958, IBM engineer H. P Luhn wrote an article saying that business intelligence is the analysis of structured and unstructured text documents. In that article, he defined business intelligence as a system that will

> utilize data-processing machines for auto-abstracting and auto-encoding of documents and for creating interest profiles for each of the "action points" in an organization. Both incoming and internally generated documents are automatically abstracted, characterized by a word pattern, and sent automatically to appropriate action points.[5]

We can even go further back in time, with the first representation of data in rows and columns in the second century in Egypt. However, with today's fast evolution and revolution of technology, software, and data mining, business intelligence has rapidly evolved since 1958. Unstructured data mining has come to life with the evolution of technology and software. Past unresolved analytics problems are now being addressed, thanks to the sophistication of tools and software. Consider Apple's voice recognition technology for the iPhone, Siri. Its origins go back to a Pentagon research project that was then spun off as a Silicon Valley start-up. Apple bought Siri in 2010 and kept feeding it more data. Now, with people supplying millions of questions, Siri is becoming an increasingly adept personal assistant, offering reminders, weather reports, restaurant suggestions, and answers to an expanding universe of questions.

From a historical perspective, consider the following timeline, which outlines milestones for how we got to the current state of unstructured data analytics:

- **Second century in Egypt:** First table with data represented in rows and columns.

- **Seventeenth century:** Two-dimensional graph invented by Descartes.

- **1756–1806:** The line graph, line chart, line bar chart, and pie chart were invented by W. Playfair.

- **Eighteenth and nineteenth centuries:** Modern statistics emerged with A. Fisher and C. Spearman introducing factor analysis and principal components analysis.

- **1958:** First definition of business intelligence as text analytics or document analysis. H. P. Luhn, an engineer from IBM, introduced the idea of basic stats analysis on text terms. He also introduced the concept of text summarization, but the software and the tools were not ready to support it.

- **1960–1980:** The focus was on database technology and relational databases.

- **1980–1990:** Business intelligence emerged as software categories and a field of expertise, but the focus was on numeric-coded data and relational databases.

- **1990–2010s:** Text analytics and data mining. Companies such as AltaVista and Teragram focused efforts on search and text mining.

- **Today:** Use of the Web, social media, and mobile technologies drives the explosion of unstructured data, requiring companies to figure out how to efficiently analyze unstructured data.

Exhibit 18.2 provides a visual timeline of the evolution of unstructured data analytics. The last step in the exhibit illustrates how semantic is really the future in the analysis of unstructured data. Some key takeovers occurred during the last three years that are worth noting:

- January 2008: Microsoft acquires FAST, an enterprise and semantic search platform.

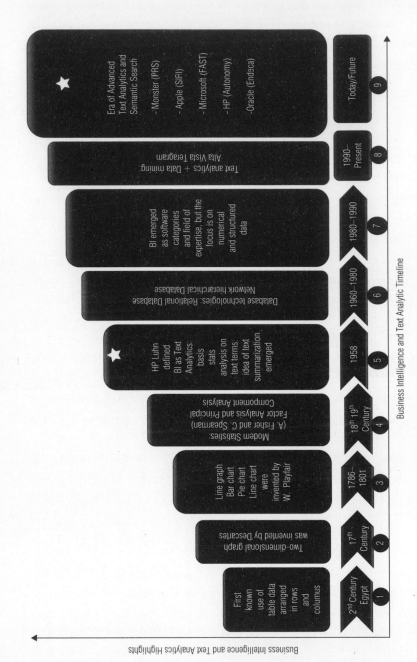

Exhibit 18.2 Evolution of Unstructured Data Analytics

Business Intelligence and Text Analytic Timeline

Business Intelligence and Text Analytics Highlights

1 — 2nd Century Egypt
First known use of table data arranged in rows and columns

2 — 17th Century
Two-dimensional graph was invented by Descartes

3 — 1786–1801
Line graph
Bar chart
Pie chart
Line chart were invented by W. Playfair

4 — 18th–19th Century
Modern Statistics:
(A. Fisher and C. Spearman)
Factor Analysis and Principal Component Analysis

5 — 1958
HP Luhn defined BI as Text Analytics: basis stats analysis on text terms: idea of text summarization emerged

6 — 1960–1980
Database technologies: Relational Database
Network hierarchical Database

7 — 1980–1990
BI emerged as software categories and field of expertise, but the focus is on numerical and structured data

8 — 1990–Present
Text analytics + Data mining:
Alta Vista Teragram

9 — Today/Future
Era of Advanced Text Analytics and Semantic Search
- Monster (PRS)
- Apple (SIFI)
- Microsoft (FAST)
- HP (Autonomy)
- Oracle (Endeca)

- July 2008: Monster acquires Trovix, a human capital and talent semantic search platform

- April 2010: Apple acquires Siri Mobile, a semantic search and speech recognition.

- August 2011: HP acquires Autonomy, an enterprise and semantic search platform.

- October 2011: Oracle acquires Endeca, an enterprise and semantic search platform.

Unstructured data analytics is the next business frontier because as we mentioned previously, data are becoming more and predominant across the globe as more people have access to Internet, mobile devices, and social media and will subsequently generate more data. As companies gather greater amounts of unstructured information regarding their customers and the market, new tools will be needed in order to turn this data into business value. We see four major drivers for the future evolution of unstructured data analytics:

1. **Voice of the market.** Leveraging the voice of the market to provide innovative services, products, and technologies to the market

2. **Voice of the customer.** Leveraging the voice of customer to increase customer intimacy, customer satisfaction, customer up-sell, and customer profitability.

3. **Scramble for semantic.** Text analytics, coupled with business intelligence, to create self-learning artificial intelligence. Using a human-like approach to leverage context and concept when searching for candidates' résumés from a résumé database or answering user questions on the weather or on directions. Recognizing the concept and the context of the words in any unstructured text or document as described in Exhibit 18.3 clearly defines semantic and sets it apart as today's and the future focus of text analytics.

4. **The integration of text analytics in predictive analytics.** Coupled with predictive analytics, text analytics transforms unstructured text, such as customer e-mails, voice-mail transcripts,

Semantic Concepts	Context
Searches on the meaning of words	Can distinguish the context in which a word is used.
Understands differences between related concepts such as job skills, industries, and education	For instance, when parsing a resume with a job seeker named Harry Ford
Understands the hierarchy of concepts	Worked for Ford Company and went to Ford Business School

Exhibit 18.3 Semantic Analytics of Résumés

and social media activities, into actionable intelligence to address the most imperative business problems companies could face in the future.

Monster worldwide has leveraged semantic search to build its SeeMore technology that helps employers perform human-like résumés search, leveraging advanced matching of job titles, skills, industries, education, and other information from job seekers' professional backgrounds. The latent semantic indexing technology provides a precise match of résumés to job requirements, ranked by actual experience, including the recency and length of skills used in a job. It has helped Monster Worldwide customers reduce by 70% the time spent searching for résumés. Also, 68% of SeeMore users claimed they were able to find résumés they couldn't find before.

INTERVIEW WITH SETH GRIMES

CASE STUDY

We had a chance to interview Seth Grimes, a pioneering leader in the field of unstructured data analytics and the founding chair of the Text Analytics Summit and the Sentiment Analysis Symposium. Here is what he had to say:

1. What are the top five benefits of text analytics in today's business environment?

Grimes: Text analytics extends business intelligence to text sources—to e-mails, survey responses, social updates, online news, financial filings, warranty claims, and scientific papers—to sources that contain immense business value that until just a few years ago couldn't be included in enterprise, government, and scientific data-analysis efforts. Text analytics delivers many business benefits. Those benefits include

- An ability to extract useful information—facts, relationships, events, sentiment—from online, social, and enterprise information, including in real time. Information extraction capabilities make for richer search and findability and also for more efficient text processing in realms that range from customer support to e-discovery.
- An ability to get at the reasons behind the numbers, at the root causes— in the customers' and stakeholders' own voices—behind the patterns that surfaced in analyzing transactional and operational data.
- The possibility of automating work with textual sources. I know of one company that reduced the time to analyze free-text responses to each employee survey it ran from five person-days to half of one person-day.
- Extended reach. Automated methods run 24/7 and are capable of ingesting and analyzing huge volumes of material, including in international languages.
- Data-mining capabilities that find patterns in large text volumes that are invisible to human analyses.

2. What companies or industries do you believe are really leveraging the power of text analytics?

Grimes: Government intelligence analysts and life sciences researchers were early text analytics adopters, with serious work that dates to the late '90s. Text analytics is more important in those domains than ever and has also proved especially compelling for customer-experience management, risk management and corporate compliance, financial services, market research and competitive intelligence, media and publishing, and also for just about anyone who's doing serious social media analysis. The global text analytics market value passed $1 billion in 2011, and I foresee strong, sustained growth in the years to come.

3. What are the key steps to implement text analytics dos and don'ts?

Grimes: As with any analytics process, the number one key step is to start with business goals and work backward to understand the insights that will help you tackle those goals, the analyses that will produce those insights, and the data—from transactional and operational and text and other sources—that you'll need to feed your analyses. Best not to start with the thought, "Text analytics sounds really interesting. How do I get going?" Better to start with an assessment that identifies the particular types of

(continued)

information, in an accessible set of text sources, that will generate high-value insights to help you optimize your business processes and decision making.

Once you've made that assess, experiment! The joy of working with text is that it was created for human consumption, so we're usually able to judge how accurately and effectively our text analysis systems are working. There are many free and low-cost solutions and very strong commercial implementations that are well suited for the range of business domains, information types, and analysis needs. Survey the options to find the best candidates for your particular needs.

4. What is the future of text analytics?

Grimes: A recent focus for text analytics has been handling the deep and complex subjective content in social, online, and enterprise sources. The field is called sentiment analysis, the application of analytical methods to discern and decode attitudes, emotions, opinions, and intent signals in the spectrum of text sources.

Expect text analytics to be built into text-rich mainstream business and consumer applications. We're seeing a consumerization in technologies such as Apple Siri, and we're seeing the creation of highly sophisticated text analysis systems such as IBM Watson, targeting large-scale problems in high-value domains such as health care. In between the extremes, text analytics will soon be pervasive for social media analyses and routine enterprise and small- to medium-business BI.

UNSTRUCTURED ANALYTICS SUCCESS STORIES

Early successes are encouraging and compel others to invest. Here are some examples of companies that have successfully taken advantage of unstructured data analytics.

Amazon.com

Amazon is a premier online shopping destination. Its customer rating system is top-notch, providing an easy-to-use application for its customers to review and comment on products and service levels of itself and partners. While some purveyors are not above writing glowing self-reviews, Amazon employs analytics to vet them, as well as exclude inappropriate posting content. New developments in unstructured analytics enable the detection and management of these reviews written under false pretenses.

Amazon's numeric categorical rating system allows customers to selectively review comments by satisfaction and level of interest. Amazon's authoritative and comprehensive product reviews attract repeat business and links to ratings from other sites. Through registration and login, as well as tracking cookies, Amazon is able to assist its customers with order status, product interest lists, possible related products and services of interest, and ease of purchase. Purchase pattern recognition using unstructured data analytics enables Amazon to determine next probable purchases, such as the follow-on book by the same author in a series, service items for products purchased, and items reviewed and not retained on a wish list.

ITA Software

ITA technology is widely used by domestic and international airlines, online and traditional travel agents, corporate and government-managed booking tools, global distribution systems, (GDSs), metasearch services, leisure packaging systems, and technology providers. It is used to quickly, consistently, and accurately identify the best available airfares without relying on high-cost, low-efficiency mainframe computers. The system provides a unique way to store, calculate and distribute seat availability and flight schedule data in order to satisfy more than one million queries per second.[6]

This software is the epitome of what is possible with a smart investment in unstructured data analytics. For instance, ask the software to quote prices on a flight from Washington to Los Angeles. Before you start the search, it will let you open the query to any airports within a mileage range you choose (25, 50, 100 miles or more) or to any airports you specify (say, Dulles or National but not BWI, to LAX or Ontario but not John Wayne . . .). You can also ask the tool to scan for flights within a time window ranging from two hours to two days, with different specifications possible for departure and return. Assimilating volumes of airline data, including current seat availability, allows ITA Software to offer a premier booking service through its deep analysis of flight and fare options.

Internet Search Engines: Bing.com, Google.com, and Others

Current search engines tackle the problem of intuiting and satisfying user intent using unstructured data analytics in a number of ways. Since the average search text is a few words, this is a very difficult endeavour. These methods include user profiling thru IP address detection, identifying interests and information needs from query text, deep analysis of query context, and probable meaning based on the popularity of other sets of queries used by other searchers. Perhaps the greatest knowledge is gained from the aggregation and analysis of all the searches performed. Since interest in a topic rises and falls over time, detecting the trend and providing options to satisfy the associated information and product need is critical for continued business viability. Last year's top Christmas toy is this year's loss leader.

Monster Worldwide

Monster Worldwide, the global leader in online recruitment solutions, manages and analyzes structured and unstructured data from employers' job descriptions to seekers' résumés' contents. At Monster we have leveraged unstructured data analytics to analyze the voice of customer and other text-based communications like e-mails and call center calls to enrich our existing customer attrition models and significantly increase the efficiency of our proactive customer retention programs.

As mentioned previously, Monster moved one step further by providing its employers with a semantic résumés search technology. Monster's 6Sense semantic search technology. powers products like *Power Resume Search* and helps recruiters to find the best candidates quicker by analyzing résumés in seconds instead of hours. It is based on semantics and language rather than keyword searches, making it a much more powerful and accurate tool. PRS enables customers to match resumes from any résumés' database to their job descriptions, leveraging artificial intelligence and machine self-learning. Monster also leveraged text analytics for its content categorization for its China branch. Launched in 1997, ChinaHR.com (a Monster company) is an innovator in online talent recruitment. It was the first company to offer online recruiting services in China, and it also offers campus recruiting and recruiting process outsourcing services. ChinaHR.com needed to manually assign meaningful occupational categories to recruitment postings. To master these needs, ChinaHR.com leveraged unstructured data analytics to provide content categorization, allowing clients to extract key information, assign categories to resumes and job postings, and store all of the information as metadata. This content categorization led to an increase in customer satisfaction and loyalty and also an increase of customer service staff productivity.

 ## KEY TAKEAWAYS

- The world's data are expected to grow by 800% during the next five years, and 80% of the data will be unstructured, creating an unprecedented need to uncover the meaning buried in unstructured data.

- To maintain their competitive edge, successful companies need to maximize business value from their unstructured data.

- We also stressed the importance of text analytics in today's business environment, which should help companies do some analysis that they couldn't do before, such as content categorization, sentiment analysis, open-ended questions analysis, e-mails, and voice of customer analysis, to enrich predictive models.

- Text analytics helps traditional predictive models' precision by providing customer feedback data to enrich the models.

- There has been a scramble for semantic search that is becoming more and more predominant for innovative organizations.

- Semantic offers the advantage of being context-, concept-, and business intelligence-driven and will be the focus in the near future.

- Text analytics enables companies to address many big data issues that arise from unstructured content by applying linguistic rules and statistical methods to automatically assess, analyze, and act on the insights buried in electronic text—such as social media content, call center logs, survey data, e-mails, loan applications, service notes, and insurance or warranty claims.

- The pace of technical improvement is rapid, in keeping with the very high value that text analytics is delivering to enterprise users. Text analytics solutions have proved capable of addressing diverse challenges, and with business intelligence integration and embedding lines of business applications, text analytics is poised for a broad market adoption.

- In today's globally connected arena, with the explosion of the Internet and social media, text analytics is no longer a choice for any forward-looking company; it is a must.

NOTES

1. Ray Paquet, "Technology Trends You Can't Afford to Ignore," Gartner, January 2010, http://www.gartner.com/it/content/1503500/1503515/january_19_tech_trends_you_cant_afford_to_ignore_rpaquet.pdf.

2. Definition of "unstructured data," pcmag.com, http://www.pcmag.com/encyclopedia_term/0,1237,t=unstructured+data&i=53486,00.asp.

3. IBM, "How has the Nature of Leadership Changed in the New Economic Environoment?" *Capitalizing on Complexity: Insights from the 2010 IBM Global CEO Survey,* IBM c-Suite Study Series 2011, http://www-935.ibm.com/services/us/ceo/ceostudy2010/index.html.

4. Sara Radicati, Emails Statistics Report, 2010, Radicati Group, Inc., http://www.radicati.com/wp/wp-content/uploads/2010/04/Email-Statistics-Report-2010-2014-Executive-Summary2.pdf.

5. H. P. Luhn, "Auto-Encoding of Documents for Information Retrieval Systems," in M. Boaz, *Modern Trends in Documentation* (London: Pergamon Press, 1959), 45−58.

6. Craig Stoltz, "The Second Coming,"*Washington Post,* December 5, 1999, http://www.itasoftware.com/pdf/05.12.99_TheSecond.coming-Washington Post.pdf.

CHAPTER 19

The Future of Analytics

"The empires of the future are the empires of the mind."

—Winston Churchill, 1943

W e foresee the analytics future to be bright. The practice of business analytics is still in its relative infancy, and technology advances are finally beginning to catch up to fulfill the promise of what analysts, statisticians, and business leaders have wanted for many years. Namely, that advanced analytic techniques can make sense of the myriad amount of data that businesses have at their disposal, simplify it, and make it accessible to the normal person, not only for those with the aptitude of the likes of Benoit Mandelbrot. It's clear we are likely progressing down this path. Already, data are everywhere. For example, even in a 2011 *Economist* article, it was clear that data production had intensified:

> Last year people stored enough data to fill 60,000 Libraries of Congress. The world's 4 billion mobile-phone users (12% of whom own smartphones) have turned themselves into data-streams. YouTube claims to receive 24 hours of video every minute. Manufacturers have embedded 30m sensors into their products, converting mute bits of metal into data-generating nodes in the internet of things. The number of smartphones is increasing by 20% a year and the number of sensors by 30%.[1]

We also believe the use of advanced analytics is intensifying and will soon become the new normal for businesses. One day soon, people will stop discussing the merits of the emergence of big data, which companies are using advanced analytics, or whether data analytics is critical to their business. It will simply be a given that every company must cope with big data, must have a data strategy, and must use various data assets and tools to augment the data it collects internally. In other words, the formal use of data within organizations will become as ubiquitous as data have become. In the same way that most companies have strategies for human capital, marketing, product, and technology, they will also have a formal strategy for analytics. In its 2011 report on big data, McKinsey Global Institute posits that companies will eventually think about their "data equity" in a way that's similar to how most companies now think of their "brand equity" to represent the value of their brand and reputation in the marketplace.[2]

Another influence of data ubiquity will be the emergence of the analytical mind-set across modern cultures. As more analytical tools develop and people begin to rely more heavily on them, their perceived necessity will increase. For example, 20 years ago there was no consumer Internet, and people needed to rely primarily on their impressions or word of mouth from friends and family when making a decision to purchase a product or a service and at what price to make that purchase. Today, most consumers use the Internet to research a product or a service, gathering data from professional reviewers, from sites that provide consumer reviews, from news stories, and from price comparison tools. As a result, consumers have become more analytical in their approach to buying products and services. We believe the continued proliferation of data and analytical tools will strengthen this trend and that consumers will have an ever-increasing reliance on the analytics that surrounds them, as well as on the technology that enables it.

A wide range of trends in technology is only just beginning to pave the way for advanced business analytics, including social computing, artificial intelligence, and data visualization. These trends are making computational analytics possible that were not possible even five years ago. In this chapter, we will discuss each of those, as well as other technology-related trends that will enable a future state of analytics.

We will also address ways in which we believe advanced analytics will help facilitate the improvement for some of the world's critical social, economic, and health challenges. We will provide examples of how this is beginning already, as well as allude to the future that is to come.

We believe the future of advanced analytics is strong and that the future holds several key trends related to analytics, each of which we will discuss in the chapter. Specifically, we think that in an advanced analytics future

- Data become less valuable.
- Predictive becomes the new standard.
- Social computing becomes essential.
- Advances in machine learning are made.
- Traditional data models evolve.
- Analytics becomes more accessible to the nonanalyst.
- Data science becomes a specialized department.
- Human-centered computing becomes part of everyday life.
- Analytics helps solve social problems.
- There is a location-based data explosion.
- A data privacy backlash occurs.

DATA BECOME LESS VALUABLE

This may seem counterintuitive, but we believe data will become less valuable in the future. Even now, data are everywhere, and people and organizations are overwhelmed with data. Basic economics dictate that when something is widely available, it becomes less valuable and when something is scarce, it becomes more valuable. In the future, having a treasure trove of data will not, by itself, hold much value. However, we do expect analytics to become *more* valuable at the same time that the supporting data become less valuable. In other words, the companies that have the ability to create actionable knowledge-based tools from data, either using their own data or using someone else's data, will see the benefits of the expected analytical economy. This will take many forms, everything from applications that sift through data for nuggets of insight to personalized algorithms that allow individual users to analyze their own data to understand something about themselves and take action.

To illustrate why we think data will become less valuable, consider the early days of the commercial Internet, the late 1990s, as an example. At that time, as it is today, almost anyone could create Internet content and allow other people to view it. At first, this was a novelty, and consumers were happy to view new Internet information as it came online. Early users of the commercial Internet took a model with its roots in traditional library science, the Gopher protocol, as a way to organize the emerging Internet content into logical categories. With Gopher, every Internet document had a defined format and type, and the typical user navigated through a single server-defined menu system to get to a particular document. This worked well for several years. However, soon the amount of data on the Internet began to expand exponentially. As a result, the amount of data and documents available on the Internet quickly became overwhelming, and navigating through using Gopher became inefficient for most uses. As a result, Web-based Internet search engines that allowed for an unstructured search of Internet content soon emerged. These analytical tools that were applied to data as a gateway to the Internet is where people eventually found the most value. Can you imagine trying to make sense of the 644 million websites without the analytical help of sites such as Google or Bing?[3] Without them, would there really be much value in adding another one million websites to the worldwide total? We think similar logic explains why data will become less valuable over time, while at the same time, effective analytical techniques will become very valuable.

PREDICTIVE BECOMES THE NEW STANDARD

We provided an overview of predictive analytics and its importance in Chapter 10. We believe that as we progress toward the future, predictive analytics will become more widespread and will evolve into the norm for all analytics. Analytical techniques will need to have a predictive component in order to be considered business relevant or effective. This will require more sophisticated statistical and machine-learning techniques and more computational power, both of which are becoming possible. It will also require the expertise of people who can develop predictive models effectively and who understand how to learn, test, and optimize using predictive analytical techniques. There are certainly many examples of predictive analytics applied to the business world, especially across Internet-based businesses, and we expect to see it become the standard across all industries in the future.

SOCIAL INFORMATION PROCESSING AND DISTRIBUTED COMPUTING

One of the challenges in the analysis of big data is the ability to process data with large velocity, volume, and variety quickly and effectively. We believe the future of analytics will enable this more effectively through two networking concepts, social information processing (SIP) and distributed computing. SIP is the idea that "computation" or analysis is carried out by groups of people. It is "an activity through which collective human actions organize knowledge."[4] It is the creation and processing of information by a group of people. Simple examples of SIP include collaborative filtering, online auctions, prediction markets, online reputation systems, and verification games. We think SIP will play a significant role in the future of analytics in several ways. One simple example is that analysts' social networks will evolve whereby they collectively share and improve algorithms and analytical techniques. Another way is that users of data themselves may create and share their own analytical models with one another, using analytical tools, thereby creating meta models that describe and predict the data patterns for the system. For example, in the future, users may use body tracking technology to record data on their activities, food intake, exercise, and health vital signs over long periods of time. The tracking technology may include a customized algorithm that allows the user to predict which factors (type of exercise, food intake, daily activities, and combinations of all three) result in healthy vital signs over time. If this information is shared in a social networking environment, the collective algorithms would provide a robust set of models that could be analyzed together to understand predictors of health over time.

Several online professional communities are already trying to facilitate the sharing, collaboration, and rapid development of analytical algorithms. One company has even taken it a step further. The site www.kaggle.com allows companies, governments, and researchers to present a data set and a problem to a community of data scientists who compete to produce the best analytical solution. At the end of a competition, the competition host pays prize money in exchange for the intellectual property behind the winning model.

A second network concept that will be leveraged in the future of analytics is the notion of distributed computing. Distributed computing refers to the use of computers connected over a network, whereby a computational problem is divided into parts and distributed across the network of computers. In other words, in distributed computing, a problem is divided into many tasks, each of which is solved by one or more computers. This enables very difficult analytical problems that cannot be easily solved using a close network of computers to be solved by spreading the computational load over multiple processors. An example of a distributed computing project currently under way is www.climateprediction.net. It is a distributed computing project run primarily by Oxford University in England to investigate and reduce uncertainties in global climate modeling by running hundreds of thousands of different models using the donated idle time of ordinary computers.[5] Through 32,000 active participants from 147 countries, the project has produced more than 100 million model years of data so far, leveraging about 35 teraflops (35 trillion operations per second) of processing power.[6]

ADVANCES IN MACHINE LEARNING

Machine learning is a branch of artificial intelligence concerned with the design and development of algorithms that allow computers to learn from processing real data and become more proficient over time. In the future, artificial intelligence will start showing up in more and more unexpected places, including all of the software used by most consumers and businesses. A major focus of machine-learning research is to automatically learn to recognize complex patterns and make intelligent decisions based on data. Some examples of the current applications of machine learning include

- Search engines
- Medical diagnosis
- Bioinformatics
- Cheminformatics
- Detecting credit card fraud
- Stock market analysis
- Classifying DNA sequences
- Speech and handwriting recognition
- Robot locomotion
- Aircraft autopilot
- Computational finance
- Sentiment analysis
- Recommender systems

Machine learning is a rapidly evolving field that has the potential to have a great impact on analytics, as well as on the experiences in human lives. However, what is not clear is how the future advances in machine learning will affect the need for trained analysts and other human resources. As machine-learning models and techniques improve over the long term, it is possible there will be a reduction in demand for humans with that specialized skill set. In addition, as sophisticated applications are developed, it will make it easier to run larger, more complex organizations with fewer people, possibly leading to corporate consolidation and the ability to do more with a smaller workforce.

TRADITIONAL DATA MODELS EVOLVE

For the last 20 or 30 years, classic data warehousing has been based on the same regimented approach. However, the future is changing this. Traditionally, processes such as identifying data lineage, documenting metadata, and being able to reconcile data across different reports coming from different data tables in different data marts have been critical to ensure that numbers are correct. This standard approach to data warehousing has been important, in order to have confidence in your data and meet regulatory and compliance requirements. However, over time businesses have become more complex and are doing things at an ever-accelerating pace, and as a result, data storage needs for analytics are changing. For example, there was a time when the core business of a retail establishment was to understand and sell a single line of products through a bricks-and-mortar presence. However, within the last 5 to 10 years, that has evolved into retail establishments needing to sell and fulfill their products through multiple online, offline, and mobile channels, while understanding the dynamic way consumers research and choose to purchase a retail product. Similar issues also exist in the telecommunications industry. In the early days of the industry, companies sold fixed lines, and the only product flavors were local, long-distance, and international calls. Today, companies must deal with mobile, data over mobile, data over different bandwidths, and all of the product permutations that people have, not to mention the increased competition. Companies also must track service switches and pricing tiers.

As a result, the predominant database storage models of today will not be the only data storage models of the future. The relational databases of the past will work alongside less formally structured database schemas, such as NoSQL, that do not require structured and logical data but lend themselves well to the fast retrieval and analysis of multiple data types. These analytical warehouses will be much more flexible and dynamic, lending themselves to ad hoc analyses and to bringing multiple disparate data sources together in order to address critical business questions. This will be essential in the future, as companies do things with data such as combine Web behavior clickstream data with Twitter feeds, customer satisfaction surveys, product purchase records, and third-party credit data, in order to use data science techniques to look for relationships.

ANALYTICS BECOMES MORE ACCESSIBLE TO THE NONANALYST

Another trend that will shape the future of analytics is that analytical techniques will become more accessible to the general business user, enabling nonanalysts to take an analytical approach to their business questions. As general knowledge of analytics spreads in the business world and software providers simplify the use of techniques such as data modeling, text analytics, Web analytics, and segmentation through automation, and the actual steps of the data analytics are more hidden from the user, it will enable people with little or no analytical background to run models and take business action from the results. We can already see instances of this occurring in certain analytical disciplines. For example, the rise of automated online survey tools during the last 10 years has led to people in all departments of the organizations creating and analyzing their own customer surveys. This is sometimes to the frustration of the marketing research experts, because survey questions are sometimes poorly worded, or statistically significant differences or margins of error not considered. However, we do believe this trend will be net positive for the influence of analytics, but we're sure there will be pain along the way. For example, the famous quote "to the man with a hammer, everything looks like a nail" has relevance. Untrained analysts are likely to apply analytical techniques improperly or in an inappropriate manner with incorrectly prepared data. As a result, there will be instances of confusion and frustration as people who know analytics help those who do not. However, we believe the resulting social pressure will eventually lead to analytics being used more effectively across the organization.

DATA SCIENCE BECOMES A SPECIALIZED DEPARTMENT

Although we expect that analytical techniques will become more available to nonanalysts across the enterprise, we also see the future of analytics being one where specialized departments are created to address the needs of data science in the organization. In the current state, analytical professionals are typically fragmented across the enterprise, often in different departments with labels such as business intelligence, marketing analytics, customer research, web analytics, CRM analytics, and so forth. Furthermore, most companies have very few, if any, true data science professionals. We expect most companies will move to centralize these functions under an umbrella analytics and data science department. The model for some companies may be to have analytics as a formal, centralized shared service, and for others, as a center of excellence where analytical professionals are kept close to the departments they serve, yet have accountability and participate in an analytics center of excellence. Regardless, the most successful companies of the future will recognize and prioritize the importance of data science and related analytics professionals, making it a formal business function in the same way that it is commonplace in many companies today to have such departments as HR, marketing, service, technology, and finance.

HUMAN-CENTERED COMPUTING

Another future trend related to analytics will be the proliferation of various forms of human-centered computing. Human-centered computing is the application of computer science, information technology, and psychology to how computers can effectively interact with humans. Human-centered computing deals with human technology interaction issues, such as algorithms, databases and information systems, artificial intelligence, information theory, software engineering, data mining, image processing, modeling and simulation, signal processing, discrete mathematics, control and system theory, circuit theory, and psychological states and motivations. Human-centered computing generates new knowledge on how humans can effectively interact with technology and on the tools to create that knowledge. Eye-tracking technology is one form of human-centered computing, whereby a camera can track the eye movement of someone viewing a computer screen, recording data about where and how often the person views different areas of the screen. It has been applied in areas as diverse as website usability testing, sports medicine, automobile testing, geriatric research, training simulators, and infant research.

As we look into the future, we expect that more devices will interact directly with the human body and, as a result, generate data from those interactions that need to be analyzed. In terms of the future applications of human-centered computing, we think the following applications will be relevant for the field of analytics:

■ Wearable computing/smart fabrics
■ Consumer health informatics

- Brainwave measurement
- Facial recognition
- Emotional recognition
- Exercise informatics
- Body scan technologies
- Gesture-based interfaces
- Motion-detection devices
- Molecular computing

ANALYTICS TO SOLVE SOCIAL PROBLEMS

One of the great promises of the future of analytics is the ability for it to help solve large-scale social problems that have previously been unsolvable. For example, will distributed analytics someday lead to a rapid cure for a new virus or diseases, as people begin to share more health analytics with one another? Will it be possible to provide early warning systems ahead of natural disasters using analytics that will save thousands of lives? Will data from sensors in the earth help us effectively manage and maintain our natural resources?

These types of applications may sounds a bit far fetched; however, the reality is that similar things are beginning to happen today. For example, a recent study by medical researchers at Harvard showed that data from Internet-based news and Twitter feeds was faster than traditional sources for detecting the onset and progression of the cholera epidemic in postearthquake Haiti that sickened almost half a million people.[7] "When we analyzed news and Twitter feeds from the early days of the epidemic in 2010, we found they could be mined for valuable information on the cholera outbreak that was available up to two weeks ahead of surveillance reports issued by the government health ministry," said Rumi Chunara, PhD, of the Informatics Program at Children's Hospital Boston, a research fellow at Harvard Medical School, and the lead author of the study. "The techniques we employed eventually could be used around the world as an affordable and efficient way to quickly detect the onset of an epidemic and then intervene with such things as vaccines and antibiotics."

Some of the same research group from the Children's Hospital Boston used the core idea that data and analytics can help address public health issues in their decision to create www.healthmap.org, launched in 2006 to provide "real-time surveillance of emerging public health threats." This site is designed to automatically capture any coverage or mentions of health issues from a variety of information sources—including news media, blogs, and discussion groups.

LOCATION-BASED DATA EXPLOSION

Another trend affecting the future of analytics is the rapid proliferation of location-based data. For example, most of the several billion cell phones in world have GPS tracking devices that have the potential to leave a continuous location data trail. Furthermore, many of the hundreds of millions of mobile apps include some type of location-based tracking. Also, stores are experimenting with location-aware services that enable retailers to communicate with or serve offers to users in a specific location. As businesses and consumers begin to leverage location-based data in greater numbers, analytics will need to cope with how to store, sort, analyze, and use these data for the benefit of organizations.

DATA PRIVACY BACKLASH

Data privacy will be a hot topic in the future of analytics, as consumers continue to grapple with the notion that many of their activities are being tracked by multiple organizations around the world and by many popular sites such as Facebook and AOL. Also, as analytics become more sophisticated and human-like, consumers may get an uncomfortable feeling when they are given insights they didn't even know were possible. Recall the case we reviewed in Chapter 1, of the father who learned his daughter was pregnant from Target when he didn't even know himself.

We expect that as the future progresses, as data and analytics become more important in our daily lives, there will be a data privacy backlash where consumers will demand more aggressive governmental involvement in consumer data privacy standards and protection. We do not know what form this will take: whether it will be a credit agency model, whereby all information is centralized in a few organizations, or whether it will be distributed across each data provider, whereby users have the ability to decide which information about them is shared, hidden, or permanently deleted. Either way, the field of analytics must take note and engage in the conversation, because our field will be directly affected by any changes in data privacy policies and standards.

 KEY TAKEAWAYS

- The future of analytics is bright, with opportunities increasing in many areas.
- Certain trends will dramatically shape the field of analytics in the future.
- Data will become less valuable, while analytical insight becomes more valuable.
- Predictive modeling becomes the new de facto standard.
- Social computing will advance analytics rapidly.
- Advances in machine learning will make analytics more powerful and actionable.
- Traditional relational database models will evolve into nonrelational models that are more dynamic and flexible and lend themselves to ad hoc analytics.
- Analytical techniques will become more accessible to the nonanalyst.
- Data science will become a specialized department within the organization.
- Human-centered computing will become part of everyday life, generating a lot of new data in the process.
- Analytics will be able to help solve important social problems.
- There will be a location-based data explosion.
- A data privacy backlash will lead to rigorous attempts at individual consumer control of one's own data.

NOTES

1. "Building with Big Data: The Data Revolution Is Changing the Landscape of Business," Schumpeter column, *Economist*, May 26, 2011.

2. James Manyika, Michael Chui, Brad Brown, Jacques Bughin, Richard Dobbs, Charles Roxburgh, and Angela Hun, "Big Data: The Next Frontier for Innovation, Competition, and Productivity" McKinsey Global Institute, May 2011, http://www.mckinsey.com/insights/mgi/research/technology_ and_innovation/big_data_the_next_frontier_for_innovation.

3. Netcraft, March 2012 Web Server Survey, http://news.netcraft.com/ archives/2012/03/05/march-2012-web-server-survey.html.

4. AAAI, "Social Information Processing," AAAI Spring Symposium, Stanford University, Stanford, CA, March 2008.

5. See www.climateprediction.net.

6. Boinc Statistics for www.climateprediction.net, as of May 8, 2012, from http://boincstats.com/stats/project_graph.php?pr=cpdn.

7. Rumi Chunara, Jason R. Andrews, and John S. Brownstein, "Social and News Media Enable Estimation of Epidemiological Patterns Early in the 2010 Haitian Cholera Outbreak," *American Journal of Tropical Medicine and Hygiene* 86 (2012): 39–45.

About the Authors

Jean Paul Isson is an internationally recognized speaker and expert in advanced business analytics. He is the global vice president of business intelligence and predictive analytics at Monster Worldwide, Inc., having built the global business intelligence team from the ground up. He has successfully conceived and implemented global customer scoring/segmentation, predictive modeling, and Web-mining applications for Monster across North America, Europe, and the Asia-Pacific.

Prior to joining Monster, Isson led the global customer behavior modeling team at Rogers Wireless, where he pioneered advanced business analytics, including conjoint analysis for new price plans offering and the Customer Life Time Value (CLTV) Segmentation that is being used to prioritize customer services sales and marketing activities. He started his career as a statistician and holds a master's degree in mathematics and applied statistics from the University of Paris 6 in France.

Isson has been a speaker for TDWI (The Data Warehousing Institute), Forbes, SAS data-mining conferences, the Premier Business Leadership Series, Measure Up, Predictive Analytics World, BusinessAnalyticsNews.com, IT World Canada, IT Business, 1to1 Media, IQCP, eMetrics Marketing Optimization Summit/SMX, and at other SAS and IDC events. He has more than 17 years of experience in advanced business analytics, focusing on customer behavior modeling, scoring, and market segmentation. Jean-Paul lives in Montreal with his family.

■ ■ ■

Dr. Jesse Harriott has been a research and analytics professional for more than 20 years and has held various client- and supplier-side analytics leadership positions. He is currently chief analytics officer at Constant Contact, an online marketing solutions company that helps more than 500,000 organizations generate repeat business and referrals through e-mail marketing, social media marketing, event marketing, local deals, and online surveys. Prior to Constant Contact, Harriott was the chief knowledge officer for Monster Worldwide, Inc., where he conceived and built a global analytics business division focused on the human capital marketplace in the United States, Europe, and Asia. Dr. Harriott also pioneered the creation of the Monster Employment Index, the first measure of online recruitment activity, which is currently in more than 30 countries and is followed by millions of people each month. He also led Web analytics, business intelligence, competitive intelligence, data governance, marketing research, and sales analytics departments for Monster.

Prior to Monster, Dr. Harriott created an analytics consulting practice for the e-commerce company Gomez, Inc., where his team led projects for Internet start-ups and well-known brands, including Orbitz.com, WebMD, and Fidelity. He has advised many private and public organizations regarding analytics and labor market issues, including the White House, the Department of Labor, the European Commission, the Federal Reserve, the National Governors Association, the Clinton Global Initiative, and various U.S. senators. He has authored several publications, including as coauthor of the book *Finding Keepers*, which has been published in North America, South America, Europe, and Asia and discusses the challenges faced by companies in today's talent market. Jesse has also taught at the University of Chicago and holds an MA and a PhD in Experimental Psychology from DePaul University. He has appeared in various media outlets, including CNBC, the *Wall Street Journal*, the *New York Times*, CBS radio, Bloomberg, and Reuters. Dr. Harriott has won several awards, including the Platinum Award from PR News and an Ogilvy Award from the Advertising Research Foundation, and was named by the *Boston Business Journal* as one of Boston's top 40 under 40. Jesse lives in New Hampshire with his wife and their two children.

Index